HOW TO VALUE YOUR BUSINESS AND INCREASE ITS POTENTIAL

JAY B. ABRAMS, ASA, CPA, MBA

McGraw-Hill

New York Chicago San Francisco Lisbon London
Madrid Mexico City Milan New Delhi San Juan
Seoul Singapore Sydney Toronto

The McGraw-Hill Companies

To my parents, my wife, and my children, who have supported me, believe in me, and root for me.

1 2 3 4 5 6 7 8 9 0 AGM/AGM 0 9 8 7 6 5 4

ISBN 0-07-139520-2

This book is printed on recycled, acid-free paper containing a minimum of 50% recycled, de-inked fiber.

Contents

Acknowledgments

I want to express my most profound appreciation to my parents, as their unceasing support above and beyond the parental call of duty brings me to tears. I am grateful to my father, Leonard Abrams, who taught me how to write, and to my mother, Marilyn Abrams, who taught me mathematics. I express my deep gratitude to my wife, Cindy, who believes in me, and to my children, Yonatan, Binyamin, Miriam, Nechamah, and Rivkah, who gave up countless Sundays with me for this book.

I am very grateful to Chaim Borevitz and Linda Feinholz, who edited every one of my chapters and who coached me to transform my writing to a much more user-friendly style, caught my mistakes, and made significant contributions to the thought that permeates this book.

I thank Daniel Jordan for his help in editing several chapters.

I am grateful to my contributors, every one of whom worked very hard to communicate their expertise to you. They all have produced excellence. In particular, I thank my contributors whose work would have appeared in this book had space permitted. Instead, their work is available to you as supplementary material on my website, www.abramsvaluation.com, under "Books: How to Value Your Business and Increase Its Potential" Thus I thank Linda Feinholz, Dan O'Connell, Jim Stump, Ed Schuck, Penelope Roeder, and Jim Ward.

I am grateful to my lovely, sweet editors, Kelli Christiansen, Ann Wildman, and Ela Aktay, who have all been patient and a delight to work with. Ela was my editor on my first book, as well as the beginning of this one. I express my gratitude to Jeffrey Krames and the McGraw-Hill team for believing in me a second time.

I thank Dr. Shannon P. Pratt for his very helpful comments on my book. Dr. Pratt is a legend in the valuation profession, and it was an unexpected great honor that he provided me with edits.

I am always grateful to my great teachers, Mr. Tsutomu Ohshima and Christopher Hunt. They modeled power and integrity and helped me draw forth my best.

Introduction

MY ASSUMPTIONS ABOUT THE READER

How to Value Your Business and Increase Its Potential will teach you just that: How to value your business "quick and dirty," and how to manage it to increase its worth. I have written it primarily for business owners, but others can also benefit. Here are some of my assumptions about the reader:

1. If you're not currently thinking of selling your business, you are nonetheless curious about how much it is worth now, and very curious about what its worth will be when you reach retirement age.
2. If you're thinking about selling your business now, you are burning with curiosity about its value. This is true as well if you are considering buying a business. This book will help you calculate the "right price" in both cases.
3. Most of you are uninterested in business valuation as a science and as an art form and would prefer to get the "easy version" of the math rather than the complete version. A few of you want the hard stuff. Therefore, I have attempted to keep mathematics out of at least the text as much as possible. Thus, the math you'll find in the chapters is there because it's necessary. Optional mathematics for quantitative connoisseurs appears in the appendixes and occasionally in documents you can retrieve on my Web site.
4. You may appreciate some humor to break up the mathematical monotony. If you don't find my humor funny, I suggest therapy, but if that doesn't work, ignore it and focus on the useful information instead. Some of the humor

is in the footnotes or in parentheses, to keep it from distracting those who prefer to stay focused on the material.

5. Some of you are comfortable with the computer. In Chapter 7 there are valuation tables created in spreadsheets in Excel format, which virtually all other spreadsheets can read. You can download these spreadsheets from my Web site, www.abramsvaluation.com, under "Books." If you have even rudimentary knowledge of electronic spreadsheets, you can follow the directions and make excellent use of the software. If not, don't worry: You can also value your company using chicken scratchings on the back of an envelope.

WHO SHOULD READ THIS BOOK, AND WHY

This book should be of benefit to the following people, or categories of people, and for the following reasons:

Business Owners

You are the primary reader. After all, it's your business, and no one cares more about its value than you.

Attorneys

Your clients need to know business values, and you have specialized knowledge that should affect our calculation of the value—if you only knew what could be relevant to a professional business appraiser,. Legal rights and restrictions often impact value, and appraisers are often knowledgeable enough about law to be dangerous. Appraisers are not attorneys, and they need your help to get it right. The better you understand valuation, the more likely it is that you can help your client receive the most accurate valuation possible.

For example, there are often restrictions on selling stock in a corporation of which the corporate attorney may be aware that the sale can depress the value of the stock were it not restricted. A partner's right of first refusal that lasts six months and provides for payment over 10 years at 5 percent interest would certainly reduce the value of the selling partner's shares. Attorneys are often more aware than a business appraiser of tax law or case law that can impact value. An attorney who does not understand the valuation process is at a disadvantage in recognizing what is relevant, and his or her client may suffer because of that.

Also, it is likely that you either occasionally or frequently are in a position of having to recommend a professional appraiser to a client and work with that appraiser. The more that you know about valuation, the better you can do both of those jobs.

Certified Public Accountants

CPAs are often a business owner's trusted adviser on financial matters—like a personal CFO. Because all businesses eventually need to transfer ownership (except in the case of liquidation), whether through sale, gift, or inheritance, you may be asked to provide valuation-related advice. This book will go into some of the mechanics of business valuation as well as examining the valuation context and environment. Understanding these, and other topics to be discussed, should make you a more competent adviser to your clients and provide more tools to help your client find the right professional when specialists are needed.

Accountants who would like to develop a valuation practice certainly can benefit from this book, which can provide and/or sharpen and increase your valuation skills. It's important to note, however, that to be a valuation professional, you'll need more quantitative tools than you will find in this book.

Insurance Agents

Learning to do "quick and dirty" valuations for your existing and potential clients can enable you to spot an underinsured actual or potential client. This could not only generate additional premiums for your existing clients, but also distinguish you from a potential client's existing agent who might have ignored his or her needs through ignorance of value.

Business Brokers

This book can sharpen and increase your valuation skills. This should enable you to do a better job of measuring and explaining values to your clients, and, ultimately, closing deals. It also should enable you to more quickly spot clients with unrealistic expectations who will waste your time trying to make impossible deals happen.

Pension Administrators and Others Who Read Valuation Reports

Too many professionals whose clients are strongly impacted by valuation results completely abdicate responsibility to the appraiser. This is unfortunate, because a professional who understands valuation can add to the accuracy of the process.

ORGANIZATION

How to Value Your Business and Increase Its Potential consists of two parts. Part One, the core of the book, contains the following general topics:

- Chapters 1 through 8: How to value your business as of today.
- Chapter 9: How to value your business as of a future date.
- How to manage your business to increase its value over time (also Chapter 9). We will analyze the future date valuation equation, and go into the elements you can manage and the tradeoffs you face in increasing the value of your business. Creating and realizing value is the long-term bottom line of owning a business.[1] By changing the questions you ask and the way you think, you can maximize your chances of increasing the value of your business.

Part Two is about the sale, financing, and taxation of a business. The first chapter in the second part consists of my tips about increasing the value of, and selling, a business. The other chapters are written by several different contributors whose areas of expertise are related to business valuation. You'll find tips by a business broker (Chapter 11) and an investment banker (Chapter 12).

[1]This is true on a personal as well as a business level, but that is largely outside the scope of this book.

There's a discussion about obtaining venture capital, and how valuation plays a part in that (Chapter 13), and about the taxation of a business sale (Chapter 14).

Howard Lewis, the author of Chapter 15, is the Internal Revenue Service's top executive in charge of valuation. He writes on the IRS perspective of valuation controversy. It's important, of course, to know how you can manage the valuation process better, in order to achieve a more satisfactory result when dealing with Uncle Sam. Much valuation controversy—whether dealing with the local agent, the IRS Appeals Division, or litigating in court—arises in estate and gift taxation, as well as over income tax.

While there are entire books devoted to the topics in each of these "guest" chapters, it's unique to find them in a book about valuing businesses. Reading about these various topics in this context will mean seeing them through valuation-colored lenses.

HOW TO READ THIS BOOK

You'll get more out of *How to Value Your Business and Increase Its Potential* if you: (1) create an extra set of copies of the tables, (2) print and read the supplemental chapters on my Web site, (3) look for updates, and (4) make sure you understand the vocabulary, which can be confusing. I'll briefly go into these four points. For your own enrichment, you can download relevant material to supplement the 15 chapters, which I'll explain below.

Create Extra Tables

It is very important to understand the tables in Part One. The explanation of the tables often spans two or more pages and often does not appear on the same page as the table. In order to make them easier to understand, I've made the tables available in Adobe Acrobat format (.pdf) on at www.abramsvaluation.com. Click on "Books," then click on this particular book, and then click on the option to download the pdf files. Once you've downloaded the tables, print them out, so you'll have them at hand. This way, you can read the explanation and have the table in front of you. Additionally, some of the tables are long, and the print will be larger and easier to read on a letter-size page, rather than the way they will appear in the book.

Print and Read the Supplemental Chapters

I strongly recommend that you go to my Web site and, as described above, click on this particular book and then print the supplemental chapters, which are listed among the resources in the back of this book. These supplemental chapters have numerous valuable insights.

Look for Updates

I'm fond of saying that valuation is an art that sits on top of a science. The scientific part of valuation moves on and changes. To make sure that you're working with the latest information I can make available, go to www.abramsvaluation.com, and again click on "Books," click on this particular book, and then look for updates.

You might find, for instance, errata sheets that list any errors in this book. With my first book, *Quantitative Business Valuation*, I produced one errata sheet with the errors organized by page number and another sheet with the errors organized by the date on which I found them. That way, you only had to look for the errors since they were last updated. I plan to produce the same type of errata sheets with this book.

It is likely that I will also update valuation spreadsheets—updated versions or entirely new versions of the valuation tables in Chapter 7. Additionally, there may be other valuation news on the Web site.

I can already speak of a particular, last-minute scientific update. I recently downloaded a working paper by finance professors whose article[2] demonstrates that a decrease in macroeconomic volatility, i.e., the volatility of the U.S. economy, has contributed to a decrease in the equity premium—a term that I explain later on in the book. This article is compelling to me, and based on it, I will post an update on my Web site, www.abramsvaluation.com, to explain to the reader how to modify his or her calculations to incorporate this new knowledge.

Thus, the discount rates in Table 5.4, 6.1, 7.1, and 7.2 need some modification. You should read the book as is, as the method-

---

[2]"The Declining Equity Premium: What Role Does Macroeconomic Risk Play?" Lettau, Martin, Sydney Ludvigson, and Jessica Wachter, January 2004. Available at Professor Wachter's Web site, http://pages.stern.nyu.edu/~jwachter/.

ology is current. After you understand what is already written in the book, it should take the reader only 30 minutes at the most to download, read, and understand how to apply the update. It takes time—sometimes many years—before we can separate the wheat from the chaff of science, and it is my experience that there must be a fair amount of research and debate before there is consensus. In the interim, while it is desirable to keep up with new research, to the extent practical, but it is also irresponsible to keep flipping methodology every two weeks with the publishing of every new article on the topic. The nuances of science at the cutting edge are beyond the scope of this book.

As I will write consistently throughout this book, when you have to make a decision based on valuation that has significant monetary consequences, get a professional appraiser to help you. This book is an invaluable tool to learn how valuation works, to perform your own "quick-and-dirty" valuation on your firm for planning purposes, and to learn how to manage your business to increase its value over time, but never rely exclusively on your own amateur skills to value a business for an actual transaction.

Understanding the Vocabulary

When I use the word "we," I picture you, the reader, sitting next to me, looking over my shoulder and doing everything together with me—whether reading an explanation of a table or typing the keystrokes on the computer. I do not use the royal "we." In the context of this book, "we" means you and I learning and doing together.

I have been careful to use phrases like "professionals agree" or "professional business valuators do x or know y" when I mean that something is standard professional thought or practice.

In contrast, when I use the word "I," that means Jay Abrams is giving you his personal and/or professional opinion or research. I have tried to use the word "I" sparingly, so you know that when I use it, I mean Jay Abrams and no one else.

I have been a major innovator in the business valuation profession, having published significant research that touches on many of the most important areas of valuation. My models for calculating discount rates and discount for lack of marketability are not universal practice. Although they are widely in use, I would not call them standard professional practice. There are other ways of doing the same thing.

Occasionally, I also use the first person to make the writing more personal and user friendly, especially when recounting one of my "war stories." Valuation tends to be a dry topic for those who are not committed to a lifetime of being true seekers of fair market value. (Probably most of us should be committed, but that is another story.) Sometimes, I found it necessary to be more personal to warm up what might otherwise be a cold topic.

I use the terms "business appraiser" and "business valuator" synonymously. The former is the more traditional term, whereas the latter is gaining more favor lately. Similarly, I use the terms "valuation" and "appraisal" as synonyms.

KNOWING THE VALUE OF YOUR BUSINESS

If you own one of the 8 million small businesses in the United States, you *must* be very curious what your business is worth. You probably want to sell it someday, and it is or will be important for you to know whether this is the golden egg upon which you can retire or an albatross around your neck that will never enable you to afford to retire.

Almost everyone wants to show their value to the IRS as being low to minimize taxes. Many small business owners for whom I have done tax-related valuations are shocked when I tell them that their businesses are *really* worth nothing. Just because your business is making a profit does not guarantee that it has a positive value. The majority of business owners overvalue their businesses due to a combination of emotional attachments to their "baby" and ignorance of how to value a business. On the other hand, a few make mistakes in the other direction—undervaluing their businesses—and I have seen some big ones. The biggest was a firm that sold to my client. My valuation, which was commissioned after the sale for tax purposes, showed the seller should have sold for four times the actual selling price—many more tens of millions of dollars! While I don't feel sorry for the sellers, and I might be delighted to trade bank accounts with them, they suffered a tremendous loss due to their ignorance of the value of their business.

MY GOALS

Considering my assumptions about you as the reader, my goals in writing this book are:

1. To teach you the fundamentals of how to do a "quick-and-dirty" valuation of your own business. Your results should be good enough for early stage life-planning purposes. The spreadsheets in Chapter 7 will facilitate the valuation process for you. After completing your valuation, you may want to hire a professional valuation firm to review it, which should be far less expensive than paying for an appraisal from scratch. Of course, the end product is not an official opinion of value, so you would be buying less than an appraisal, which should be fine for early stage planning for many people. Then, when you need the additional accuracy, you can have a professional appraiser value your business.
2. To keep Part One—the valuation "core" of the book—relatively short, so you'll read it and use it. (One of the biggest challenges in writing this book has been what *not* to say.) There are competent books on valuation written for professional business appraisers, including my own.[3] They are beyond the patience of the layman to read and use. It is not worth your time to read a 500-page book to value your business; it would be cheaper to pay $5000 to $20,000 for a professional appraisal. CPAs who want to become professional appraisers should read this book, but will still need to read the encyclopedic books on appraisal. *How to Value Your Business and Increase Its Potential* is valuable, however, because it is so short and simple. It provides an overview of professional appraisal before diving into myriad details and variations.
3. To give you insights on how to increase the value of your business.
4. To help you "groom" your business for sale.
5. To help you understand when you must increase your profitability or consider closing your business.
6. To provide you with some rudimentary knowledge in financial planning, so you can create a lifetime financial

[3]Jay B. Abrams. *Quantitative Business Valuation: A Mathematical Approach for Today's Professionals.* New York: McGraw-Hill, 2001.

plan and include your valuation in it. To do this, I show you (in Chapter 9) how to value your business at a future date, e.g., at your expected retirement age, not just at this moment. You can supplement this with the additional chapters on my Web site, which has material on estate planning and exit strategies in more depth.

7. To enable you to understand the broader context of valuation well enough to interface more effectively with a professional appraiser when you need that kind of help. There are many reasons why people hire professional appraisers: buying or selling a whole business or part of a business, establishing a buy-sell agreement, estate taxes, gift taxes, income taxes, Employee Stock Ownership Plans (ESOPs), litigation, etc. When the business owner understands the valuation process, he or she becomes an invaluable part of the process. Professional business valuators are human and make mistakes. They may not find an important piece of information, one that has a large impact on the forecast of sales, for example. Or they might make technical errors in the valuation process. Knowledge of valuation will sensitize you to the type of information that may be important. The more knowledgeable you are, the more likely it is that you'll be an important, active participant in the valuation. You may even be able to prevent your professional appraiser from making a mistake, or catch a mistake when he or she makes one.
8. Last, and certainly far from least, I've written this book to have fun. Believe me, business appraisal could be one of the most boring topics on Earth. To spice it up, as I said, I've added a few laughs along the way. We can start with the definition of an appraiser: an accountant without the charisma. Remember Mary Poppins: "A spoonful of sugar helps the medicine go down"? The valuation equivalent is: "An optimistic growth rate makes the value go up, the value go up, the value go up. . . ."[4]

---

[4]Sung to the same tune, of course.

More on Laughter

I have been accused of having an off-the-wall sense of humor, which is why I never worked on Wall Street, and I have decided not to spare you from it. If you don't like it, as I suggested earlier, try therapy. Otherwise, you can always ignore it. My wife does. Why should you be any different? Do I hear Rodney Dangerfield in the background?

My fond hope is that this book should be enough fun that students and housewives will also want to read this for the humor alone. Besides, you never know when valuation formulas will become a popular game show topic, and the ability to whip out a Gordon Model formula will enable you to bludgeon those ignorant savages who will be your opponents on *Family Feud* who never had the good sense to buy this book.

It is important to understand that the purpose of the off-the-wall humor in this book is to make your learning process fun, and in doing so, hopefully, you'll learn the material better than if your eyeballs were hanging down to the floor in boredom. The humor notwithstanding, I am a first-rate scientist in my field, and this material can enable you to make wise decisions that could easily save you tens of thousands or even millions of dollars. Let my humor enhance your learning; if you don't respond to it, then ignore it and don't let it get in your way of some very important knowledge.

Dear Reader,

I have struggled, strained, and groaned in order to give you the wisdom I have gathered, and created, on the value of a business. It is my great hope that you will value this wisdom and take it seriously—and have a few laughs along the way. For some of you, it may help turn your lives around and change your retirement from a dreary trial to be endured to a golden age to be enjoyed. I wish you much success in that and pray that this book is a turning point in achieving that for many of you.

—Jay B. Abrams, September 17, 2003

Part One

BUSINESS VALUATION

Part One encompasses the first nine chapters of this book. It is the core of *How to Value Your Business and Increase Its Potential,* being strictly about business valuation.

The first two chapters are nonquantitative and lay the foundation for understanding what value is, the various approaches that one can use in valuing a business, and which approaches are most appropriate for you to use.

You will find in Chapter 2 that the Discounted Cash Flow (DCF) method is the primary recommended valuation method. The DCF method consists of the following steps:

1. Forecast cash flow
2. Discount to present value
3. Adjust the value for the appropriate level of control and marketability

Chapter 3 teaches you how to forecast sales and net income, and Chapter 4 teaches you how to forecast cash flows. Together they comprise a unit that will enable you to forecast cash flow, the first step listed in the DCF method, above.

Chapters 5 and 6 teach you how to discount your cash flows to present value: the second step. Chapter 5 deals with discount rates, present values, and present value factors and will enable you to discount annual cash flows to present value. Chapter 6, the Gordon Model, will enable you to calculate the present value of an infinite stream of cash flows that have constant growth.[1] That is a necessary shortcut to greatly reduce the number of calculations necessary to produce a valuation. For an already mature business, using the Gordon Model can enable you to do a valuation with very few calculations on the back on an envelope.

My Web site, www.abramsvaluation.com, contains valuation spreadsheets that you can download and use to value your business. Chapter 7 describes how to download the spreadsheets and use them. Thus, Chapter 7 is the culmination of the valuation process.

You might have noticed that we "finished the process," but we only covered steps 1 and 2, above. Chapter 8 deals with two main topics: defining the valuation assignment and adjusting the valuation for the control and marketability of your company, or a business interest in your company. The material in defining the valuation assignment will help you think more like a professional business valuator, and much of the purpose of presenting it is to enable you to interface more effectively with a professional when you need one.

The portion of Chapter 8 that focuses on adjusting for control and marketability is the third step of the DCF process. It was the subject of considerable debate as to whether this chapter should have come before or after Chapter 7. I finally chose to place adjustments for control and marketability after the valuation spreadsheet because:

- The magnitude of the combined adjustments for both control and marketability for most 100 percent interests in privately held companies should be small—around 5 percent.[2] Given the inherent inaccuracies of the valuation process, this is not enough of an adjustment to be concerned about. Therefore, for most business owners,

[1]Don't worry if this phrase puts you into a trance. You should understand its meaning after reading Chapter 6.

[2]The adjustments for minority interest are large and outside of the scope of this book.

the numbers from Chapter 7 should be accurate enough for your "quick-and-dirty" valuation needs.

- The actual calculations of the discount for lack of marketability are very complex and technical and are beyond the capabilities of most nonprofessionals. Chapter 8 also contains important strategic recommendations for readers to protect themselves when considering an investment in a private business as a minority owner.[3]

In Chapter 9, I present a valuation formula to value your business as of a future date. Then I analyze the formula to show that there are only a few categories of actions you can take to increase the value of your business. For most readers this should be the most important chapter of the book. Understanding it can change your future. It should clarify why you should manage your business with a "valuation thinking cap." You should be able to analyze any business decision with this framework in mind, i.e., you'll know how your decision will affect the growth rate of sales, profit structure, Payout Ratio[4] and cash flow, growth rate, and business risk.

---

[3]The "minority" status means less than a 50 percent shareholder and has nothing to do with race or gender.

[4]This term is explained in Chapter 4.

Chapter 1

What Is Value?

There are many different concepts and definitions of value, and it is important to understand how to sort through and make sense of them. While the theory and mechanics of measuring value will take several chapters, in this introductory chapter we present different definitions of value, and note how value itself can change with the definition and the context.[1]

There are many reasons why you will want or need to know the value of the stock in your company.[2] First and foremost, readers need to understand how to do a "quick-and-dirty" valuation, in order to manage your business over time to maximize its value and to plan your retirement and exit strategies. However, there are other business and personal life cycle events that can require you to obtain a professional valuation. For example: the imminent sale of your business, either whole or in part;[3]

[1]Unless otherwise noted, all definitions of value in this chapter come from the *International Glossary of Business Valuation Terms.* In subsequent footnotes we will merely indicate the source as *International Glossary*. This glossary may be downloaded from www.bvappraisers.org/glossary.

[2]For ease of expression, we assume a corporate form, although the essential meaning remains the same whatever the form of the business entity.

[3]While a professional appraisal is not mandatory, it is unwise to rely solely on your own valuation skills in the face of an actual sale.

participating in a merger; making an initial public offering; gifting shares of stock to your family; litigation of various types (divorce, shareholder dissolution, business damages, etc.); initiating and maintaining an Employee Stock Option Plan; spinning off a portion of your business; entity restructuring; and other reasons.

The term "value" in and of itself can mean many things in different contexts. *Webster's Dictionary*[4] has two relevant definitions: (1) A fair return or equivalent in goods, services, or money for something exchanged; and (2) the monetary worth of something, i.e., its marketable price.

Both definitions are somewhat general, and we will need to be more specific. Eskimos have dozens of different terms for snow, as it comprises such an important part of their lives—and indeed their lives may depend on the precise understanding of what kind of snow is falling on the tundra. So, too, the valuation profession uses several different terms to describe value. They are called *standards of value*.

Each standard of value has its own unique definition, context, and set of underlying concepts. Many of them have specific legal definitions and contexts in which they apply. It is vital to understand the differences of the various standards of value. Failure to do so can cost you a lot of money. Just as the question of what value is does not have a simple one-dimensional answer in our complex world, how we measure value also has multiple possibilities.

STANDARDS OF VALUE

The *International Glossary of Business Valuation Terms* defines a standard of value as "the indication of the type of value being used in a specific engagement; e.g., Fair Market Value, Fair Value, Investment Value."

A standard of value is a definition of value and a statement of the context in which it applies—whether implicitly or explicitly. While there are perhaps half a dozen standards of value, there are two—*Fair Market Value* and *Investment Value*—that

[4]www.m-w.com/cgi-bin/dictionary.

will apply to virtually all readers, i.e., they apply to the "quick-and-dirty" valuations you all want to do. Typically, the contexts in which the other definitions of value are important are legally determined. They include situations such as shareholder dissolution suits, divorce, other litigation, etc., in which a professional business valuator is needed. These contexts are outside of the main scope of this book. I mention them to accentuate the point that in a legal context, failure to understand and use the appropriate standard of value can be costly and painful.

Fair Market Value

The most common term for value is "Fair Market Value," often shortened to FMV. (Note: You will see the FMV abbreviation frequently throughout the valuation chapters in this book, so it is wise to "burn this into your memory.")

The definition of Fair Market Value is as follows.

> The price, expressed in terms of cash equivalents, at which property would change hands between a hypothetical willing and able buyer and a hypothetical willing and able seller, acting at arm's length in an open and unrestricted market, when neither is under compulsion to buy or sell and when both have reasonable knowledge of the relevant facts.[5]

The term "property" can be a 100 percent interest in the stock of your company—or a partnership interest in a General Partnership or Limited Partnership, or a member interest in a Limited Liability Company—a partial interest in the same, or it can be the assets of your business if you are not selling the legal business entity.

There are two important concepts buried in this definition for you to understand. The first concept is the hypothetical buyer and seller. FMV is measuring the amount that a financial buyer would pay for the firm. It is not specific to any particular buyer's fit with the company. If there are synergies with one or more particular buyers, FMV is less than "Investment Value," defined

[5] *International Glossary.*

later, which includes the synergies. Thus, a more informal definition of FMV could be: "The amount that any buyer would pay for your business."

The second important concept implicit in the definition of FMV is in the term "cash equivalents." Frequently, small businesses are sold with a down payment of approximately 40 to 60 percent of the purchase price, with the seller financing the rest. If the interest rate on the loan is the same rate that a bank would charge the buyer of the business, then the sales price is identical with the "cash equivalent." However, the most common scenario is that the interest rate on the loan from the seller to the buyer is below the market rate that a bank would charge. When this is the case, the "cash equivalent" price is lower than the nominal sales price. Because most small business sales are financed by loans, the sales price for most small businesses most commonly is inflated.

FMV is the legally required standard of value for estate and gift tax valuation reports. It is also required for valuation for income tax purposes and for Employee Stock Ownership Plans.

Investment Value

The definition of Investment Value:

> The value to a particular investor based on individual investment requirements and expectations.[6]

Again, Investment Value takes synergy into consideration. In acquisitions of publicly held businesses, i.e., in the Mergers & Acquisitions (M&A) market, synergies add average premiums of 35 to 65 percent over the minority interest trading price. There are instances of synergies that are much larger. Thus, it is best if you can sell to a strategic buyer who is willing to pay for the synergies. For example, if a financial buyer should be willing to pay $1 million for your company, then a strategic buyer might be willing to pay $1.35 to $1.65 million.

---

[6]*International Glossary.* Note: In Canada the definition is "Value to the Owner."

Fair Value

Fair Value is the standard of value currently used in at least two legal contexts. The first use of Fair Value is that it is the standard of value used in financial statement accounting for publicly traded companies. The Financial Accounting Standards Board (FASB) made its pronouncements of Statement of Financial Accounting Standards 141 and 142 dealing with the original measurement of and possible subsequent impairment to goodwill.[7] The Securities Exchange Commission oversees this aspect of valuation. This is a national standard used throughout the United States. Since this is a very specialized use of this valuation standard, we will not present that definition.

The second context in which Fair Value is the standard of value is in shareholder dissolution suits. When one or more shareholders are suing to dissolve a corporation, Fair Value is the standard of value. Unlike the financial accounting use above, here Fair Value is controlled by the states. There is no uniform definition of Fair Value in this context. It has been interpreted by case law. Generally, Fair Value has been interpreted the same as Fair Market Value, except some states allow a discount for lack of control and other states do not. If you are involved in a shareholder dissolution suit, you will want to make sure your attorney and your business valuator both understand these points and are working with the correct definition of Fair Value for your state.

Other Standards of Value

There are several additional terms for value. Some of them are specific to certain legal contexts and purposes. It is vital to be clear on the operating definition of the type of value relevant to you, since the definition usually has underlying assumptions that can affect the numerical calculations. Frequently, the appropriate definition will determine which valuation discounts or premiums (a concept we will cover later in the book) are permitted in the calculations.

---

[7]SFAS 141 deals with the original measurement of goodwill, and SFAS 142 with testing for possible impairment to the value of goodwill.

For example, in San Diego County, "Marital Value" is the standard of value for valuing the family business in divorce cases. It is virtually the same as Fair Market Value, except that it does not permit a "Discount for Lack of Marketability." Thus, if the family business is located one block inside the border of San Diego County, its "Marital Value" would be 10 to 35 percent more than if it were one block away, outside the county. As you can see, it is imperative to understand and use the appropriate standard of value in any particular valuation context.

CONCLUSION

In this introductory chapter we have said:

- There are several different standards of value.
- The way we measure value depends on the standard of value. Thus, the standard of value actually affects the measurement of value.
- It is vitally important to be clear about the appropriate standard of value, given the reason you need a valuation.

In the next chapter we will explain the different valuation approaches and methods.

Chapter 2

Valuation Approaches: How We Value a Business

A Valuation Approach is "a general way of determining a value indication of a business, using one or more valuation methods."[1] Notice the word "general." In fact, a Valuation Approach is not a specific technique for calculating value. Specific techniques are called *Valuation Methods,* which is defined by the *International Glossary* as "within approaches, a specific way to determine value."

THREE VALUATION APPROACHES

The three Valuation Approaches are:

- Asset Approach
- Income Approach
- Market Approach

Two or more Valuation Methods fall under each Valuation Approach.

The Asset Approach seeks to measure value through the calculation of assets net of liabilities.[2] The Income Approach at-

[1] The full definition from the *International Glossary* is "a general way of determining a value indication of a business, business ownership interest, security, or intangible asset using one or more valuation methods."
[2] The amounts can be either historical or market values.

tempts to measure value by converting a stream of expected economic benefits (net income, cash flow, or dividends) into a present single amount. The Market Approach seeks to measure value by comparison to recent transactions of similar businesses. It is important to understand the strengths and weaknesses of the various different valuation approaches. As for Valuation Methods, when we finish analyzing the three approaches and the various methods in this chapter, I think you'll see why there is only one method—Discounted Cash Flow—that I recommend and teach at length in this book.

The Asset and Income Approaches are based on the Subject Company's financial statements. (The Subject Company is the company we are trying to value. Throughout most of this book, we will assume that we are trying to value your company.) The Market Approach[3] is based on the valuation of similar firms, and not on the Subject Company's financial statements, although it still makes use of financial statement data. Another way of looking at this is that the Asset and Income Approaches are internally focused, while the Market Approach is externally focused.

ORIGINS OF BUSINESS VALUATION

Business valuation developed from real estate valuation. Many more of us are familiar with real estate value than business value because real estate is so tangible, while businesses contain many intangible assets that most of us never think about. These include an assembled and trained work force, a customer list, technical know how, trade secrets, intellectual property, and goodwill—even though it is rare to see any of those assets on the company's balance sheet. Certainly, businesses are far more than their visible bricks, mortar, desks, chairs, and computers.

In real estate, there are the same three valuation approaches we find in business valuation: Cost, Income, and Market.

A simple explanation of the Cost Approach is that it focuses on how much it would cost to replace a house or a building with one that is functionally the same. Or we ask: "How much did

[3] Also known as the Market-Based Approach.

this house or building cost to build?" We adjust that for depreciation, obsolescence, and inflation, but the simple essence is: "How much did and/or will it cost?" That concept in business valuation relates to equity on the balance sheet, which is, more or less, the depreciated costs of the various assets net of liabilities.

In the Income Approach to real estate valuation, the appraiser may perform a Discounted Cash Flow—or, more commonly, a shortcut capitalization of cash flow[4]—to value the property based on its cash flow–producing capacity. This is the fundamental valuation approach that we cover in this book for business valuation. The Income Approach requires that we focus on the income statement and the statement of cash flows.

In the Market Approach in real estate valuation, real estate appraisers find comparable homes or buildings to the subject property. They tabulate how much they sold for, their square footage, lot size, and a host of other independent variables. They develop ratios,[5] make adjustments for differences of the comparable properties to the subject property, and perform their mathematics to calculate the Fair Market Value of the property. In business valuation, the Market Approach involves valuation by comparison to the values of other businesses—public and private. However, the principle of the Market Approach is the same in real estate and business valuation.

ASSET APPROACH

The Asset Approach is "a general way of determining a value indication of a business, business ownership interest, or security using one or more methods based on the value of assets net of liabilities."[6] We will discuss three methods under this ap-

---

[4] The *International Glossary of Business Valuation Terms* defines capitalization as "a conversion of a single period of economic benefits into value." Thus, capitalization of next year's forecast cash flow for an office building or a business involves a mathematical procedure to convert that cash flow into a value. There is normally an underlying assumption of a constant growth rate in the cash flows.

[5] Ideally they should use multiple regression analysis, but I have only known one real estate appraiser who does that.

[6] *International Glossary.*

proach: the Book Value Method, the Adjusted Net Book Value Method, and the Liquidating Balance Sheet Method.

Book Value Method

A *balance sheet* is a listing of the assets, liabilities, and equity of the business. It is possible to use the net book value of equity (a.k.a. "book value") as a measure of Fair Market Value (FMV). This is known as the Book Value Method. However, accounting balance sheets are based on Generally Accepted Accounting Principles (GAAP), such as the principle of conservatism, in which accountants use the lower of historical costs, or "market value," in reporting asset values. This leads to a book value that is conservative, but does not represent Fair Market Value if it is higher than book value. If your company has real estate with a book value of $1 million and a FMV of $30 million, it is obvious that the net book value of the company will be significantly less than its FMV. Thus, using the net book value of equity from your balance sheet is almost never appropriate to calculate FMV. It is surprising how many shareholder buyout agreements specify book value as the agreed-upon buyout value, given how inappropriate it is.

Adjusted Book Value Method

A variation of a balance sheet valuation approach is to substitute the FMV of each asset and liability on the balance sheet to create a "Fair Market Value" balance sheet. Also known as the Adjusted Book Value Method, this is a more serious candidate to be a legitimate valuation approach since it eliminates the unadjusted balance sheet problem of the Book Value Method described above.

Even so, the Fair Market Value Balance Sheet is still not the best primary valuation approach for valuing an operating business. The reason for this is that it's likely to miss valuable intangible assets that are not currently on the balance sheet. Let me give you an example.

In 1984, I valued many radio stations. One of them had an unusual, cost-efficient manner for gathering information to relay traffic conditions. Most radio stations send a helicopter over the city to gather information to report traffic. This particular station, however, had a network of people who would call in on a regular basis and report traffic conditions on "their stretch of road." Every year, the station would provide them with gifts. The cost of these gifts, and of gathering information this way, was many tens of thousands of dollars less per year than the cost of owning, maintaining, and flying a helicopter. The lifetime value of this cost savings was many hundreds of thousands of dollars—perhaps close to $1 million in today's dollars. However, such an unusual intangible asset would never appear on a balance sheet. Thus, even the Fair Market Value balance sheet is not usually good enough to be the primary approach to value an operating company.[7]

Liquidating Balance Sheet

Nevertheless, we still use one variation of the balance sheet approach in every valuation, and that is a Liquidating Balance Sheet. The purpose of this valuation approach is to determine whether the company is worth more "dead or alive." By dead, we mean liquidating the company and turning it into cash. By alive, we mean valuing the business as a going concern. Normally we assume that companies have infinite lives as a going concern, unless there is a specific reason to assume a finite life. The Liquidating Balance Sheet is our valuation of the company "dead," and we compare that to other methods for valuing the firm "alive." If the firm is worth more dead, it means you're better off liquidating the firm, investing the cash that remains after liquidation, and getting a job elsewhere.

To create a Liquidating Balance Sheet, we restate all the assets and liabilities to their net realizable value if the company were to liquidate. In doing so, it is necessary to add a liability to the Liquidating Balance Sheet to measure the cost of performing the liquidation itself. The company will still have to pay one or more employees to liquidate the company and wind up

---

[7] The balance sheet is often the best approach to value a holding company, i.e., a firm that owns either other companies or real estate, where the business valuator is either supplied with the FMVs of the other assets or uses other approaches to value them.

its affairs, and frequently there can be costs to buy out of the company's lease. Additionally, there are typically legal and accounting costs of liquidation. (See Table 2.2 in the appendix to this chapter for an example of a Liquidating Balance Sheet.)

INCOME APPROACH

The Income Approach—also known as the Income-Based Approach—is "a general way of determining a value indication of a business, business ownership interest, security, or intangible assets using one or more methods that convert anticipated economic benefits into a present single amount."[8]

This is the single best valuation approach. It's far superior to using the balance sheet to value an operating company as a going concern, because it is logical that investors are willing to pay for anticipated income or cash flows. If a company has significant value in its intangible assets—even assets that do not appear on the balance sheet—the Income Approach, properly performed, will incorporate the value of those assets. It does so because those intangible assets have value to the extent that they produce net income and cash flow, which the Income Approach includes in its valuation calculations, while the Asset Approach is likely to miss that component of value and undervalue the firm.

There are three different valuation methods under the general category of the Income Approach: Discounted Future Dividends, Discounted Cash Flow, and Discounted Future Net Income. In all three, we forecast future returns (profits, dividends, or cash flow) and adjust the returns for perceived risk and the time value of money. This adjustment is called *discounting,* which I will explain in detail in Chapter 4.

All three of these methods measure income in a different way, and there are advantages and disadvantages to each.

Discounted Future Dividends

Also known as DFD, this method of valuation only considers the cash distributions to owners. It ignores cash held by a business

---

[8] *International Glossary.*

that could be dispersed to its owners but is not. The DFD method measures the cash flows at the individual owner level. Therefore, it is mostly applicable for minority ownership interests. Valuing such interests are very complex and in the domain of the professional valuator, and therefore we won't focus on this method. In addition, most private firms do not payout dividends, so the DFD method is not applicable when valuing the whole firm.

This method could work well for a business that distributes all or at least most of its income, like Real Estate Investment Trusts (REITs), which by law must pay virtually all of their earnings in dividends. However, businesses that pay little or no dividends are usually undervalued using DFD. For example, Microsoft Corporation pays no annual dividend, but it has a market capitalization of approximately $250 billion.

Discounted Cash Flow and Discounted Future Net Income

The DCF and DFNI methods are the same techniques applied to different measures of future economic benefits. The DCF forecasts future cash flows and discounts them to present value. The DFNI forecasts net income and discounts that to present value. Thus, we can narrow the question of which method is superior down to which measure of future economic benefits is superior: cash flow or net income.

Here are the reasons cash flow is superior:

1. As we will discuss in detail in Chapter 4, cash flow includes net income, but net income does not include cash flow. Thus, cash flow is a more complete measure.
2. In simple down-to-earth language, you cannot pay your bills with net income, and you cannot deposit net income in your bank account. Therefore, cash is king in business, and it is universally recognized in finance that cash flow is the best basis from which to measure value.
3. The rates of return that professional business valuators use, and that you will use, are calculated based

on publicly traded firms, and those are based on cash flows, not net income.[9] There are no known rates of return based on net income. Thus, it is internally consistent to discount cash flows with these discount rates, and it is inconsistent to use the discount rates to discount net income.

4. As you will see in the story of "Leonardo Meets the Snakeman," below, net income actually can be harmful, whereas cash flow is always beneficial.

There is one disadvantage of discounting cash flow: Forecasting cash flow requires the extra step of multiplying our forecast of net income by a percentage called the Payout Ratio, and calculating the Payout Ratio can be very involved for professionals. As a result, many business valuators "cheat" and use DFNI on some assignments. But the DFNI is a flawed shortcut that almost always leads to mistakes and should not be used. It trades the convenience of sweeping the conversion of net income to cash flow under the rug for the disadvantages that come with it.[10] Since this book is not for professional business valuators, I teach a reasonable shortcut that one can use in estimating the Payout Ratio.

The following is a true story that dramatically demonstrates the superiority of cash flow over net income. The names and a couple of minor factual details are changed to protect the innocent and the guilty—or is that the good, the bad, and the ugly?

Leonardo Meets the Snakeman

My friend Leonardo opened a business with a partner, Victor Snakeman. They both worked in the business

---

[9] See Chapter 5 for further explanation.

[10] It hides the assumption of the Payout Ratio, which is the percentage of income available to be paid out to the business owners as cash distributions. If the Payout Ratio is less than 100 percent and the valuator has not adjusted the discount rates, then he or she has just overvalued the company, because discount rates (a topic we will cover in Chapter 5) are calculated based on cash flows of publicly traded stocks. They are not based on net income.

full-time. Victor Snakeman was the moneyman, so they were 75-25 percent shareholders in an S corporation.[11]

After 10 years, Leonardo was taking home about $130,000 a year, plus he was due a substantial amount of profit sharing that was to be distributed "when there was plenty of money." Leonardo was on top of the world—at least as viewed from Australia. Then he walked into work one day, and Snakeman fired him, changed the locks, and booted him out.

They spent two years in lawsuits. Leonardo lost. The judge said it was legal for Snakeman to fire him. His reason for doing so was that income was down and that he couldn't afford Leonardo. Interestingly, the year after Leonardo was fired was the best year the company ever had, with net income of $1 million.

To add insult to injury, Snakeman paid out cash dividends of $5000—probably the minimum amount necessary to make it look like he was not blatantly trying to wreak his revenge on Leonardo, since there was still other litigation pending. In the meantime, Leonardo owed taxes of $25,000 on the net income.

Snakeman was sitting pretty. His salary covered his living needs and his taxes, so he was able to make the corporation show the maximum net income possible, generating the maximum possible tax liability for Leonardo, who had $5000 to pay $25,000 of income taxes. Obviously, Leonardo was not sitting pretty. He was facing imminent bankruptcy, due to a combination of the taxes, litigation costs, and his other living expenses.

Leonardo was eventually compelled to make an unfavorable deal to stave off bankruptcy. He received far less for his stock than the Fair Market Value, which I had calculated on his behalf. Of course, that transaction was not taking place at FMV, since the definition of Fair Market Value says that the buyer and seller are acting

[11] An S corporation is taxed primarily like a partnership. There is no corporate tax. The net income flows through to the shareholders, who are responsible for personal taxes.

> at arm's length. That implies that the buyer is not pummeling the seller with brass knuckles while his henchman has him locked in a half nelson.[12]

This story illustrates two principles. The first principle—and the one we're concerned with in this chapter—is that cash is king.[13] If the company had been a C corporation instead, Leonardo only would have been responsible for personal income taxes on dividends paid to him. Then he would have been fine, even though the C corporation arguably would be worth less than the S corporation to the collective ownership, because of corporate taxes.[14] Or, if Victor Snakeman were a nicer guy, Leonardo never would have been dispelled of his illusion that he was on top of the world.

It should be obvious, from this story, that cash flow is more important than net income. It turns out that net income is the most important component of cash flow, and it is the starting point in our calculation of cash flow. The reverse is not true. Cash flow is not a component of net income.

What's less obvious from the story, but no less important, is that in extreme circumstances, net income in the absence of cash flow actually can be harmful to a business owner.

MORE ON DISCOUNTED CASH FLOW

The advantages to the DCF method are straightforward. Logically, investors should be willing to pay more for a business with higher expected cash flows than one with lower expected cash flows, all other things being equal. Also, investors should be willing to pay more for a business with less risk associated with achieving the forecast cash flows compared to a firm with the same expected cash flows but with higher risk.

In general terms, performing a DCF involves the following four steps:

---

[12] Where was Willie when we needed him? Probably singing, "Suddenly, I'm not half the man I used to be," with apologies to the Beatles.

[13] This story illustrates a second principle, which comes later in the book, and that is the need for a discount for lack of control, a.k.a., the minority interest discount.

[14] This is a source of considerable controversy in the valuation profession and will be the subject of research for years to come.

1. Forecast cash flows.
2. Discount cash flows to present value. This is the essential valuation arithmetic.
3. Adjust for the level of control, i.e., a control interest or a minority interest.
4. Adjust for the level of marketability.

The first two steps—forecasting cash flows and discounting them to present value—are fundamental and primary in valuing your business. In fact, the size of cash flows is the primary determinant of value. Chapter 3 focuses on forecasting net income, and in Chapter 4 we will define and analyze cash flow and explain why it is so fundamental to valuation. In Chapter 5, we will discuss discounting cash flows to present value. The valuation adjustments in the final two steps, above, are part of the "fine-tuning" of the valuation and will be discussed in Chapter 8.

For those readers who like to ponder the unity of the universe, notice that the Liquidating Balance Sheet is also in its essence a Discounted Cash Flow Method. The difference is the underlying assumption of whether the business is more valuable dead or alive. With the Liquidating Balance Sheet, we are valuing the business "dead" by assuming we liquidate it and turn it into cash. The cash flow happens nearly immediately—usually over a three- to six-month period. Indeed, we may even discount the liquidating cash flows to present value and use that valuation for different assets and liabilities on the Liquidating Balance Sheet, depending on how long it takes to liquidate.

For example, suppose we estimate that it will take one month to liquidate inventory and three months to liquidate machinery and equipment, and that each one has the same net realizable value of $300,000. While it is too early in this book to have developed the financial theory to explain the present value calculations, please take it on faith at the moment that the present value of the inventory is $295,476, while the present value of the machinery and equipment is $286,633.[15] Intuitively, it

[15] That is assuming a 20 percent discount rate. In Chapter 4 we cover how to calculate present value.

makes sense that even though we expect to receive the same nominal amount of cash for both assets, it's the inventory that's more valuable. This is because we expect to receive the cash for inventory two months earlier than the cash we expect to receive for the equipment, and we can invest the $300,000 cash from the inventory for two months—which we will not be able to do for the equipment. Thus, at the end of three months, we should have $300,000 for the equipment, but more than that for the inventory.

In other words, the curtain that separates the Liquidating Balance Sheet and the Discounted Cash Flow is much thinner and more transparent than one would have first thought.

Hybrid Method: Excess Earnings

The Excess Earnings Method is a hybrid valuation method using the income statement and the balance sheet. It is an inferior method and generally should not be used.[16] However, because it is somewhat mechanical and relatively simple, it frequently is used, and it's even unofficially required in valuation for property settlement in divorce proceedings in some jurisdictions.

We will only briefly go into this method, but it's important to know that it suffers from theoretical and empirical problems that can produce serious distortions of value if handled improperly, and even if handled properly for high-growth firms! For small, low-growth firms, its weaknesses matter much less. It is not a tool for a business owner; but be forewarned: If you are involved in a divorce proceeding and the company being valued is a high-growth firm, it's extremely important to have a top-notch business valuator. Too many small practitioners do not fully understand the limitations and the distortions in valuation that this method can produce.

The Excess Earnings Method involves calculating a "normal" return on tangible assets, then calculating "excess returns" by subtracting the required return on tangible assets from net

[16] It requires two discount rates instead of one, and generally neither of them are empirically observable.

income. The excess returns are attributable to the presence of intangible assets. One would then value the intangible assets by dividing the excess returns by a rate of return between 20 and 100 percent. That means multiples of one to five of excess returns.

For example, if excess returns are $100,000, then the Excess Earnings Method calculation of the intangible asset component of value would be between $100,000 and $500,000 ($100,000/20% = $500,000, and $100,000/100% = $100,000). That is a huge range of multiples, and there is no empirical evidence of what it should be, since we can only see stock market returns on entire equity interests in publicly traded companies; we do not get to see the return on intangible assets. Finally, we add the value of the intangible assets to the book value of tangible assets to compute the value of the business using the Excess Earnings Method.

In a divorce, the "in-spouse's" (spouse who owns the business) valuator may be tempted to use the highest possible rate in order to lower the indication of value (however defined)—thus having to pay less in a property settlement—while the "out-spouse's" valuator may be tempted to do the opposite. Less sophisticated valuators rarely have the know-how to demonstrate that the weighted average cost of capital implied by the final product may be empirically inconsistent with historical market returns. If it is a small business, the distortion may not be too material. The larger the business and the higher its forecast growth rate, the more important it is to have a sophisticated valuator.

The reason some courts[17] love the Excess Earnings Method and dislike the Discounted Cash Flow is that former makes no use of forecasts. It is a mechanical extension of the past. This eliminates haggling over what is likely to occur in the future, and overworked judges relish the opportunity to reduce the grounds for argument and abuse. It is easy to abuse the process by using unrealistically optimistic or pessimistic sales forecasts, and it's clear why judges would prefer not to have to sort through technical arguments when each side has its own agenda. In the

[17] Some divorce courts in particular are known for this.

real world, it is our perception of the future that drives value, and sweeping that under the rug is convenient, but it's not the most accurate valuation method.

MARKET APPROACH

The definition of the Market Approach—also known as the Market Comparison Approach or "Comparable Companies"—is "A general way of determining a value indication of a business, business ownership interest, security, or intangible asset by using one or more methods that compare the subject to similar businesses, business ownership interests, securities, or intangible assets that have been sold."[18] Under the Market Approach, the most common methods are those of Guideline Companies. There are two types of Guideline Companies: publicly held and privately held.

We will spend relatively little space in this book on the Market Approach, as it has theoretical and practical problems that render it impractical for most business owners. However, due to its popularity, I will discuss it briefly, and I provide an example of the Guideline Public Company Method in the appendix to this chapter.

Guideline Public Company Method

The definition of the Guideline Public Company Method (which we'll shorten to GPCM, for convenience) is "A method within the Market Approach whereby market multiples are derived from market prices of stocks of companies that are engaged in the same or similar lines of business, and that are actively traded on a free and open market."[19] The GPCM works well when the following conditions exist:

1. The subject company being valued is relatively the same size as the Guideline Companies. I would feel uncomfortable if the Guideline Companies are more

---

[18] *International Glossary.*
[19] *International Glossary.*

than triple the size of the subject company, although some professionals feel comfortable with an average size that is 10 times the subject company.[20]

2. There are many Guideline Companies in the same industry as the subject company. The more the better. Statistically, there is a huge difference between having three or four versus even seven or eight.
3. There is data on historical and/or forecast growth (forecast is more important) on the Guideline Companies.
4. The multiples are either very consistent (meaning they do not vary in magnitude by much) or their variations can be explained by known factors such as different forecast growth rates.

The less these conditions are met, the less reliable the GPCM will be. It is ridiculous and dangerous to use public company multiples, which are typically in the 15 to 33 range for Price Earnings (PE) multiples, on small, private companies, which normally should have PE multiples in the 2 to 6 range unless they are expected to be very high growth firms. Also, remember that the stock of publicly traded firms is almost instantly marketable—you can sell today and receive cash in three days—while ownership of a private firm is very illiquid and requires a discount for lack of marketability to put it on a level playing field with ownership of publicly traded securities.

Guideline Private Company Method

This is mechanically identical to the Guideline Public Company Method except the nature and cost of the data that are avail-

[20] There are mathematically sophisticated ways that may be able to control for differences in size, but they are complex and beyond the scope of this book. See Jay B. Abrams, *Quantitative Business Valuation: A Mathematical Approach for Today's Professionals*, New York: McGraw-Hill, 2001, 46–52. Even so, these methods do not always work. In regression analysis, I prefer that the guideline companies be within the range of one-half to twice the size of each other and the Subject Company, because of heteroscedasticity—correlation of the valuation errors to the size of the guideline companies.

able and the level of value of the Fair Market Value calculations are different.[21]

Individual private companies do not have the benefit of being tracked by millions of investors. Suppose your company is Vaporware, Inc., a software developer. There are no stock analysts tracking it. The Securities Exchange Commission has no jurisdiction over it, and its financial statements do not have to be audited and are not subject to SEC regulation.

There are a few private databases that record sales of private businesses. They cost money to obtain, and I don't think they're worthwhile for "quick-and-dirty" valuation purposes. If you have a legal reason to need a valuation, you'll probably have a professional business valuator working for you, and he or she will have access to at least one of the private transactional databases. I am not much of a fan of any of them, except for valuing very common, prosaic businesses like restaurants. There is usually too much data that is not present—especially historical and forecast growth—for them to be useful to me as a professional. Other professionals disagree. For those of you who are interested in the business databases, you can see their Web sites at www.bizcomps.com, www.instbusapp.org/, and www.bvresources.com/. The latter Web site sells several private databases and offers a single-inquiry option at a fraction of the annual subscription price.

If you do use a private database, you would perform the calculations in the same way as in Table A2.1, the Public Company Method sampled in the appendix to this chapter. The major difference is that private databases at least theoretically provide much more of an apples-to-apples comparison than public databases. Vaporware is actually a mid-size business, not a small business. If it had sales of $750,000 instead of $7.5 million, it would be the same size as the majority of the transactions in the Institute of Business Appraisers' database. The firms in the database have more resemblance to most private

---

[21] The level of value is a concept we will present later in the book. It is part of the fine-tuning of the valuation, and it deals with the level of control and marketability of the business interest being valued. It is not part of getting us in the right ballpark of value to begin with.

firms than publicly held firms, and the multiples are more reasonable for application to private firms. The sales are of 100 percent interests in illiquid, privately held businesses—most likely just like yours. In contrast, the multiples of the publicly held firms are highly liquid minority interests in huge firms with lots of resources that most privately held firms could only dream of.

However, my disappointing experience is that for most types of businesses, these transactional databases are still too small, and consequently they have too few transactions per SIC (Standard Industrial Classification) code to be of significant help in the valuation process. Of course, there are exceptions, but they are exceptions, not the rule. There are further comments about the disadvantages of this valuation method in the next section.

Rules of Thumb

Rules of thumb are ad-hoc valuation rules, the sources of which are almost always unknown. Examples of rules of thumb that I've heard "on the street" (I always picture some 350-pound guy in a trench coat, chomping on a cigar, and telling me this in a Brooklyn accent)[22] are: "The business is worth one and a half times gross." Or, "It's worth three times net plus inventory." Continuing the "thumb" metaphor, I like to think of rules of thumb as "valuation hitchhiking," with results being about as safe and reliable as hitchhiking across the country in the year 2004. Just make sure your thumbs are still attached after you've used one of the rules of thumb. And, of course, you're likely to have two left thumbs in using a rule of thumb, and you are likely to get nailed!

More seriously, if you hear of a rule of thumb for your industry, use it as a sanity check on the results from a Discounted Cash Flow valuation. It is not meant to be a primary valuation method. The reasons for that are (1) It has no basis in financial theory, and (2) it implicitly relies on averages, e.g., average profit

[22] How's that for being politically incorrect? Actually, my wife is from Brooklyn, and she looks good in a trench coat. However, she is nowhere near 350 pounds, and she gave up cigars years ago.

margins in an industry—and to the extent that the subject company will vary from the average, the valuation will be inaccurate.

DANGERS OF THE MARKET APPROACH

There are several dangers in using the Market Approach. The first one is that businesses are more diverse than homes, or even office buildings, and thus the comparability of businesses is weaker than real estate. Homes and office buildings all do the same thing, even if one is a little nicer than the other.

Also, there are hundreds or thousands of homes and office buildings in the area of almost any real estate that one might want to value. Usually, dozens of them have sold in the past six months, and their selling prices and other important data are easily available. That is not true of businesses. The number of transactions in most of the transactional databases of privately held firms is in the low thousands. To my knowledge, the Institute of Business Appraisers has the largest private transactional database, and it numbers less than 20,000 transactions over 20 years throughout the United States. Remember, that covers hundreds of Standard Industrial Classification (SIC) codes. My experience is, if I'm valuing restaurants, there are hundreds of guideline transactions, although far fewer that are local and recent; but if I'm valuing a distributor of airplane parts, there are perhaps three—and none of them are local. So, there are very few truly comparable transactions in business valuation.

Using the Guideline Private Company Method, my typical experience has been to find three or four companies in SIC codes that are reasonably similar to any client. One has net losses, which makes a PE multiple impossible to use. The other three have PE ratios of 2, 7, and 35.[23] What is one supposed to do with that? Some valuators grit their teeth and average it, some delete the outliers and average the remaining Guideline Company observations. I trust my DCF far more than three highly

---

[23] Large Price Earnings multiples generally arise for one reason—the market expects high growth from the firm. However, that can happen for positive reasons when the company is doing well and is expected to do even better, or it can happen for the negative reason that it was barely profitable. In the latter case, its earnings base is very small, which pushes the PE multiple high. This is by far the more likely explanation of high PE multiples in private firms.

disparate business sales. More often than not, I either discard the GPCM, or I weight it perhaps 5 or 10 percent, at most, in the final calculation and conclusion of Fair Market Value. When the private databases contain 100,000 transactions, including historical and forecast growth for the firms sold, then I will become more enthusiastic about that valuation method.

The second danger of the Market Approach is in using guideline companies—public or private—that are substantially different than the subject company. They can be different in industry, market niche, size, expected growth, and risk (later you will see that size is an important component of risk). As mentioned previously, if the Guideline Companies are significantly different in size than the subject company, then the answer is likely to be very wrong in the absence of sophisticated adjustments that are beyond the scope of this book.

In real life there can also be vast differences in risk and growth rates for companies of similar size. For example, consider two biotechnology companies of a comparable size to public biotech firms. Mechanically using the GPCM, they would be treated the same. But the reality may be that one of them has five blockbuster drugs almost finishing FDA approval, while the other has only two not very exciting drugs close to FDA approval. In this case, using average multiples in the GPCM would grossly undervalue the company with five blockbusters waiting to hit the market and grossly overvalue the company with the two so-so drugs about to enter the market, because mechanically using average multiples is tantamount to assuming that we should apply the industry average growth to the subject company being valued.

Failing to adjust for differences in risk can also lead to incorrect valuations. Suppose that one of the companies is facing a huge lawsuit and the other is free of such problems. Mechanically applying average multiples usually will lead to wrong valuations. However, detailed research of the Guideline Companies to understand if company-specific adjustments are appropriate is a significant task that is time consuming, expensive, and may not be worth the effort, depending on the situation. Additional accuracy comes with a cost, and it is wise to weigh the probable costs and benefits before embarking on any additional research.

The third danger in the Market Approach is that it may well be a case of the blind leading the blind. If you're using guideline sales where people made bad deals or especially good deals, you may get an unrealistic picture of the amount for which you can sell your business.

Think back to the dot-com boom and bust. The dot-com company valuations were astronomical, but almost none of them had positive earnings. So, there was no PE multiple, no price-to–cash flow multiple, etc. Valuators were using exotic multiples like price-to-R&D, price-to–star scientists, and perhaps even price-to–employee parking spaces multiples. (That last one was just sarcastic humor—don't take it literally.) Valuators were straining to learn Real Options Pricing to explain the higher values that Discounted Cash Flow could not explain, and in the end the market was wrong. At the heart of it, the Internet was a new phenomenon, and there was a great deal of uncertainty as to how much companies could make selling over it and providing Internet services. The entire process was externally driven. Once people lost sight of the present value of forecast cash flows, there were no limits on value—until reality set in and all of a sudden there were limits. That illustrates the danger of an externally focused valuation approach.

CONCLUSION

In this chapter we have examined and explained the following:

- The three valuation approaches.
- That methods are specific techniques under an approach.
- Why Discounted Cash Flow is the best single method.
- The Guideline Company Methods valuation.
- The Liquidation Balance Sheet Method valuation.
- The dangers of the Market Approach.

Now that we've concluded the nonquantitative introduction to the topic of valuing businesses, as explained in the first two chapters, we will discuss forecasting net income. From there, in Chapter 4, we'll go on to converting our forecast net income to forecast cash flow, which is a precursor to performing a Discounted Cash Flow method valuation.

Appendix to Chapter 2

In this appendix, we present sample calculations, with accompanying tables, for two Valuation Methods we discussed in Chapter 2: the Guideline Public Company Method valuation and the Liquidating Balance Sheet Method.

GUIDELINE PUBLIC COMPANY METHOD

Suppose your company is Vaporware, Inc., a software developer. We would begin to implement the Guideline Public Company Method by doing a search of publicly held software developers and find those that most closely match your business. Since their market capitalization—price per share times the number of shares outstanding—is their Fair Market Value, we could then develop mathematical relationships between their FMVs and various important measures of economic power that can translate into value: gross sales, net income after tax (earnings), cash flow, earnings before interest and taxes (EBIT); earnings before interest, taxes, depreciation, and amortization (EBITDA); book equity, the market value of invested capital (MVIC), etc. The most commonly known resulting ratio is the Price Earnings (PE) multiple.

Table A2.1 is a very simple example of using a Guideline Public Company Method. Suppose we find five guideline com-

	A	B	C	D	E	F	G	H
1	**TABLE A 2.1**							
2	Sample Guideline Public Company Method							
3								
4	**Step 1: Develop Valuation Ratios**							
5								
6								
7			**Independent Variables**			**Valuation Ratios**		
8		**Mkt Cap = FMV = P**	**Sales**	**Net Income**	**Book Value**	**P/S**	**PE**	**P/BV**
9	Guideline Company #1	$15,000,000	$20,000,000	$1,000,000	$12,500,000	0.750	15.000	1.200
10	Guideline Company #2	$30,000,000	$40,000,000	$3,000,000	$15,000,000	0.750	10.000	2.000
11	Guideline Company #3	$45,000,000	$30,000,000	$3,000,000	$36,000,000	1.500	15.000	1.250
12	Guideline Company #4	$10,000,000	$18,750,000	$750,000	$5,714,286	0.533	13. 333	1.750
13	Guideline Company #5	$36,000,000	$75,000,000	$2,500,000	$17,142,857	0.480	14.400	2.100
14	Average	**$27,200,000**	**$36,750,000**	**$2,050,000**	**$17,271,429**	**0.803**	**13.547**	**1.660**
15								

	A	B	C	D	E	F	G	H
16	**Step 2: Application to Subject Company**							
17								
18		**Subject Company**	**Avg Ratio**	**Indication of FMV**	**Weighting [1]**	**Wtd FMV**		
19	Sales	$7,500,000	0.803	$6,020,000	0.25	$1,505,000		
20	Net Income	$700,000	13.547	$9,482,667	0.50	$4,741,333		
21	Book Value	$4,000,000	1.660	$6,640,000	0.25	$1,660,000		
22	**FMV**					**$7,906,333**		
23	**FMV-Rounded**					**$7,906,000**		
24								
25	[1] This is subjective, based on judgment							

panies that we feel are very similar to Vaporware, Inc. Since these are software developers, the different companies could be well-known names such as Microsoft, or they could be lesser known names. Since Vaporware has sales of $7.5 million, Microsoft is too large to be an appropriate Guideline Company. Instead, we use data from firms in the same size category as Vaporware, as measured by sales and book value.

The above table contains two sections. In the first section, Step 1, we develop the valuation ratios, and in the second, Step 2, we apply the average valuation ratios (in real life we frequently make adjustments to the ratios, so we are often not using unadjusted averages) to Vaporware, Inc. We begin with the data on the first Guideline Company (GC), i.e., GC 1, which has a market capitalization of $15 million (cell B9), sales of $20 million (C9), net income after taxes of $1 million (D9), and net book value of $12.5 million (E9).

Next we develop the valuation multiples. The market capitalization is the FMV of the firm, which we denote as P, for price. We divide the $15 million FMV for GC 1 by its sales of $20 million to calculate a Price-to-Sales multiple (P/S) of 0.750 (F9). Similarly, we divide the FMV by net income and book value to calculate the Price-to-Earnings (PE) multiple of 15.000 (G9) and the Price-to-Book Value multiple (P/BV) of 1.200 (H9). Then we repeat the calculations for the rest of the Guideline Companies in rows 10 through 13.

Row 14 shows the averages for all of the raw data and calculated ratios. Let's focus on column F. The high Price-to-Sales ratio is 1.500 (F11), while the low is 0.480 (F13), which is less than one-third of the high P/S ratio. It is fairly common to find a wide dispersion in ratios, which is one reason why there may be a lot of inaccuracy in using this method.

In any case, let's proceed with the valuation in Step 2. In B19 through B21 we list Vaporware's sales, net income, and book value, respectively. In C19 through C21 we list the average valuation ratios from F14, G14, and H14. We then multiply column B times column C to calculate each variable's "Indication of Fair Market Value." An indication of FMV is not necessarily our conclusion of FMV. It is merely the calculation of FMV using one valuation ratio or one valuation method. Using the Price-to-Sales ratio, we multiple Vaporware's sales of $7.5 million (B19) times the average P/S ratio of 0.803 (C19, transferred from F14) to calculate an indication of FMV of $6,020,000 (D19). We then repeat the same procedure with Vaporware's net income and book value in rows 20 and 21, which result in indications of FMV of $9,482,667 (D20) and $6,640,000 (D21).[1]

Which is the "right" Fair Market Value? The truth is, none of them will ever be exact, since valuation is almost always imprecise. We are financial analysts—whether professional or amateur—dealing with incomplete and sometimes conflicting information that is changing and evolving over time.

However, even though it will never be divine truth, we still have to do our best to calculate FMV. Suppose we subjectively decide—based on education, training, experience, and judgment—that we feel net income is the most important measure, and the sales and book value are less important. We might select weights of 25 percent for sales and book value (E19 and E21) and 50 percent (E20) for net income. We then multiply the indication of FMV in column D by the weighting in column E to calculate the weighted (indication of) FMV in column F. Thus, $6,020,000 × 0.25 = $1,505,000 (D19 × E19 = F19). Similarly, we do the same procedure in rows 20 and 21. Finally, we add F19 + F20 + F21 = $7,906,333 (F22).

This is an example of calculating the indication of FMV using the Guideline Public Company Method. To finish off the valuation, we would proceed to calculate the indication of FMV for each method we use, decide on a weighting among methods, and calculate the weighted average of those in order to calculate the our actual opinion of Fair Market Value.[2] It is also appropriate to round off the answer to the nearest $1000 or even $10,000, since it's ridiculous to pretend that valuation of an operating

[1] A multiple regression analysis incorporating these independent variables and forecast growth would be a more sophisticated and accurate means of applying this approach, but that is beyond the scope of this book.

[2] This is very simplified. Professionals would need to adjust for the level of control and marketability of the interest being valued—topics we will address later in the book.

business is so precise that we present our final answer to the nearest dollar. Thus, we round to \$7,906,000 (F23), but it would be entirely reasonable to round to \$7,900,000—and even possibly to \$8 million.

LIQUIDATING BALANCE SHEET METHOD

Liquidation valuation is a method that is necessary to use in all valuations to determine whether the company is worth more dead or alive. Below, in Table A2.2, column B shows book values. In column C, we estimate the percentage of book value that we forecast will be realized in liquidation. It is possible that percentage can be over 100%—especially for real estate and marketable securities, which are the most common assets that appreciate. However, most assets realize less than their book value in liquidation. Column D is the liquidation value and equals column B × column C.

	A	B	C	D
1	**TABLE A2.2**			
2	Sample Liquidation Valuation			
3				
4		**Book**	**Percent**	**Liquidation**
5		**Value**	**Realized**	**Value**
6	Cash	30,000	100%	30,000
7	Accounts Receivable	1,500,000	80%	1,200,000
8	Inventory	7,000,000	50%	3,500,000
9	Prepaid Expenses	50,000	50%	25,000
10	Property, Plant & Equipment	2,000,000	25%	500,000
11	Leasehold Improvements	150,000	0%	0
12	Total Assets	**10,730,000**	NA	**5,255,000**
13	Liabilities	300,000	100%	300,000
14	Cost to Liquidate [1]	0		100,000
15	Capital	10,430,000	NA	**4,855,000**
16	Total Liabilities & Capital	**10,730,000**	NA	NA
17				
18	[1] Assume 1/2 Year * Salary of \$100,000 = \$50,000 + expenses of			
19	\$50,000 = \$100,000.			

Usually, the more liquid is the asset, the higher the percentage realized. The liquidation value of cash is always 100 percent (C6). It is common for receivables to lose some value in liquidation, since some customers who know the company is going out of business will take unfair advantage and not pay their bills. This is a subjective estimate, as are almost all of the items in column C. Note that leasehold improvements rarely have any liquidation value—hence the zero percent (C11).

The book value of Total Assets in our sample liquidation is $10,730,000 (B12), while we have estimated liquidation value of Total Assets to be $5,255,000 (D12). Liabilities typically carry their book value through, as the company or its owner must still pay what it owes. If the company has a large loan at interest rates that are substantially different than current market rates, then the market value of the liability may be materially different than its remaining principal. To value such debt, you will need to read Chapter 4 and perform a Discounted Cash Flow calculation on it.

It is necessary to estimate liquidation costs. An orderly liquidation takes more time than a "fire sale." The liquidator's time is an opportunity cost, as are out-of-pocket expenses. He or she could just abandon the business or do a fire sale and begin working elsewhere immediately. In this example, we assume the owner will spend six months to liquidate the business. If the appropriate arm's length salary is $100,000 per year, a six-month effort costs $50,000 and is an economic liability of the business. We further assume it will cost $50,000 in out-of-pocket costs to liquidate the firm, for a total of $100,000 (D14). The total liquidation value liabilities are $400,000 (D13 + D14). Subtracting that from assets of $5,255,000 (D12) leaves liquidation value capital of $4,855,000 (D15).

The next step is to compare the value of the business dead and alive. It is worth $4,855,000 dead (Table A2.2, D15) and $7,906,000 alive (Table A2.1, F23). Thus, the live value dominates, i.e., Vaporware is worth more as a going concern than it is in liquidation. This is true even though the book value of equity, $10,430,000 (Table A2.2, B15) is higher than the Guideline Public Company Method valuation.

If the opposite would have been true, i.e., that its liquidation value were higher than the Income Approach, then the ownership should liquidate the firm, and liquidation value would dominate if we are valuing a control interest. If we're valuing a minority interest, it does not have the power to force the liquidation of the firm, and the valuation can get complicated, since then the valuation will depend on our assessment of the intentions of the control shareholder. That is better left to a professional appraiser.

Chapter 3

Forecasting Sales and Economic Net Income

In the last chapter we established that the Discounted Cash Flow Method is the single best valuation method. The DCF Method contains three steps: (1) forecasting sales and economic net income, (2) transforming forecast economic net income into forecast cash flow, and (3) discounting forecast cash flow to present value. In this chapter we will discuss the first of these three steps, and we'll go into the others in Chapters 4 and 5, respectively.

It is critical to understand that in business valuation the past in and of itself is completely irrelevant. Only the present and the future matter. That being said, however, the past is usually the best guide to forecast the future.

To begin the process of forecasting economic net income:

1. Analyze historical sales growth—annual and average growth rates.[1] Select appropriate growth rates to forecast the future. (For an example of this, see Table 3.1.)
2. Analyze historical income statements and make adjustments to economic net income. Calculate average

[1] More mathematically sophisticated readers may also want to analyze compound growth rates. We have not included compound growth rates in the text, due to their complexity.

and weighted average economic profit margins. Analyze the time pattern of the margins, and select the appropriate margin(s) to forecast the future. (For an example of this, see Table 3.2.)

Then you can forecast sales and economic net income. (After examining and analyzing the abovementioned tables, we will see the forecasting in Table 3.3).

HISTORICAL SALES GROWTH

The easiest way to illustrate the historical analysis of sales and sales growth is by example. Let's take the (obviously) fictitious Billabong Boomerang company, a manufacturing firm. It is a C corporation, and we will assume a 40 percent corporate income tax rate.

Table 3.1 shows the company's historical sales and annual growth for the past five years. In valuation, it is normally best to have at least five years of historical financial statements for analysis, and more years is generally better. However, there is the danger of older results becoming increasingly "stale," i.e., conditions may change, and using data that is too old may weaken the forecast rather than strengthen it. This is a matter of judgment.

Sales, which appear in row 6, rose from $10 million in 1998 to $13 million in 2002. Row 7 shows the annual sales growth.

	A	B	C	D	E	F	G
1	**TABLE 3.1**						
2	Billabong Boomerangs						
3	Historical Sales Growth						
4							
5		**1998**	**1999**	**2000**	**2001**	**2002**	**Avg**
6	Total Sales	10,000,000	9,820,000	11,150,000	12,200,000	13,000,000	
7	Annual Sales Growth		−1.8%	13.5%	9.4%	6.6%	**6.9%**
8							
9	**Spreadsheet Formulas:**						
10	Cell C7: =(C6/B6)-1						

In 1999, sales declined by 1.8 percent (C7). The average sales growth for 1998-2002 was 6.9 percent (G7), or approximately 7 percent per year. Growth in 1999 was negative. In 2000 it was very high, and the last two years show a declining trend. There is no absolutely clear trend in sales, as there would have been if sales growth were rising or declining every year. Thus, it is reasonable to use the average as a starting place to forecast for 2003.

In the absence of information that future sales growth will be materially different than historical growth, it is reasonable to forecast sales growth at 7 percent for 2003, 6 percent for 2004 and 2005, and 5 percent thereafter. There is no magic formula to forecasting sales. It requires sound judgment. It would be reasonable to forecast 6 percent for 2003 instead of 7 percent, and indeed it would be reasonable to forecast 6 percent for every year, which would be simpler. However, the downward trend of sales growth in the last two years indicates that perhaps 5 percent might be a better long-term forecast.

It is important to also switch from thinking about sales in nominal dollars to sales in constant dollars. Inflation in the United States has averaged around 3 percent. Therefore, sales growth of 6 percent in nominal terms means 3 percent for inflation and 3 percent real sales growth. As a benchmark, Gross Domestic Product in the U.S. economy has grown at a compound average of 3.4 percent from 1947 to 2001.[2]

ADJUSTMENTS TO HISTORICAL NET INCOME

There are a number of standard adjustments that professional appraisers typically make to convert historical net income to economic net income. "Economic net income" and "economic cash flow" are my own personal terminology. The more standard industry terms are "adjusted net income" and "adjusted cash flow." I use the term "economic" to convey the intrinsic, long-term earning power of the business, devoid of the effects of discretionary decisions and infrequent or unusual income or expense items. I

[2] My calculations based on data in www.economic-indicators.com/gdphist-table.xls.

define "economic net income" as net income with the following adjustments:

1. Adjust owners' compensation to arm's length.
2. Add back discretionary and personal expenses and unreported cash receipts.
3. Add back onetime losses and subtract onetime gains.
4. Allocate periodic expenses appropriately.
5. Adjust for nonoperating assets.

We will discuss each of these below.

Adjusting Owners' Compensation to Arm's Length

"Arm's length" refers to financial transactions performed without the influence of bias causing relationships. An arm's length salary is the compensation that a company would pay to an employee no matter who he or she is, based entirely on talent, effort, and accomplishment.

Family members often are paid more than arm's length salaries for tax reasons. For example, a business owner may include one or more of his children on the payroll, even though the children do not contribute to the business operations. This is especially true in C corporations. In such cases, we must reduce owners' compensation to arm's length, net of entity level income tax effects, i.e., corporate income tax or LLC income tax, because if the business only produces enough cash flow to pay the owners the same salary they would have to pay someone else to do the same work, then the business is just a job.

A few business owners pay themselves salaries that are lower than arm's length in order to make the business "look better." Also, family members may not receive a paycheck, even though they do provide real service to the business. For example, a business owner's spouse may not receive a paycheck even though the spouse acts as a bookkeeper, office manager, administrative assistant, etc. Obviously, the value of the business should not vary just because of the owner's arbitrary decision how much to pay him or herself and family. In this case we would increase the owner's and the family's compensation to an arm's length level.

Another way of looking at the issue of arm's length salary is that if the owners cannot make any more money in their own business than they could by working for someone else, then the business has no value as a going concern. You wouldn't pay someone else money for the opportunity to work for them. The employer would pay you.

Adding Back Discretionary Expenses

We add back discretionary expenses—as well as personal expenses and unreported cash— because the owner has the choice whether to spend this money. Charitable contributions are one of the two types of common discretionary expenses. However, not all charitable expenses are the same.

Let's consider two types of charitable contributions. One type is apparently discretionary, but not really so. That type is the donation because one of your clients asked you to support his or her favorite charity, and you fear that not doing so might lead to losing the client. The second type of charity is the donations you make of your own free will. These are truly discretionary. A potential buyer of your company would not be able to eliminate the first type of charitable contributions, but he or she could eliminate the second type. Also, you could choose to give personal rather than business checks for such donations. Therefore it is not only unfair, but also incorrect to penalize the business valuation by using the lower economic net income with truly discretionary expenses left in.

We also add back to net income the second type of discretionary expense, which is personal expenses charged to the business, e.g., charging flowers for your wife or your personal phone bills (except to the extent that you make business calls from home) to the company.

There is one caveat with charging personal expenses to the business. Even using a purely Machiavellian approach, you should stop this practice at least three to five years before you want to sell the company, as buyers are always wary of sellers trying to pull a fast one on them. They may not believe that your expenses really are personal, or they may only partially believe you. This will cause them to discount your claims, and you will probably sell your business for less than you otherwise could without the fun and games.

This caveat applies all the more so to unreported cash income. If you show your valuation analysis with unreported income and/or personal expenses added back to income, you run the risk that your potential buyer may threaten to report you to the IRS. Again, all I can recommend is that if you are "hooked" on living off of unreported income, go to a 12-step program to come off of it five years before you want to sell your business—certainly if it's a more mainstream business.

Certain types of businesses are known for being "cash businesses," and they typically sell for rules of thumb such as "x times gross." Buyers can never verify expenses and net income. The tax returns are nearly meaningless. All a buyer can do is verify sales activity. In relying on the rules of thumb, they assume the business will be of average profitability in that industry. I am not recommending this, but merely reporting what I hear tends to happen "on the street." In fact, I have never personally valued any business of this kind, because they're typically either too small or they're insufficiently legitimate to work with.

Adding Back Onetime Losses

The most common onetime loss is loss from discontinued operations, such as closing a location, product, or a line of business. Financial statements that are in accordance with Generally Accepted Accounting Principles (GAAP) require showing the gain or loss from a discontinued operation as a separate line item below net income from operations. That should help make your life easier in knowing how to adjust your financial statements to show the company's ongoing earnings capacity.

However, suppose you're analyzing five years of historical financial statements, and the operation was discontinued in the third year. The obvious adjustment is to add back that loss in year three. That leaves years three through five showing your ongoing earnings capacity. However, years one and two still contain losses that are probably intermingled in your income statements. It is important to add back the losses (or, less likely, subtract the gains) from the discontinued operation that are included in net income for years one and two.

Allocate Periodic Expenses

Most expenses occur on a fairly continuous basis. However, there are some that occur periodically. Examples are moving expenses and losses from lawsuits. Most companies move locations every five to ten years, and the move is expensive, and many firms will have losses from lawsuits. Most small- and medium-size businesses, however, experience such losses infrequently—perhaps once every five to 15 years. Therefore, it is necessary to allocate the expense properly during the period of analysis. We will cover an example of how to do this in Table 3.2.

Losses from discontinued operations should be allocated as if they were periodic expenses, if it is your best forecast that your business will continue to try new products or services, and some of them will succeed, and some will fail. Then you cannot say that the discontinued operation is a loss that will never happen again. This is a more difficult area of financial analysis, and if it is unclear how to forecast, seek professional help.

Adjusting for Nonoperating Assets

Adjusting for nonoperating assets can be a complicated topic, and depending on how material the asset is, you might need professional help to deal with it. If your company owns a nonoperating asset, such as a condo in Aspen used primarily for personal pleasure, you should remove any expenses paid by the business on it—for example, mortgage interest—and add the appraised value of the condo to the fair market value of the business, whether as an operating entity or in liquidation. If the condo is an integral, indispensable part of the business because it generates so much sales activity, then it is an operating asset. Because it is complex and unusual, we won't cover this adjustment category in the example in Table 3.2.

HISTORICAL AND ADJUSTED STATEMENTS

Table 3.2 shows the company's historical and adjusted income statements for 1998-2002. We will discuss the detail in the first

	A	B	C	D	E	F	G
1	**TABLE 3.2**						
2	Billabong Boomerangs						
3	Historical and Adjusted Income Statements						
4							
5		**1998**	**1999**	**2000**	**2001**	**2002**	**Avg**
6	Total Sales	10,000,000	9,820,000	11,150,000	12,200,000	13,000,000	
7	Cost of Sales	6,500,000	6,900,000	7,200,000	8,000,000	8,600,000	
8	Gross Profit	**3,500,000**	**2,920,000**	**3,950,000**	**4,200,000**	**4,400,000**	
9	Total Expenses	2,200,000	2,400,000	2,900,000	3,100,000	3,800,000	
10	Net Income Before Taxes	**1,300,000**	**520,000**	**1,050,000**	**1,100,000**	**600,000**	
11	Adjustments to Net Income:						
12	+ Connie's Actual Comp	250,000	300,000	260,000	200,000	300,000	
13	+ Bobby's Actual Salary	50,000	50,000	60,000	60,000	75,000	
14	− Connie's Arm's Length Salary	(85,480)	(88,900)	(92,456)	(96,154)	(100,000)	
15	− Bobby's Arm's Length Salary	–	–	–	–	–	
16	+ Charitable Contributions	25,000	15,000	20,000	30,000	35,000	
17	+ Loss From Discontinued Operations	10,000	25,000	20,000	15,000	500,000	
18	+ Moving Expense		25,000				
19	− Allocate the Moving Expense 10 Years	(2,500)	(2,500)	(2,500)	(2,500)	(2,500)	
20	= Total Adjustments	**247,020**	**323,600**	**265,044**	**206,346**	**807,500**	

	A	B	C	D	E	F	G
21	**Economic Net Income Before Taxes**	**1,547,020**	**843,600**	**1,315,044**	**1,306,346**	**1,407,500**	
22	Corporate Income Taxes @ 40% [1]	(618,808)	(337,440)	(526,018)	(522,538)	(563,000)	
23	Economic Net Income After Corporate Taxes	**928,212**	**506,160**	**789,027**	**783,808**	**844,500**	
24	Economic Profit Margin	**9.3%**	**5.2%**	**7.1%**	**6.4%**	**6.5%**	**6.9%**
25	Sum-of-the-Years' Digits	**1**	**2**	**3**	**4**	**5**	**15**
26	Sum-of-the-Years' Digits- % [2]	**6.7%**	**13.3%**	**20.0%**	**26.7%**	**33.3%**	**100.0%**
27	SYD Weighted Profit Margin	**0.6%**	**0.7%**	**1.4%**	**1.7%**	**2.2%**	**6.6%**
28							
29	[1] Even for a nontax entity, we still calculate corporate income tax. Then we later add back a valuation premium for						
30	nontax entities. The federal corporate tax rate is approximately 35%, depending on net income. State corporate tax						
31	rates vary. When precision is important, this number should be tailored to the relevant tax rate for your state.						
32							
33	[2] The percentages equal 1/15, 2/15, 3/15, 4/15, and 5/15, respectively when working with five years of historical data.						

year, 1998. The logic of the calculations in the remainder of the columns is identical to 1998—even if the numbers change.

We begin with sales of $10 million in 1998 (cell B6). Cost of sales were $6.5 million, leaving gross profit of $3.5 million (B8). Total expenses were $2.2 million, which leaves net income before taxes of $1.3 million (B10). So far, all of these numbers are historical and are merely a listing from the company's annual income statements.

The next section, from rows 12 to 20, contains our adjustments from historical to economic net income. Before we can explain these adjustments, you will need some background to the company.

Constance Billabong, owner of the company, pays herself $250,000—the total sum of salary, bonuses, pension payments on her behalf, and any other perquisites—and she pays her son Bobby $50,000 to sit around and play cards all day. (Maybe she can hire my son and give him a raise?)[3] If Connie were to sell the business to you, you would immediately fire the son (hers, not mine). You would have to pay someone to do Connie's work. It could be you, her, or someone else. The relevant question is: "How much would you have to pay for someone with Connie's skills and efforts, who does not have ownership in the firm, to do that work?" Let's say the answer is $100,000 per year in the year 2002. If so, we adjust net income by adding back hers and Bobby's actual salaries and subtracting their arm's length salaries.

We add back Connie's actual total compensation of $250,000 and Bobby's $50,000 in B12 and B13, and we subtract their arm's length compensation in B14 and B15. Bobby's arm's length compensation is easy—zero (row 15). (Of course, my son's arm's length compensation would be huge. Such genius is rare to find.)

Connie's arm's length salary requires a little more explanation. We show her $100,000 arm's length compensation in

[3] Actually, her son did design one product—a boomerang that does not return. With his great marketing expertise, he came up with the trademarked name "The Stick." (Rim shot, please, maestro.) This is why his arm's length salary is zero. It is also why I haven't yet revealed my comic talents at amateur night at The Comedy Store or the Improv.

2002 in F14, and we have to deflate that number going backward. We do this by dividing $100,000 by 4 percent per year. Thus, her arm's length compensation for 2001 is $100,000/1.04 = $96,154 (E14), for 2000 it is $96,154/1.04 = $92,456 (D14), etc., until we reach 1998, which is $88,900/1.04 = $85,480 (B14). Alternatively, we can calculate 1998 as $\$100{,}000/1.04^4 = \$85{,}480$.

Next we add back charitable contributions, which were $25,000 in 1998.[4] In 2002 the company had a loss of $500,000 (F17) from discontinued operations. Upon investigation, we find that losses in 1998-2001 from the discontinued operation were $10,000, $25,000, $20,000, and $15,000, respectively.

The final adjustment in this example is to add back a moving expense of $25,000 that occurred in 1999. We add that back in cell C18. Then we estimate that the company will move every 10 years, which means the moving expense should be $2500 per year, which we subtract in row 19 from all five years of the proforma analysis.

Total adjustments to net income in 1998 are $247,020 (B20), which we add to net income to calculate economic net income before taxes of $1,547,020 (B21). Next we calculate income taxes at 40 percent,[5] which are $618,808 (B22), leaving economic net income after taxes of $928,212 (B23). The economic profit margin after tax is 9.3 percent (B23/B6 = B24).

The logic of the adjustments in 1999-2002 is the same as 2001, so we will not repeat the blow-by-blow description of each adjustment. Let's focus on the economic profit margins in row 24.

---

[4] Here I mean the truly discretionary charitable contributions, not the forced kind.

[5] If you are a nontax entity, normally you still should calculate a corporate tax and later add a valuation premium. This is a topic of high controversy in the valuation profession, and there is no consensus yet. Probably the majority of business appraisers do not add any premium. I disagree with this. In my opinion the appropriate premium should be in the 15 to 22 percent range. For small businesses with relatively low values, it is likely that your potential buyer would be an individual, and it is reasonable to eliminate the corporate tax entirely.

The Pattern of Economic Profit Margins

The economic profit margin began at its five-year high of 9.3 percent (B24) in 1998, declined to its low of 5.2 percent in 1999, then settled into a middling pattern of 7.1, 6.4, and 6.5 percent in 2000 through 2002, respectively. The significance of this is to gain insight into how to forecast the future.

When there is a lot of money at stake, it can be worthwhile to look at a detailed income statement and calculate every expense item as a percentage of sales for the five years. You would want to look for material changes in each category over time. For example, if liability insurance were 2 percent of sales for 1998 through 2001 and suddenly jumped to 5 percent in 2002, that would scream for investigation. You would want to ascertain if that is a permanent or temporary change and adjust your financial statements accordingly. However, this level of detail in financial analysis is beyond most amateurs, and it would strain the patience of most readers, so we will not do it in this book.

Instead, we will proceed assuming we do not have any particular information on how to interpret and forecast the pattern of profitability. Just looking at the pattern of profitability, it looks like the "good old days" of 1998, with its 9.3 percent (B24) economic profit margin, are not likely to be repeated. That appears to be true of the low time of 1999, with its 5.2 percent margin. The trend of the past three years is somewhere in the middle.

Let's look at two types of averages. A simple average of the past five years' economic profit margins is 6.9 percent (G24). A common method to weight the most recent years most heavily and the more distant years' less heavily is to use the sum-of-years' digits (SYD) method. Accountants use SYD frequently. We are analyzing five years of historical data, so we add 1 + 2 + 3 + 4 + 5 = 15. That is, we weight 1998, the oldest year, as 1, 1999 as 2, etc. (row 25). The denominator for the weight equals the sum of the years added together.[6] The weights for 1998-2002 appear in row 26 (1/15 = 6.7%, 2/15 = 13.3%, 3/15 = 20%, 4/15 =

---

[6] For analysis of n years, the denominator equals $n(n + 1)/2$ years.

26.7%, and 5/15 = 33.3%). The weights always total 100 percent, as long as there are no mistakes.

We multiply the economic profit margins in row 24 by the weights in row 26 to calculate the SYD weighted profit margin in row 27, which adds to 6.6 percent (G27). Thus, the weighted average profit margin is slightly lower than the simple average profit margin for the past five years.

Now, which one should we use? In the absence of more specific information (the type I mentioned above, that can come from detailed, line-by-line expense analysis), I think the trend is clear that the weighted average of 6.6 percent is a better forecast of the future than the simple average in this example.

It is possible to calculate other averages. We could, for example, calculate an average excluding 1998, which is 6.3 percent (it does not appear in Table 3.2). That appears too low to me, so I wouldn't use it. Also, we could average 2000 through 2002, which is 6.7 percent, also not shown in the table. That appears too high to me.

When there is a clear long-term upward or downward trend, it makes a lot of sense to use the economic profit margin of the last year—unless you expect the trend to continue, in which case you may want to use a more extreme amount. For example, if the economic profit margins were instead percentages of 9, 8.5, 8, 7.5, 7, and 6.5 for 1998-2002, respectively, then the likely candidate for your forecast in the valuation is 6.5 percent. However, suppose you expect the trend to continue downward and stop at 5 percent after three years. Then you would want to forecast 6 percent for 2003, 5.5 percent for 2004, and 5 percent for 2003 and beyond. If you prefer to use one long-term growth rate, I would suggest something like 5.3 percent, because it's a little higher than 5 percent but not by much.

In Table 3.2 we do not have a completely clear trend. I would use the weighted average of 6.6 percent (G27) or perhaps the 2002 margin of 6.5 percent (F24) for forecasting. As you can see, this is detailed work, but it is not rocket science. Let's select the 6.6 percent.

Forecasting economic net income is probably the greatest source of valuation error—especially for amateurs. Think ahead to what may change in the future before you settle on your forecast. This is the area where an amateur—and occasionally even a professional—may err by missing something very important. Perhaps you'll forget that you will exceed your office space in two years, which will cost considerably more going forward, or perhaps you won't foresee that new competition will squeeze your margins more, starting next year. When there's a lot of money at stake in a transaction, at a minimum you should get a professional to review your valuation. Even so, you must tell the professional valuator the trends that you see, since you know more about your business than he or she does, and your expertise is very important to the valuation process.

FORECAST OF ECONOMIC NET INCOME

Now we're ready to forecast economic net income. As noted at the beginning of this chapter, our analyses in Tables 3.1 and 3.2 have led to the forecast in Table 3.3.

In Table 3.1 we see that Billabong Boomerangs had an average annual sales growth rate of 6.9 percent for 1998-2002, but annual growth was slowing down in 2001 and 2002. In the ab-

	A	B	C	D	E	F
1	**TABLE 3.3**					
2	Billabong Boomerangs					
3	Forecast Economic Net Income					
4						
5		**2003**	**2004**	**2005**	**2006**	**2007**
6	Forecast Total Sales	13,910,000	14,744,600	15,629,276	16,410,740	17,231,277
7	Forecast Sales Growth	7%	6%	6%	5%	5%
8	Economic Net Income After Corporate Taxes	**918,060**	**973,144**	**1,031,532**	**1,083,109**	**1,137,264**
9						
10	Economic Profit Margin (Table 3.2, G27)	**6.6%**				

sence of any specific market intelligence—and, of course, it is always preferable to have as much market intelligence as one can afford to obtain—it is reasonable to forecast sales growing 7 percent in 2003, 6 percent in 2004 and 2005, and 5 percent thereafter. Remember, 5 percent growth in sales in the United States is about 3 percent inflation and 2 percent real growth. This is slightly high long-term growth for a healthy, small- to mid-size business, as long-term growth in the U.S. has been about 3.4 percent, and approximately 1 to 2 percent of that growth would have come from new businesses, net of bankruptcies.

We begin with sales in 2003, which we forecast as 1.07 (1 + B7) × $13,000,000 (2002 sales, per Table 3.1, F6) = $13.91 million (B6). Our forecast for 2004 equals $13.91 million × 1.06 = $14,744,600 [B6 × (1 + C7) = C6]. The sales forecast for the remaining years follows the same pattern as the 2004 forecast.

Our forecast of economic net income is merely the sales forecast in row 6 times the economic net profit margin of 6.6 percent (B10, which we calculated in Table 3.2, G27). Thus, our forecast of economic net income after corporate taxes is $918,060 (B8) in 2003, and rises every year to $1,137,264 (F8) in 2007.[7]

CONCLUSION

In this chapter we began our dive into the quantitative side of business valuation. We analyzed historical sales, discussed and demonstrated how to forecast economic profit margins, and demonstrated how to forecast economic net income.

In the next chapter you will learn how to calculate cash flow and, hopefully, how to manage it as well.

[7] If you forecast economic net income is such that income tax rates vary by year, as will happen if economic net income is between $100,000 and $335,000 for a C corporation, then it is better to forecast pre-tax economic net income and apply the appropriate tax rate year-by-year.

Chapter 4

Defining and Measuring Economic Cash Flow

In Chapter 2, we established the Discounted Cash Flow (DCF) Method as the single best valuation method. In Chapter 3, you learned how to forecast sales and economic net income. The focus of this chapter is defining and measuring cash flow. As cash flow is a somewhat complex topic, we will proceed in gradual steps of increasing complexity:

- A shortcut definition of cash flow
- Net working capital
- The complete cash flow definition
- Economic cash flows
- Required cash and net working capital
- Payout and Retention Ratios

Ultimately, you will learn a simple method to convert your forecast of net income to a forecast of cash flow.

CASH FLOW: THE SHORTCUT EQUATION

Our shortcut definition of cash flow can be expressed in the following equation:

Cash flow = Net Income + Depreciation − Capital Expenditures − Increases in Noncash Net Working Capital[1]

Let's analyze this definition and understand it. In spite of net income's limitations, which we detailed in Chapter 2, it is the beginning of our calculation of cash flow.

Net income is the engine powering cash flow. Although a company temporarily could have positive cash flow with zero or negative net income, this is not sustainable in the long run. This is because the only way positive cash flow can be created without positive net income is by depleting current and fixed assets.[2]

If you use ordinary net income in the above equation, then the equation produces ordinary cash flow. If you use economic net income, it produces economic cash flow.

The next two terms after net income are depreciation and capital expenditures. These two items really form one unit. Together they account for the changes in cash resulting from changes in the fixed assets of the business. Depreciation expense[3] is a deduction from net income, but it is a noncash expense. Since no cash actually changes hands, we must add back depreciation. Capital expenditures are the mirror image of depreciation. They do not appear on the income statement, yet they are a use of cash. Therefore, we must subtract capital expenditures from net income in calculating cash flow.

Even in a stagnant business, the dollar amount of capital expenditures will outpace depreciation by the average amount of price increases separating the two, and this is a drain on cash. For example, if you need to replace the machine that you bought

---

[1] If any of the items are negative, we add the negative amount. For example, if noncash net working capital decreased by $10,000, then we subtract a negative $10,000, which is the same as adding $10,000 to cash flow.

[2] I'm referring to cash flow as defined in the shortcut equation. A complete cash flow equation will indicate that there are other ways to create positive cash flow, e.g., increases in long-term debt, sale of new equity, sale of fixed assets, etc.

[3] Amortization expense operates in the same way as depreciation. For simplicity, we will discuss only depreciation, but in fact it is depreciation and amortization that we add back in calculating cash flow.

five years ago for $1000, last year's depreciation expense would have been $200 ($1000 ÷ 5-year life). However, the next machine, assuming 3 percent per year growth in equipment cost, will cost $1159. Thus, capital expenditures "run ahead" of depreciation by the price increases in the equipment, which itself is mostly driven by inflation in the U.S. economy.

This is all the more true for a growing business, where capital expenditures will exceed depreciation by the inflationary rise in prices and the real increase in the amount of property, plant, and equipment (PP&E) the business will buy. For a business in decline, capital expenditures may be greater than, equal to, or less than depreciation, depending on the degree of the decline. Later in the chapter, I will explain how to easily forecast the difference between capital expenditures and depreciation expense.

Increases in net working capital, the final term in the shortcut equation, are an adjustment that accounts for the cash drain of increasing current assets (receivables, inventory, etc.) more than current liabilities (accounts payable, short-term notes payable, accrued salaries, etc.). As businesses grow, they need to stock more inventory, extend more credit to customers (this means more receivables), and maintain larger cash balances to pay bills. Increasing these current assets requires cash. This cash can come from sources of debt, like suppliers (accounts payable), banks (notes payable), or it can come from the company's own pockets, i.e., from its profits.

NET WORKING CAPITAL

Let's begin by illustrating the dynamics of changes in net working capital. Suppose your sales increased from $1.2 million per year ($100,000 per month) in 2001 to $1.5 million per year ($125,000 per month) in 2002. Let's also suppose that your customers pay their bills in 30 days, on average. Then your accounts receivable should have increased from $100,000 on December 31, 2001, to $125,000 on December 31, 2002, i.e., receivables increased $25,000. If you use accrual based accounting, you will be showing all of your sales, but you did not collect $25,000 of those sales.[4] Thus, using the shortcut equation above as our starting point to calculate cash flow, net income overstates cash flow by $25,000, and we have to subtract it to calculate cash flow. Accounts receivable is part of net working capital, and therefore the increase in receivables is part of the increase in net working capital in the equation.

Let's look at inventory. If inventory increases, let's say, $50,000, that increase does not show up in net income, as we have not yet sold the inventory. But we did have to use cash to buy it. Therefore, we would have to subtract the $50,000 from net income to calculate cash flow.

Now let's look at the right-hand side of the balance sheet. Increases in liabilities are a source of cash. Increases in accounts payable are an increase in cash flow, because we have bought inventory or services on credit, but we have not paid for them yet. Or, if we borrowed (short-term) money from the bank, the increase in the current liability indicates that we increased our cash. Thus, if your supplier finances the $50,000 purchase of inventory with credit, you will have a corresponding $50,000 accounts payable, which is a source of cash. In this case, the $50,000 use of cash from the increase in inventory and the $50,000 source of cash from the increase in accounts payable will cancel each other out, for a net zero effect.

It is important to note that we add only the *increase* in the balance sheet items, i.e., the net working capital (if they decrease, then we subtract them), while we add the full amount of depreciation expense and subtract the full amount of capital expenditures.

Effect on Cash Flow

A business with large working capital needs will generally have larger changes in net working capital. These larger changes will

[4] If your accounting is cash basis, then accounts receivable and accounts payable always equal zero, and you might think that this is a "free" ticket to not lowering cash flow. That is not true, however, since your net income on a cash basis will be lower than on an accrual basis, because you are not recording sales made but not paid for. Thus, cash flow is identical regardless of your choice of cash or accrual accounting.

have a more profound influence on a company's value, because the net working capital component of the cash flow equation will be larger. On the flip side, a business with small working capital requirements will usually have small changes in net working capital, and consequently its net income will more closely approximate cash flow. By reviewing the typical items that comprise net working capital, we will gain insight into which types of firms will tend to have high versus low net working capital.

The typical current assets are cash, accounts receivable, and inventory. The typical current liabilities are accounts payable and other accrued liabilities. Firms with high net working capital as a percentage of sales will be those with a high percentage of current assets to sales and a low percentage of current liabilities to sales. Let's clarify which types of businesses will have high or low net working capital requirements:

1. Firms with high net profit margins will have a low percentage of costs and expenses to sales. Therefore their required cash as a percentage of sales will tend to be low, which leads to a lower required net working capital as a percentage of sales, which means smaller increases in net working capital as the business grows. This, in turn, raises the value of the business. Of course, the converse is true. Low margin firms will tend to have higher required net working capital as a percentage of sales, which leads to larger increases in net working capital as the business grows, and this decreases the value of the firm.
2. Considering the effects of credit policies:
   a. If your credit policies match those of your suppliers—e.g., both bill net 30 days—then your receivables and payables have the same cycle, and the difference between the two will be based only on your gross profit margin.[5] Firms with high gross

[5] It will also depend on how fast you pay your suppliers versus how fast your customers pay you. If you pay your suppliers, on average, in 28 days, and your customers pay you in 32 days, that will tend to increase receivables and decrease payables, which increases required net working capital. In other words, the actual deviation from the credit policies affect the size of net working capital, but usually not by much.

margins will have relatively higher receivables than payables, and thus required net working capital will be higher, which lowers the valuation. This seems counterintuitive, but such a firm will "make up" for that in higher net income. Thus, a high gross profit margin is still desirable, even if it increases net working capital.

b. If your credit policies are more lenient than your creditors' policies—e.g., you give your customers 60 days to pay, while your creditors give you an average of 30 days—then your receivables will tend to be that much higher than your payables, and required net working capital is higher. As sales grow, this gap will grow in dollars. In addition, this gap will increase as a business adopts more lenient credit policies. Of course, a business owner with such a policy should be experiencing a corresponding increase in business and profitability to offset the negative effect on cash flow. If not, then it is time to change the policy. (See Jim Ward's chapter on my Web site for managing cash flow.)

c. The opposite is true if your credit policies are less lenient than your creditors, e.g., you give 30 days and they give you 60 days. This would lead to a smaller required net working capital as a percentage of sales. In this case, working capital requirements will not be a significant drain on profitability as sales grow.

3. If you are a service business, your "accounts payable" is not really money owed to suppliers (of raw materials or products), it is salaries payable to your employees. There's probably not much you can do to change the "credit policy" on wages significantly. Probably the best you can do is pay your employees every two weeks instead of every week. Few employees are willing to work for employers that pay as infrequently even as once per month. That leaves your credit policy as the major variable in determining required net working capital.

4. Firms with high inventory tend to have high required net working capital, and the opposite is true of firms with low inventories. Thus, product-based firms will tend to have higher required net working capital, larger changes in net working capital, and less cash flow than service based firms with similar sales and profitability.

CASH FLOW: THE COMPLETE EQUATION

The shortcut equation teaches us that cash flow is equal to net income with adjustments for the cash costs of fixed assets and increases or decreases in required net working capital. For your own internal planning and amateur valuations, that equation is probably adequate. Depending on the nature of the business and the purposes of the valuation, however, a more complete cash flow equation may be necessary.

The equation below includes all operating, investing, and financing transactions that affect cash flow. It is rather long, but it's useful in acquiring a more complete understanding of cash flow.[6]

$$\text{Cash Flow} = \text{Net Income} + \text{Depreciation} - \text{Capital Expenditures} - \text{Increase in Required Net Working Capital} + \text{Cash Received for Sale of Fixed Assets} - \text{Gain on Sale of Assets} + \text{Increase in Long-Term Debt} + \text{Sale of Stock} - \text{Purchase of Stock} - \text{Dividends Paid}$$

The first three terms on the right-hand side of the equation are the same terms as in the shortcut equation, so let's look at the additional terms and try to understand them.

Cash received from the sale of fixed assets is not included in net income, yet it is a source of cash, and hence we must add it to net income to calculate cash flow. The gain on sale of fixed

[6] For a detailed mathematical derivation, see "Cash Flow: A Mathematical Derivation," *Valuation*, January 1994. To download, go to www.abramsvaluation.com, select "Articles," then "Articles in .pdf." *Quantitative Business Valuation*, Chapter 1, contains a slightly more extensive derivation and explanation.

assets is the mirror image term, since it is included in net income, yet it is not a source of cash. (In that sense it is like depreciation in its relationship to capital expenditures, and indeed is the mirror image.) Since the gain on the sale is included in net income, now we must subtract it from net income to calculate cash flow. If the company experienced a loss on its sale of fixed assets, then it reduced net income, but it does not reduce cash flow and hence you must add it back to calculate cash flow. Increasing long-term debt and selling stock in the company are sources of cash, while purchasing stock back from shareholders and paying dividends are uses of cash.

From this longer equation, we can understand why the shortcut equation is useful and usually sufficient. If a business does not have any equity transactions, sale of assets, or increases in long-term debt, then the long equation becomes the shortcut equation. Sales of assets and the related gains or losses are normally immaterial in amount, and most businesses other than venture capital–backed startups are not selling or buying equity on a regular basis.

Also, we can see why net income is the only long-term source of cash flow that provides a stable existence for a business. While increasing debt is a short-term source of cash, and it creates an immediate positive cash flow, debts have to be paid back, and they create a long-term negative cash flow. While selling stock creates an immediate cash inflow, it dilutes ownership of the firm, and the original shareholders will receive a smaller portion of future profits. Thus, net income is the only safe source of cash flow in the long run.

Nevertheless, it is important to manage all of the elements of cash flow on a regular basis. There are times when it's appropriate to borrow or sell stock. These actions must be done with wisdom and should not be viewed as a cheap panacea to generate cash.

DEFINING ECONOMIC CASH FLOW

For valuation purposes, we need to calculate "economic cash flow," which I define as ordinary cash flow with the following adjustments:

- Use economic net income instead of ordinary net income in the shortcut and fuller cash flow equations.
- Use "required cash" in the calculation of required net working capital.

We already covered the first point in Chapter 3. We will discuss the second point next.

Using Required Cash

In valuation, it is very important to distinguish between required cash and "free cash." The former is cash that is necessary for paying the company's bills (of all types—for inventory, payroll, overhead, etc.) and is properly included in net working capital. Free cash, on the other hand, is the amount of cash the company holds above what is necessary for paying its bills. In other words, it's the cash available to distribute as dividends—whether or not the company chooses to do so.

For example, if you forecast cost of sales and total expenses to be $1.2 million next year, that equals $100,000 per month. It is reasonable to expect that at any time, you should have cash in your checking account equal to about 5 to 10 days of expenditures—let's say 10 days, which is one-third of one month.[7] That means maintaining an average checking account balance of about $33,000. This amount is unavailable for distribution to shareholders as dividends, and you should include it in your calculation of net working capital.

It follows that any cash you have above the $33,000 for the first forecast year is potentially available for distribution as dividends. If you mistakenly include all cash that you have maintained historically as part of your forecast of required net work-

[7] There is no magic number. This is strictly a matter of judgment as to what is a reasonable amount of cash to keep in the checking account. From a valuation standpoint, the ideal is to keep only as much as necessary to be able to pay the bills smoothly without running out of cash. Keeping any cash above that on a regular basis is a waste, since it either should be invested in productive assets (PP&E or in people) or paid as dividends to the shareholders, whose present value of their investment rises when they receive dividends sooner than later.

ing capital, you're likely to end up with a zero value coming out of your Discounted Cash Flow analysis, because your required net working capital will appear to "suck up" all cash the company will ever produce.

Calculating Economic Cash Flows

It is easiest to illustrate the calculation of economic cash flows by example. As in Chapter 3, we will use Billabong Boomerangs for our examples. We adjust cash flows to economic cash flows in Table 4.1A. Some of this will be a repeat from Chapter 3; however, we will use the numbers in different ways here.

In Table 4.1A, we begin with net income before taxes of $1 million (cell B5). From this, we subtract $400,000 (B6) of corporate taxes to arrive at net income after taxes of $600,000 (B7). We add back depreciation expense of $75,000 (B8)[8] and subtract capital expenditures and the increase in net working capital of $125,000 (B9) and $50,000 (B10), respectively, to calculate the cash flow of Billabong Boomerangs of $500,000 (B11).

Now we make the adjustments to arm's length salaries. We add back Connie's and Bobby's actual salaries of $250,000 (B13) and $50,000 (B14), and we subtract their arm's length salaries of $100,000 (B15) and zero (B16). The net adjustment is to add back $200,000 (B17) to economic cash flow. However, if we were to add that back to net income, the company would have been taxed an additional $200,000 × 40% = $80,000 (B18), so the net addition is $120,000 (B19). Thus, economic cash flow is $500,000 + $120,000 = $620,000 (B11 + B19 = B20).

There is an alternate calculation in the bottom half of the table that, besides verifying this result, also will enable us to calculate the Payout Ratio.[9] In Section 2 we repeat net income before taxes of $1 million from B5 in B23. We add back the $200,000 (B24, which comes from B17) of excess compensation, for economic net income before taxes of $1,200,000 (B25). We

---

[8] It was already included in expenses—the detail of which is not shown in this table—that are part of the calculation of the $1 million net income before taxes.

[9] The Payout Ratio is the percentage of net income distributed to owners.

	A	B	C
1	**TABLE 4.1A**		
2	Calculation of Economic Cash Flow, Net Inc & Payout Ratio		
3			
4	**Section 1: Calculation of Economic Cash Flow**		
5	Net Income Before Taxes	1,000,000	
6	Income Taxes	(400,000)	
7	Net Income After Taxes	**600,000**	
8	+ Depreciation Expense	75,000	
9	− Capital Expenditures	(125,000)	
10	− Increase in Net Working Capital	(50,000)	
11	Cash Flow	**500,000**	
12	Adjustments		
13	+ Connie's Actual Comp	250,000	
14	+ Bobby's Actual Salary	50,000	
15	− Connie's Arm's Length Salary	(100,000)	
16	− Bobby's Arm's Length Salary	–	
17	Total Adjustments	**200,000**	
18	Less Tax Effects of Adjustments	(80,000)	
19	Adjustments, After Tax	**120,000**	
20	Economic Cash Flow (B11+B19) | ECF/Econ Net Inc (B20/B27)	**$620,000**	**86.1%**
21			
22	**Section 2: Calculation of Economic Net Income**		
23	Net Income Before Taxes (B5)	1,000,000	
24	+ Total Adjustments (B17)	200,000	
25	Economic Net Income Before Taxes (B23+B24)	**1,200,000**	
26	Income Taxes (B25 * 40%)	(480,000)	
27	Economic Net Income After Taxes (B25 + B26)	**720,000**	**100.0%**
28			
29	**Section 3: Calculation of Payout Ratio**		
30	Capital Expenditures (B9)	125,000	
31	− Depreciation (B8)	(75,000)	
32	+ Increase in Net Working Capital (B10)	50,000	
33	Total Income Retained | Retention Ratio (B33/B27) [1]	**100,000**	**13.9%**
34	Economic Cash Flow (B27-B33) | Payout Ratio (B34/B27)	**620,000**	**86.1%**
35			
36	[1] Per Equation [9] in the article, "Forecasting Cash Flow: Mathematics of the Payout Ratio,"		
37	Jay B. Abrams, Retention Ratio = [(Cap Expenditures − Depr) + Increase in NWC] / NI		

	A	B	C
1	**TABLE 4.1B**		
2	Calculation of Payout Ratio-With Unadjusted Income & Cash Flow [1]		
3			
4	**Section 1: Calculation of Cash Flow**		
5	Net Income Before Taxes	1,000,000	
6	Income Taxes	(400,000)	
7	Net Income After Taxes	**600,000**	
8	+ Depreciation Expense	75,000	
9	− Capital Expenditures	(125,000)	
10	− Increase in Net Working Capital	(50,000)	
11	Cash Flow	**500,000**	
12	Adjustments		
13	+ Connie's Actual Comp	–	
14	+ Bobby's Actual Salary	–	
15	− Connie's Arm's Length Salary	–	
16	− Bobby's Arm's Length Salary	–	
17	Total Adjustments	–	
18	Less Tax Effects of Adjustments	–	
19	Adjustments, After Tax	–	
20	Cash Flow (B11 + B19) | CF/Net Inc (B20/B27)	**$500,000**	**83.3%**
21			
22	**Section 2: Calculation of Net Income**		
23	Net Income Before Taxes (B5)	1,000,000	
24	+ Total Adjustments (B17)	–	
25	Net Income Before Taxes (B23 + B24)	**1,000,000**	
26	Income Taxes (B25 * 40%)	(400,000)	
27	Net Income After Taxes (B25 + B26)	**600,000**	**100.0%**
28			
29	**Section 3: Calculation of Payout Ratio**		
30	Capital Expenditures (B9)	125,000	
31	− Depreciation (B8)	(75,000)	
32	+ Increase in Net Working Capital (B10)	50,000	
33	Total Income Retained | Retention Ratio (B33/B27) [2]	**100,000**	**16.7%**
34	Cash Flow (B27-B33) | Payout Ratio (B34/B27)	**500,000**	**83.3%**
35			
36	[1] This table is identical to Table 4.1A, except the adjustments in		
37	B13 through B16. Thus, we calculate the Payout and Retention Ratios for ordinary in-		
38	come and cash flow, not economic income and cash flow.		
39			
40	[2] Per Equation [9] in the article, "Forecasting Cash Flow: Mathematics of the Payout Ratio,"		
41	Jay B. Abrams, Retention Ratio = [(Cap Expenditures − Depr) + Increase in NWC] / NI		

subtract income taxes at 40 percent of $480,000 (B26), which leaves economic net income after taxes of $720,000 (B27).

In Section 3 we add capital expenditures and the increase in net working capital and subtract depreciation expense, which is our shortcut calculation of income retained according to the shortcut equation. Those three items add up to $100,000 (B33). The income retained of $100,000, divided by economic net income of $720,000 (B27), is the Retention Ratio of 13.9 percent (C33). Subtracting the income retained of $100,000 from economic net income of $720,000 leaves us with economic cash flow of $620,000 (B34). The Payout Ratio is the $620,000 economic cash flow divided by the $720,000 economic net income, or 86.1 percent (B34/B27 = C34).

Table 4.1B is identical to Table 4.1A, except we work with ordinary net income and ordinary cash flow. All of the adjustments to economic net income in rows 12 through 17 are missing. This table demonstrates that the Payout Ratio formula works even when using ordinary net income instead of economic net income, since the result of 83.3 percent in cell C34 equals the result in C20.

PAYOUT AND RETENTION RATIOS

We can derive cash flow from net income in an alternate format, i.e., as a percentage adjustment to net income. Usually this will be a much easier calculation than forecasting all the elements of cash flow, i.e., depreciation, capital expenditures, and net working capital changes. For valuation purposes, the Payout Ratio (POR) is the portion of net income that can be distributed to owners—ideally without impairing operations.[10] The portion of net income required for operating and growing the business is called the Retention Ratio (RR), which equals one minus the Payout Ratio. In algebraic form, we can calculate cash flow through the Payout Ratio, as shown in the following equations:

[10] In calculating the Payout Ratio historically, it is simply dividends paid divided by net income. Even if the owner did impair operations by paying out too much in dividends, one does not distinguish whether or not operations were impaired. However, for valuation purposes, in forecasting ahead, we consider only the dividends that can be paid without impairing operations.

$$CF = NI \times POR$$

Where CF = Cash Flow, NI = Net Income, and POR = Payout Ratio

$$CF = NI \times (1 - RR)$$

Where $1 - RR = POR$

Since both of these equations calculate cash flow, they are both equivalent to the shortcut equation. I will assume you understand net income, so we need to understand the Payout Ratio and the Retention Ratio.

The Retention Ratio is the percentage you withhold from net income for the maintenance and growth of the business. Let's consider the investment needs of a stagnant business. Suppose Connie's boomerang business has no real growth. It sells the same number of boomerangs year after year, has the same number of employees, etc. Sales and probably wages will show only inflationary growth, which has been approximately 3 percent per year in the United States. Such a business will not need much new equipment. It can probably do with just replacing existing equipment when it wears out. Thus, in our shortcut equation, capital expenditures will only exceed depreciation expense by growth in the costs of boomerang carving equipment. If we forecast the business to decline, then if it declines by just the inflationary difference, capital expenditures will equal depreciation expense in dollars. If it declines by more than that, capital expenditures will be less than depreciation expense.

On the other hand, an expanding business will require capital expenditures in excess of depreciation expense for two factors: the inflationary increase in prices, and the real increase in the amount and quality of machinery in the business.

Payout Ratios of Publicly Held Firms

There is a logical connection between the Retention Ratio and the growth of the business. The faster you expect your business to grow, the larger the percentage of net income you'll need to retain in order to fuel that growth. As a benchmark, the Dividend Payout Ratio = (1 − RR) for publicly held firms was 47 percent at the beginning of 1926 and decreased to 32 percent by the end of 2000.[11] However, a new working paper by Boudoukh, et al.[12] suggests that stock repurchases have taken up the slack for the drop in the Payout Ratio. This means that publicly traded firms retain on average 1 − 47% = 53% of their income for cash flow and growth. Publicly held firms experienced an average growth of approximately 6 to 8 percent, which is much faster than private firms—certainly due to their much larger Retention Ratio and greater business opportunities.[13]

Growth in cash flows is not the same as sales growth. Often during periods of high sales growth, the firm's profit margin declines. Thus, it is not only possible but common to find high sales growth coupled with stagnant profits and cash flows. The cash flows of most healthy privately held firms grow from 1 to 6 percent per year. The 1 percent nominal growth is really a 2 percent decline, after subtracting 3 percent for inflation, while the 6 percent growth represents 3 percent for inflation and 3 percent real growth. It is a rare privately held firm that can reasonably be expected to grow forever at an average rate of 8 percent per year. That rate is more typical of a young firm, especially one with a very exciting or unusual product.

It's important to note that it is growth in cash flows—not growth in sales—that count in valuation. If sales grow by 15 percent per year but the business is losing its profit margins and cash flows decline, it is the decline in cash flow that we use in our valuation formula, not the increase in sales.

---

[11] Roger G. Ibbotson and Peng Chen, "The Supply of Stock Market Returns," Yale ICF Working Paper No. 00-44, page 7 and Figure 4.

[12] Boudoukh, Jacob, Roni Michaely, Matthew Richardson, and Michael R. Roberts, "On the Importance of Measuring Payout Yield: Implications for Empirical Asset Pricing," available on the Social Science Research Network, 12/16/03.

[13] According to Ibbotson and Chen (cited above), page 5, equation 6, geometric average capital gains in the public equity markets from 1926 to 2000 were 3.02 percent in real terms and approximately 6.2 percent in nominal terms. Arithmetic returns are always higher than geometric returns, and the former is the correct measure for valuation purposes. This suggests nominal capital gains of approximately 7 to 8 percent. The author wishes to thank Dr. Shannon Pratt for pointing out new research by Roger Grabowski using two-year instead of the traditional one-year arithmetic average returns that suggests that the arithmetic averages may be even slightly lower, perhaps 6 to 8 percent (see Dr. Pratt's editorial in *Business Valuation Update*, November 2003). Income returns in the Ibbotson and Chen article were 4.28 percent.

Calculating the Payout Ratio

There are two ways to calculate the Payout Ratio: the easy way, which is using a benchmark guesstimate of the Payout Ratio, and the more technical way, which is my own invention and should be more accurate and firm-specific. However, my way is far too mathematical for all but the most quantitative readers.[14] Thus, we will stick to the easy way.

Moskowitz and Vissing-Jorgensen[15] guesstimate an average 60 percent Payout Ratio for privately held C corporations and 80 percent for privately held S corporations and other nontax entities. MVJ emphasize that external financing is more expensive for privately held C corporations than for publicly held C corporations, because of their smaller size. They further state that the nontax entities tend to be smaller yet, and external financing should be even more expensive for them than for the larger, privately owned C corporations. However, counterbalancing this is the likelihood that the smaller, nontax entities probably have fewer growth opportunities than the larger firms, which is why they assume a lower retention.

It is clear from reading between the lines in their article that the main determinants in the earnings retention decision are size and cost of external financing, not the form of organization. Thus, a one-person C corporation should retain as little—and pay out as much—as a sole proprietorship with no employees.

I have valued no-growth clients with historical Payout Ratios as high as 99.8 percent. On the other hand, high-growth startup firms typically have net losses for one to two years, and then need to retain all of their net income for the next several years before they have a positive Payout Ratio. Thus, the Payout Ratio is often zero—or at least very low—until the company matures. It is important to use common sense. The bottom line is that the higher your forecast growth rate, the lower your Payout Ratio should be, and vice versa.

---

[14]Interested readers should refer to Jay B. Abrams, "Forecasting Cash Flow: Mathematics of the Payout Ratio," *Business Valuation Review*, June 2003, available on www.abramsvaluation.com in "Articles."

[15] Tobias J. Moskowitz and Annette Vissing-Jorgensen, "The Private Equity Premium Puzzle," *American Economic Review*, September 2002, vol. 92, no. 4. See especially page 755, second column.

TABLE 4.2

Benchmarks for the Payout Ratio

Firm Size, Type, and Growth	Long-Run Growth	Payout Ratio
Large public firms (all C corporations)	6 to 8%	32 to 47%
Large private firms	5 to 8%	60%
Small to medium private firms—moderate growth	3 to 4%	80%
Small to medium private firms—no growth	0%	90 to 99%

Table 4.2, summarizes the various benchmarks we discussed in the chapter and should help you select a reasonable Payout Ratio, given your forecast of growth.

The estimates in the long-run growth rate column are based on my experience. Only the 6 to 8 percent growth figure for large public firms is primarily a fact, and even that requires a guesstimate of the difference between the arithmetic and geometric growth rates. Thus, though the estimates in this table are reasonable, they are not divine wisdom cast in stone.

It's important to remember that our earlier discussions in this chapter also affect the Payout Ratio. For example, if your credit policy is very liberal and your accounts receivable therefore tend to be high compared to other firms with the same sales, then your required net working capital will be high, and consequently your Payout Ratio will be lower. Thus, it is reasonable to use your judgment to make adjustments to the benchmarks in Table 4.2 or to select in which range your firm belongs—low, medium, or high.

CONCLUSION

In this chapter, we have defined ordinary and economic cash flows. We have demonstrated how to make economic cash flow calculations, introduced Payout and Retention Ratios, and provided formulas to calculate these ratios.

In the next chapter we will cover the topic of discounting cash flows to present value, another important building block in the skill set necessary to value your company.

Chapter 5

Discounting to Present Value

In Chapter 2 we explained why the Discounted Cash Flow Method is the preferred valuation method. In Chapters 3 and 4 we focused on defining and calculating economic cash flow, which is the CF in DCF. In this chapter you will learn about discounting cash flow to present value, which is the D in DCF.

Present value can be a difficult concept for people with no exposure to the topic. It is easier for most people to understand how compound interest works to calculate future values. Once you have that understanding, it will be much easier to understand present value, which is the reverse process.

Before learning compound interest, it is first necessary to understand Return on Investment, since the ROI is the interest rate you will use both for calculating future values and for discounting your company's forecast cash flows to present value.

RETURN ON INVESTMENT

Return on Investment (ROI) is a measure of the profitability and efficiency of your investment. It is also known as rate of Return on Investment, Return on Equity (ROE), rate of return, and just "returns." It is equal to your cash flow divided by the amount of your investment. It is easier to understand this concept by explaining it in the context of publicly traded stocks. Then we will apply that to investment in privately held firms.

Suppose you own shares in the XYZ Corporation, which is publicly traded. Let's assume the stock was selling for $100 per share on December 31 of Year One. During Year Two it paid dividends of $2 at the end of the year, at which time the stock price was at $108 per share, which means you had an $8 capital gain. Your return would be the dividends plus the capital gain divided by the beginning market price, or ($2 + $8)/$100 = 10%.[1] Here our measure of return is cash flow, as you actually received $2 of dividends, and if you wish you can sell your stock at the end of Year Two and receive $108 of cash and the $8 capital gain included in that. Our measure of equity is the market value of equity, not book value.

Calculating ROI for a private firm requires making decisions on the measure of returns as well as the measure of equity. Most privately held firms do not pay dividends, so that part of cash flow usually does not exist. Being private means there is no market price with which to calculate the capital gain.[2] Therefore, most people measure ROI (or ROE) in private firms as net income divided by book equity. It is important to keep in mind that this is merely a substitute for ROI, not the real thing. It is not directly comparable to the ROI of publicly held firms.

CALCULATING FUTURE VALUES

To make a fairly dry topic more interesting, let's use a well-known historical event—the purchase of Manhattan Island—as the scenario to understand how to calculate future values, which, again, is the precursor to being able to calculate present values.[3]

---

[1] It can get more complicated than this when dividends are paid quarterly, but we won't go into that here.

[2] It is possible to calculate this by having annual valuations.

[3] The version of the purchase you'll read below (with some sections deleted) is from www.tlc.discovery.com/tlcpages/newyork/1626.html.

Historical Background of the Manhattan Purchase

In the land of city slickers and Donald Trump, the myth of Manhattan's purchase is one that New Yorkers love. Legend has it that in 1626, Dutch Governor Peter Minuit bought Manhattan Island from the local Lenape Indians for various goods. According to a copy of Minuit's deal, the Indians received "some Diffles duffel cloth, Kittles kettles, axes, hoes, wampum, drilling awls, Jews harps, and diverse other wares." Total value of the Manhattan deal? Around $24.

But this swindle was not really all that cut and dry. To begin with, the Indians weren't the rubes this story makes them out to be; trinkets were exceedingly valuable to the Lenape.[4] They invested much time and energy acquiring them, polishing them, and trading them. But why would they sell acres and acres of land for Diffles duffel cloth? Because the Indians had no concept of land ownership. The Lenape thought they were merely granting rights to use the island. Imagine their surprise when the Dutch proceeded to drive the Lenape off the land they were now "trespassing" on.

And where did the $24 amount come from? According to the 17th century Dutch, the value of the trinkets was 60 guilders. However, a historian in 1847 converted this number to $24, neglecting to take into account events like inflation.

But in the end, who's to say that selling Manhattan for $24 was a bad deal? According to Wall Street maven Peter Lynch, if the Indians had invested the $24 at 8 percent, they "would have built up a net worth of more than $20 trillion. Enough to give Donald Trump a run for his money." Hopefully, this is not the American version of Marie Antoinette's, "Let 'em eat cake" remade into, "Let 'em eat wampum."

---

[4] According to www.vny.com/cf/city/Citydetail.cfm?QID=44, Peter Minuit bought Manhattan Island from the Algonquin Indians in 1626. There are other versions of the story too.

Economic Analysis of the Purchase

In the last paragraph of the Web page article from which the version above was taken, Peter Lynch compares the values across time. If we assume there were alternative places to invest the $24 at an 8 percent rate of return, which is a question that is outside of the scope of this book, let's work to understand his comment, since it will enable us to apply the underlying principle to business valuation.

It is not important that you understand the mathematics—especially the mechanics of manipulating the equation of the time value of money that you'll see in the next paragraph—since the valuation spreadsheets in this book, and those you can download, will do the present value math for you. However, in order to understand valuation, it's important to grasp the intuition behind the math.

The "Time Value of Money" equation, using compound interest, is:

$$FV = PV(1 + r)^n$$

Where FV is the future value of the money, PV is the present value of the money (the amount you are investing today), r is the rate of Return on Investment, and n is the number of years you will invest the money.

Applying this equation to the purchase of Manhattan, we are assuming the settlers and their descendants would keep reinvesting the entire amount, never withdrawing any of the proceeds of the investment.

Let's apply the equation to Peter Lynch's quoted statement. The amount invested (i.e., the present value as of the year 1626) is $24, the rate of return is 8% = 0.08, and the investment will be from 1626 to 2002, or 376 years. Substituting those values into the equation, the value in 2002 would be:

$$FV = \$24 \times 1.08^{376} = \$24 \times 3.693 \text{ trillion} = \$88.6 \text{ trillion}$$

It looks like we have a discrepancy with Peter Lynch. Table 5.1 will enable us to see the numbers and possibly explain the difference.

	A	B	C	D	E	F	G
1	**TABLE 5.1**						
2	A. Value of $24 for Manhattan Island						
3							
4		**Years**			**Interest Rate**		
5	**Year**	**Passed**	**3%**	**5%**	**8%**	**10%**	**12%**
6	1626	0	$24	$24	$24	$24	$24
7	1650	24	$49	$77	$152	$236	$364
8	1983	357	$918,545	$880,624,998	$20,534,869,656,733	1.44E + 1 6	8.93E + 18
9	2002	376	$1,610,674	$2,225,295,512	$88,622,358,726,450	8.79E + 16	7.69E + 19
10							
11	B. Value of Each $1 for Manhattan Island						
12							
13		**Years**			**Interest Rate**		
14	**Year**	**Passed**	**3%**	**5%**	**8%**	**10%**	**12%**
15	1626	0	$1.00	$1.00	$1.00	$1.00	$1.00
16	1650	24	$2.03	$3.23	$6.34	$9.85	$15.18
17	1983	357	$38,273	$36,692,708	$855,619,569,031	5.99E + 14	3.72E + 17
18	2002	376	$67,111	$92,720,646	$3,692,598,280,269	3.66E + 15	3.21E + 18

The Value of Manhattan Island

Table 5.1, Section A, columns C through G, shows the value of the \$24 invested in Manhattan Island in various years beyond the purchase date, and various rates of return.[5] Section B shows the same thing for each \$1 the settlers paid the Indians. In other words, the numbers in Section B are 1/24 of the corresponding numbers in Section A.[6] All of the amounts in Section A, columns C through G, are calculated using our Time Value of Money equation.

Let's begin with row 7 in the table, i.e., in the year 1650 (cell A7). Twenty-four (B7) years had passed since the purchase. If the \$24 were invested at a constant rate of return of 3 percent (column C), its value after 24 years would be $\$24 \times 1.03^{24} = \$49$. If instead the settlers made a constant return of 12 percent (column G), the \$24 initial investment would be worth \$364 (G7).

Now let's roll the clock forward to the year 1983 (A8), 357 (B8) years after the purchase. At an 8 percent (column E) rate of return for 357 years, the \$24 would be worth $\$24 \times 1.08^{357} = \$24 \times \$855.6$ billion = \$20.5 trillion (E8), which matches Peter Lynch's quote. So it would seem that he made that statement in 1983.[7] Also note that as of the end of 1626 (cell A6), zero years (B6) had passed since the purchase, and the purchase was worth \$24 (C6 through G6) at all interest rates.[8]

We can gain several insights about future values from our analysis of the Manhattan purchase:

1. Looking down columns C through G, we can see that the effect of time on the amount of investment is profound. This occurs because compound interest causes

---

[5] We will assume the sale took place on December 31, 1624, and that all values in the future are as of December 31 of the various years.

[6] Section B values are calculated for each \$1.00 invested, i.e., when $PV = \$1.00$.

[7] If not, perhaps he had other complicating factors in mind, such as taxes, when he made the statement. The point is not to research Peter Lynch, of course, but to understand compound returns.

[8] Mathematically, that occurs because n, the number of years of the investment, equals zero. When we substitute $n = 0$ in our equation, the future value equals the present value at all values of r, the rate of return.

the principal invested to increase exponentially, not linearly.

2. Moving to the right across the rows, we can see that the effect of the interest rate on the final value is huge. At a 3 percent return after 376 years, the Indians' $24 would grow only to $1.6 million (C9): enough to buy a condo in Manhattan, and certainly not worth having sold all of Manhattan. At a 12 percent rate of return, which is the average return on the New York Stock Exchange for the past 75 years, the $24 received for the sale of Manhattan would be worth $\$7.69 \times 10^{19}$ (G9), which is probably enough to buy the world. (You can send me your check to my P.O. box in Tahiti.)
3. The effects of time and the rate of return are interactive. In 1650 the difference between a 3 percent rate of return and a return of 12 percent is only $364 (G7) – $49 (C7) = $316, while in 2002 the difference (G8 minus C8) is enough to buy the world. Thus, a long time span and a high rate of return leads to much larger accumulations of wealth than either one without the other.[9]

DISCOUNTING TO PRESENT VALUE

Discounting to present value is the reverse process of calculating future values. In calculating future values, we are going forward in time. In discounting, we go backward in time, normally from the future to the present.

Suppose Ardath Bigbucks, a wealthy woman you know, asks you for a business loan. She promises to repay you $100,000 in one year. How much would you be willing to loan her? If you are willing to loan her $100,000, then you would have no profit from the loan when she repays $100,000 in one year. If your motivations are business and not personal, then you would loan her somewhat less than $100,000—let's say, for the moment,

[9] This occurs because the interest rate is the rate of curvature of the curve. Over short spans of time, the differences in value from different interest rates are not very material, but over long spans of time small differences in the degree of curvature will translate to enormous differences in value.

$90,000, which means you expect to make $10,000 interest income in one year.

How would your answer change if Johnny Middlebucks asks for the same deal? Well, you know that Johnny doesn't have the same killer portfolio that Ardath has. He is a riskier loan. To compensate you for the risk, you would want a higher expected return, which means you want to make a higher expected profit on the loan. So perhaps you might be willing to lend him $85,000, and expect to make $15,000 in interest income after one year. You need the extra $5000 with Johnny compared to Ardath because there's a better chance that he'll come back to you after one year with a sob story instead of the cash.

The point of these scenarios is that $1.00 tomorrow is worth less than $1.00 today. How much less? We will develop a precise answer in the equation below. Again, it's not important that you understand the mechanics of the algebra, since the valuation spreadsheets will do that for you. But it is more important to understand the concepts and the intuition, in order to think about values clearly and correctly.

If we divide both sides of the above, Time Value of Money, equation by $(1 + r)^n$, and switch the left and right hand sides of the equation, we get:

$$PV = \frac{FV}{(1 + r)^n}$$

As you can see in the above Present Value equation, the present value of an amount of cash to be received in the future is equal to the future amount divided by one plus the rate of return—which we now call the *discount rate*—to the nth power. We call the rate of return the discount rate because we are reducing the future expected cash flow in size for the time value of money, which includes both the risk of the investment and the investment's length of time.

Present Value Factors

It is convenient to calculate present values for each $1.00 of expected future cash flows. This is called a *present value factor* (PVF), and it equals $\frac{1}{(1 + r)^n}$. We can do this by splitting up the right-hand side of our Present Value equation into two factors. Thus, the equation below states that the present value equals the future value times the present value factor.

$$PV = FV \times \frac{1}{(1 + r)^n}$$

The present value factors for the first 30 years of cash flows for a variety of different discount rates can be seen in Table 5.2. Column B is a 5 percent discount rate (again, this is the rate of return), which is a fairly typical rate of return for a 30-year U.S. Treasury bond. The U.S. Treasury is the largest borrower in the world, and it always repays. In finance, the Treasury rates are known as the "risk-free rate" of interest, because there is no risk of default on the loan. The 8 percent rate in column C is a fairly typical interest rate on corporate bonds.

The remaining discount rates, 12 to 30 percent in columns D through M, are equity rates of return for ownership of a business. Business owners have more risk than lenders, since lenders are paid before shareholders are entitled to receive dividends. We will cover this in more detail later in the chapter, but for the meantime, 12 to 16 percent are typical rates of return for large publicly traded stocks. The 18 to 20 percent rates of return are typical for small, publicly traded stocks; 22 to 26 percent are typical for private business; and 30 percent is fairly typical for valuing a startup business.[10]

As I statistically demonstrated in my first book,[11] this is a logical progression; on average, the smaller the business, the more volatile its returns. In mathematical finance, risk is defined as the volatility of returns.[12] Since investors like predictability, they will prefer bonds to stocks, large stocks to small

---

[10] These are long-term stock market returns. Returns in any year or any decade, for that matter, can vary considerably from these returns. There is reasonable professional opinion that one should use somewhat lower discount rates than these.

[11] Jay B. Abrams. *Quantitative Business Valuation: A Mathematical Approach for Today's Professionals.* New York: McGraw-Hill, 2001, Chapter 4.

[12] This is measured by the variance or the standard deviation of returns. In statistical parlance, volatility usually means the latter; however, I have seen it used both ways, and it is best to double-check the specific meaning the user has in mind if the difference is important.

	A	B	C	D	E	F	G	H	I	J	K	L	M
1	**TABLE 5.2**												
2	Present Value Factors (the Present Value of $1)												
3													
4		**Discount Rate**											
5	**Years**	**5%**	**8%**	**12%**	**14%**	**16%**	**18%**	**20%**	**22%**	**24%**	**26%**	**28%**	**30%**
6	**1**	0.95	0.93	0.89	0.88	0.86	0.85	0.83	0.82	0.81	0.79	0.78	0.77
7	**2**	0.91	0.86	0.80	0.77	0.74	0.72	0.69	0.67	0.65	0.63	0.61	0.59
8	**3**	0.86	0.79	0.71	0.67	0.64	0.61	0.58	0.55	0.52	0.50	0.48	0.46
9	**4**	0.82	0.74	0.64	0.59	0.55	0.52	0.48	0.45	0.42	0.40	0.37	0.35
10	**5**	0.78	0.68	0.57	0.52	0.48	0.44	0.40	0.37	0.34	0.31	0.29	0.27
11	**6**	0.75	0.63	0.51	0.46	0.41	0.37	0.33	0.30	0.28	0.25	0.23	0.21
12	**7**	0.71	0.58	0.45	0.40	0.35	0.31	0.28	0.25	0.22	0.20	0.18	0.16
13	**8**	0.68	0.54	0.40	0.35	0.31	0.27	0.23	0.20	0.18	0.16	0.14	0.12
14	**9**	0.64	0.50	0.36	0.31	0.26	0.23	0.19	0.17	0.14	0.12	0.11	0.09
15	**10**	0.61	0.46	0.32	0.27	0.23	0.19	0.16	0.14	0.12	0.10	0.08	0.07
16	**11**	0.58	0.43	0.29	0.24	0.20	0.16	0.13	0.11	0.09	0.08	0.07	0.06
17	**12**	0.56	0.40	0.26	0.21	0.17	0.14	0.11	0.09	0.08	0.06	0.05	0.04
18	**13**	0.53	0.37	0.23	0.18	0.15	0.12	0.09	0.08	0.06	0.05	0.04	0.03
19	**14**	0.51	0.34	0.20	0.16	0.13	0.10	0.08	0.06	0.05	0.04	0.03	0.03
20	**15**	0.48	0.32	0.18	0.14	0.11	0.08	0.06	0.05	0.04	0.03	0.02	0.02
21	**16**	0.46	0.29	0.16	0.12	0.09	0.07	0.05	0.04	0.03	0.02	0.02	0.02
22	**17**	0.44	0.27	0.15	0.11	0.08	0.06	0.05	0.03	0.03	0.02	0.02	0.01
23	**18**	0.42	0.25	0.13	0.09	0.07	0.05	0.04	0.03	0.02	0.02	0.01	0.01
24	**19**	0.40	0.23	0.12	0.08	0.06	0.04	0.03	0.02	0.02	0.01	0.01	0.01
25	**20**	0.38	0.21	0.10	0.07	0.05	0.04	0.03	0.02	0.01	0.01	0.01	0.01

	A	B	C	D	E	F	G	H	I	J	K	L	M
26	**21**	0.36	0.20	0.09	0.06	0.04	0.03	0.02	0.02	0.01	0.01	0.01	0.00
27	**22**	0.34	0.18	0.08	0.06	0.04	0.03	0.02	0.01	0.01	0.01	0.00	0.00
28	**23**	0.33	0.17	0.07	0.05	0.03	0.02	0.02	0.01	0.01	0.00	0.00	0.00
29	**24**	0.31	0.16	0.07	0.04	0.03	0.02	0.01	0.01	0.01	0.00	0.00	0.00
30	**25**	0.30	0.15	0.06	0.04	0.02	0.02	0.01	0.01	0.00	0.00	0.00	0.00
31	**26**	0.28	0.14	0.05	0.03	0.02	0.01	0.01	0.01	0.00	0.00	0.00	0.00
32	**27**	0.27	0.13	0.05	0.03	0.02	0.01	0.01	0.00	0.00	0.00	0.00	0.00
33	**28**	0.26	0.12	0.04	0.03	0.02	0.01	0.01	0.00	0.00	0.00	0.00	0.00
34	**29**	0.24	0.11	0.04	0.02	0.01	0.01	0.01	0.00	0.00	0.00	0.00	0.00
35	**30**	0.23	0.10	0.03	0.02	0.01	0.01	0.00	0.00	0.00	0.00	0.00	0.00
36	**Total**	**15.37**	**11.26**	**8.06**	**7.00**	**6.18**	**5.52**	**4.98**	**4.53**	**4.16**	**3.84**	**3.57**	**3.33**
37													
38	**Years**	**Present Value of $1 per Year for each 10-Year Period**											
39	**1-10**	7.72	6.71	5.65	5.22	4.83	4.49	4.19	3.92	3.68	3.46	3.27	3.09
40	**11-20**	4.74	3.11	1.82	1.41	1.10	0.86	0.68	0.54	0.43	0.34	0.28	0.22
41	**21-30**	2.91	1.44	0.59	0.38	0.25	0.16	0.11	0.07	0.05	0.03	0.02	0.02
42	**Total**	**15.37**	**11.26**	**8.06**	**7.00**	**6.18**	**5.52**	**4.98**	**4.53**	**4.16**	**3.84**	**3.57**	**3.33**
43													
44													
45	**Years**	**Percentage of Present Value for each 10-Year Period**											
46	**1-10**	50%	60%	70%	74%	78%	81%	84%	87%	89%	90%	92%	93%
47	**11-20**	31%	28%	23%	20%	18%	16%	14%	12%	10%	9%	8%	7%
48	**21-30**	19%	13%	7%	5%	4%	3%	2%	2%	1%	1%	1%	0%
49	**Total**	100%	100%	100%	100%	100%	100%	100%	100%	100%	100%	100%	100%

stocks, and publicly traded firms to privately owned firms—unless they are compensated for the additional risk in the form of a higher expected return. That is what happens—at least on average over the long run.

Now let's understand the table. At a 5 percent rate of return, you should be willing to pay $.95 (cell B6) today for the right to receive $1.00 in one year. Why? Because you can take the $.95, invest it at 5 percent, making $.05 interest, and end up with $1.00 in one year.[13] Moving one column to the right, you should be willing to pay only $.93 (C6) today for the promise of $1.00 in one year if you require an 8 percent rate of return. Again, you can invest the $.93 for one year at 8 percent, earn $.07 interest ($.93 × .08 = $.07), and end up with $1.00. Of course, as you move to the right in the table, the discount rate rises—which means the risk also increases—and the amount you should be willing to pay for each dollar of cash in one year decreases. This is consistent with the intuitive explanation of Ardath Bigbucks versus Johnny Middlebucks.

Now let's move down a column to see how the present value factor behaves over time. We will use the 20 percent discount rate (column H), since that is a reasonable discount rate for midsize privately held businesses, and the mathematics are easy.

Assuming a 20 percent rate of return is appropriate, you should be willing to pay $.83 (H6) for the expectation of receiving $1.00 in one year, $.69 (H7) for the expectation of receiving $1.00 in two years, and $.58 (H8) for the expectation of receiving $1.00 in three years. If you take the $.58 today and invest it and receive an annual return of 20 percent, you will have $.69 at the end of Year One ($.58 × 20% = $.11, plus the original $.58, equals $.69),[14] $.83 at the end of Year Two ($.69 × 20% = $.14, plus the $.69, equals $.83), and $1.00 at the end of Year Three ($.83 × 20% = $.17, plus the $.83, equals $1.00). Thus, if 20 percent is

[13] There is some apparent—but not real rounding error in this process. If Table 5.2 were shown to three or four decimal points, that problem would disappear. I chose two decimal points because it is simpler and most people are not familiar with fractions of a cent.

[14] Again, there is an apparent but not real rounding error that would go away with more decimal points.

the relevant rate of return of your business, you should be indifferent to receiving $.58 today, $.69 in one year, $.83 in two years, or $1.00 in three years—since they are all equivalent in present value terms. Valuation is a way of financial thinking across time.

Perhaps this seems counterintuitive, all the more so because this is so mathematical and ethereal. You might be asking why a dollar today is not the same as a dollar 1, 5, or 10 years from now. After all, George Washington still looks the same. To bring it down to earth, let's look at Table 5.3, which shows the price behavior of various foods over time.

At the end of 1980 a one-pound loaf of white bread cost $.52 (B6). Ten years later, at the end of 1990, the same loaf cost $.70 (C6), and at the end of 2000 it cost $.99 (D6)—for a price increase of 90 percent (E6) over 20 years. That means that for $.52 you could have bought a loaf of white bread in 1980, but only slightly more than half a loaf in 2000. So in real terms,

	A	B	C	D	E
1	**TABLE 5.3**				
2	Food Prices over Time				
3					
4			**December**		**% Increase**
5	**Items: (per lb.)**	**1980**	**1990**	**2000**	**1980-2000**
6	Bread, white	0.52	0.70	0.99	90%
7	Ground chuck, 100% beef	1.86	2.02	1.98	6%
8	Chicken, fresh, whole	0.76	0.86	1.08	42%
9	Grade A, large, per doz.	1.03	1.00	0.96	−7%
10	Apples	0.50	0.77	0.82	62%
11	Oranges	0.45	0.56	0.62	38%
12	Bananas	0.35	0.43	0.49	40%
13	Tomatoes	0.66	0.86	1.57	137%
14	Orange Juice, per 16 oz.	1.12	2.02	1.88	67%
15	Coffee, 100%, ground roast	2.82	2.94	3.21	14%
16	Lettuce	0.48	0.58	0.85	76%
17	Total	**10.56**	**12.75**	**14.44**	**37%**
18	Average	**0.96**	**1.16**	**1.31**	**37%**
19					
20	Source: http://data.bls.gov/cgi-bin/surveymost?ap				

$1.00 today and $1.00 in 1, 5, or 10 years from now are all different.[15]

Referring back to Table 5.2, we can conclude that the longer it will take to receive that dollar, the less we should be willing to pay for it now.

Present Value of an Annuity

Now let's take a look at the present value of receiving one dollar every year for a specified number of years. That is called an *annuity*. Besides showing the present value factors for each year, by adding down the columns, Table 5.2 also shows the present value of a 30-year annuity.

As we saw before, at a 20 percent discount rate, you should be willing to pay $.83 (H6) for each dollar we expect to receive in one year, $.69 (H7) for each dollar you expect to receive in two years, etc. For the dollar that you expect to receive in 30 years, you would not even be willing to pay one penny, i.e., cell H35 shows a zero value.[16] Adding up all of the present values in cells H6 through H35, the total is $4.98 (H36). In other words, at a 20 percent discount rate, for the right to receive $1.00 every year for 30 years you should only be willing to pay $4.98. What a cheapskate you are! So, timing is everything. Thirty dollars received as one dollar once a year for 30 years is worth less than five dollars at a 20 percent discount rate.

Let's look at the 10-year patterns. The present value of the first 10 years of cash flows is $4.19 (H39), the second 10 years is $.68 (H40), and the last 10 years is $.11 (H41)—again totaling $4.98 (H42 = H36). In percentage terms, the first 10 years accounts for 84 percent (H46) of the present value of the 30-year annuity, the second 10 years for 14 percent (H47), and the last

---

[15] Note that the percentage increase from 1980 to 2000 varies widely among the different foods, as food prices are affected not only by the general level of inflation, but also technological changes in farming, manufacturing, and distribution; weather, nutritional trends, and food tastes; and other supply and demand conditions.

[16] In fact it is worth a fraction of one cent, but with only two decimal points, it appears as zero.

10 years comprises only 2 percent (H48) of the present value of the annuity.

Of course, the amounts and the percentages change with the appropriate discount rate. At a 5 percent discount rate—again, that is appropriate for discounting U.S. Treasury bonds—the present value is $15.37 (B36), which is more than three times the present value at a 20 percent discount rate. Intuitively, this is reasonable, because, as noted earlier, the U.S. Treasury is a risk-free[17] loan, and we require less interest income—and thus a lower discount rate—to part with our money than we would with investing in a private business. For the 5 percent discount rate, the last 10 years accounts for 19 percent (B48) of the present value of receiving one dollar every year for 30 years, which is much higher than the 2 percent (H48) at a 20 percent discount rate. Since the U.S. Treasury is a risk-free loan, we discount the future much less than we do for a private business. Thus, it makes intuitive sense that the more distant cash flows in Years 21 to 30 matter more to us when we loan to the U.S. Treasury than when we invest in a private business.

Another way of looking at it is that with an investment in a private business, we are much more likely to discount the "pie-in-the-sky" forecasts of having sales in the hundreds of millions of dollars 30 years now and focus on "the bird in the hand," i.e., the forecast cash flows in the first 5 to 10 years. In valuing a startup business, where a 30 percent discount rate is appropriate, 93 percent (M46) of the present value comes from the first 10 years of forecast cash flows, and the last 10 years contribute no material present value, i.e., M48 appears as zero percent (which means that it is less than 0.5 percent of the present value of the 30 years of cash flows).

[17] It is risk-free in the sense that there is no material risk of the U.S. Treasury defaulting on its loans. There is still term risk in the longer loans. For example, a 30-year Treasury bond paying 5 percent when originally purchased would become an unattractive investment if interest rates rise to 6 percent. In hindsight, it would have been better for the investor to buy a short-term Treasury bill until interest rates rose, then buy the long-term bond. This is covered in greater detail later in the chapter.

The next step mechanically in the mathematics is to multiply the PVF by the forecast cash flow(s). If we expect \$1 million of cash flow every year for 30 years, and 20 percent is the appropriate discount rate for the specific investment we are valuing, then its present value is \$1 million × \$4.98 (H36) = \$4.98 million. If we are expecting cash flows only for two years, then we would be willing to pay \$1 million × \$.83 (H6) = \$830,000 for the first year's expected cash flow, plus \$1 million × 0.69 (H7) = \$690,000 for the second year's cash flow, for a total of \$1,520,000, which is the present value of the two years of expected cash flows.

CALCULATING DISCOUNT RATES

Calculating discount rates is a topic about which many hundreds of thousands of pages of scholarly and professional literature have been written. For the sake of practicality, we will keep it relatively short and useful.

In this section, we discuss some fundamentals of finance that will be helpful in understanding business discount rates on a deeper level. Later in this chapter you will see that small firms are more volatile and therefore riskier than large firms. For starters, we'll look at the components of equity returns.

One of the few and most powerful laws of finance is the greater the risk, the greater the expected reward that investors will demand. Note that there is a significant difference between the expected reward (return) on a security before we invest in it and the actual return after the fact.

Bonds

A bond is a contract between a borrower and a lender. For a simple bond, the usual form is that the borrower—also known as the "issuer"—promises to pay a specific series of interest payments to the lender over time, plus the return of the principal at the end of the term of the bond.

The interest payments are stated at a nominal rate, also known as the "coupon rate." For example, if a \$1000 bond carries a 7 percent coupon rate and pays annually, the borrower must pay interest of $70 per year. The coupon rate remains fixed throughout the life of the bond.

The market rate of interest—also called the "yield to maturity"—can fluctuate on a daily basis. If the market rate equals the coupon rate, then the bond will sell for its face value—$1000 in the current example. If the market interest rate rises above 7 percent for the issuer, then the bond price will decline. Suppose the market rate rises to 8 percent on new bonds being issued for borrowers of the same risk. Investors would prefer to invest in the new bond rather than the old one, preferring to receive $80 interest per year instead of $70. Therefore, investors will bid down the price to less than $1000 to compensate for the below-market nominal interest rate on the bond. The opposite will be true if market interest rates decline. For example, if the bond price declines to 6 percent, then new $1000 bonds will pay only $60 interest per year. Consequently, this bond will be very attractive, and investors will bid up the price to yield 6 percent.

The lowest bond interest rate is that of a 30-day U.S. Treasury bill. Since the risk of default on this bill is virtually zero, its real return, which is the return above inflation, is also close to zero.

The next step up the ladder in risk is a Long-Term Treasury bond. While there is still virtually no risk of default, there is a new risk in this type of a bond. If you buy a 30-year bond, for example, your coupon rate is "locked in" for 30 years. If you buy a new 10 percent bond today and one day later interest rates on the same type of bond rise to 12 percent, then you're stuck for 30 years earning 2 percent a year less than if you'd bought a 30-day Treasury bill, followed by a 30-year bond after interest rates rise. You can sell the bond, but, as you will soon see, you will suffer a capital loss in doing so. When interest rates rise, the value of your existing bonds go down, and when interest rates decline, the value of your existing bonds rises—and the longer the time horizon of the bond, the more widely the prices swing. That is why the interest rates usually rise as the time horizon increases: because of the greater risk of price swings.

The interest rate differential between a Short-Term and a Long-Term Treasury bond is called the *horizon premium*. Corporate bonds are riskier than U.S. Treasury bonds because they carry a real risk of default. The interest rate differential between these bonds and government bonds is called a *default premium*. Moody's and Standard & Poor's both rate corporate bonds for their risk. The highest-rated bonds carry lower interest rates, because investors are less worried about losing their money than they are with junk bonds, and consequently they require a lower return to compensate them for their lower risk than investors in low-grade bonds.

Stocks

Stocks, also called *equities*, are riskier yet. Stockholders get paid after bondholders, and that is true whether the company is solvent or insolvent. Investing in equities, being riskier, should promise higher returns on average than investing in bonds. Otherwise a rational investor would always invest in bonds. The average differential in returns on equities compared to corporate bonds is called the *equity premium*.

Therefore, we could calculate the expected return on an equity as the expected return on a Short-Term Treasury bill + Horizon Premium + Default Premium + Equity Risk Premium. More commonly, business valuators usually use a shortcut and calculate an equity risk premium over the Long-Term Treasury bond rate. Beyond the equity risk premium, those who invest in the stock market know there is also a small stock risk premium to quantify the higher return that small-cap stocks experience in the very long run (and not necessarily in the short run) over large-cap stocks.[18]

Research in my first book and in prior articles that were published indicates that the smaller the firm, the higher the discount rate should be, all other things being equal, because the returns on small firms are more volatile than those on large firms. Other researchers also found that small firms have more

---

[18] In any particular year or even over periods of time as long as 20 years, large stocks may outperform small stocks. Indeed, there is debate in the academic and professional literature as to whether there really is a small stock premium. However, the dominant opinion is that there is, and we will go by that school of thought in this book.

volatility in their operating margins than large firms.[19] Since investors prefer stability, they prefer to buy large firm stocks—all other things being equal—which causes the price of large firm stocks to rise relative to small firm stocks. This lowers the returns on the large firm stocks and raises the returns on the small firm stocks. Thus, investors demand and receive higher returns on the latter investments to compensate them for the undesirable volatility.

Discount Rates According to Firm Value

My calculation of historical average rates of return in the stock markets from the years 1938-2001 can be seen in Table 5.4, which is a good starting point to use for discount rates.[20] Again, it isn't necessary to understand the mathematics behind the calculations since the valuation software that can be downloaded from my Web site, (included with the purchase of this book) will perform the mathematics for you automatically. You can relax and do your best to understand the material without any performance pressure.

The table is very simple. Column A shows various levels of market capitalization—which is price per share times the number of shares—and is the FMV of publicly traded firms, and column B shows the average rate of return experienced in the stock markets[21] from 1938 to 2001, i.e., for the past 64 years. For ex-

---

[19] Roger Grabowski and David King, "New Evidence on Size Effects and Rates of Return," *Business Valuation Review*, September 1999, 108–113.

[20] I excluded 1926 to 1937 because those years, which included the Roaring 20s and the Great Depression, were extremely volatile, and such extreme volatility is unlikely to recur.

[21] The "semi-raw" data comes from Ibbotson Associates SBBI Yearbook for the year 2002. However, Ibbotson's ultimate source for data is the Center for Research in Security Prices (CRSP) from the University of Chicago. CRSP divides the New York Stock Exchange into 10 groups of firms—called deciles. Each decile contains 10 percent of the firms in the NYSE, grouped by market capitalization, i.e., size. Decile 1 contains the largest 10 percent of the NYSE firms, decile 2 contains the next largest 10 percent and decile 10 contains the smallest 10 percent. Then CRSP adds in American Stock Exchange and Nasdaq firms into the respective decile groups by size. The net result is, the CRSP data—and hence my regression—is sized by NYSE deciles, but contains data from all three U.S. stock exchanges.

	A	B
1	**TABLE 5.4**	
2	Discount Rates According to Firm Value	
3		
4	**Mkt Cap 12/31/01 = FMV**	**Discount Rate [1]**
5	10,000,000,000	13.7%
6	1,000,000,000	16.0%
7	100,000,000	18.2%
8	50,000,000	18.9%
9	35,388,037	19.2%
10	25,000,000	19.6%
11	20,000,000	19.8%
12	10,000,000	20.5%
13	5,000,000	21.2%
14	3,000,000	21.7%
15	1,000,000	22.8%
16	500,000	23.5%
17	250,000	24.1%
18	125,000	24.8%
19	100,000	25.0%
20	50,000	25.7%
21	25,000	26.4%
22		
23	[1] Based on Abrams' regression of the SBBI-2002 Yearbook 1938-2001	
24	results.	

ample, $10 billion firms averaged a 13.7 percent (B5) rate of return over the 64 years, while $1 billion firms experienced a 16 percent (B6) average return. The difference between the two size groups is 2.3 percent. That difference extends to smaller firms too. When we go down in size by another factor of 10, i.e., from $1 billion firms to $100 million firms, the discount rate increases another 2.3 percent, to 18.2 percent (B7).[22] A $10 million firm had average returns of 18.2% + 2.3% = 20.5% (B12).

---

[22] It is actually 2.27 percent. Using one decimal point is simpler; however, it causes an apparent, but not real rounding error.

Similarly, reducing firm size by one-half increased the average rate of return by 0.7 percent. You can see this by looking at the $20 million firms, which had an average return of 19.8 percent (B11), while $10 million and $5 million firms had average returns of 20.5 (B12) and 21.2 percent (B13).

Of the various firm sizes, $35,388,037 (A9) is the average size of the 10th decile, which is the smallest of the publicly traded firms. The discount rates for all firm sizes below that (B10 through B21) are my extrapolations of the results from the publicly traded stocks.

Most privately held firms are smaller than $35.4 million in FMV. Therefore, it was necessary to extrapolate the results to forecast discount rates for smaller firms, which accounts for rows 10 through 21 in the table.[23]

Circularity of the Calculation

While publicly held firms have an objective stock price, which is the FMV in Table 5.4, privately held firms do not. Therefore, it's possible to choose a discount rate that is inconsistent with the value of your firm, and it is imperative to ascertain that the assumed discount rate used in the Discounted Cash Flow Method is consistent with the value calculated. If not, you must update the discount rate in order to force consistency in the assumption and the result.

This is necessary because we must first estimate a value of the firm in order to calculate a discount rate, which we use to calculate the value of the firm! This is circular reasoning and is only valid if the assumption is consistent with the result, as mentioned above. Table 5.4 provides guidance, so your initial guess is likely to be close to the correct discount rate, and the iterations are done semiautomatically with our valuation software, with clear instructions on how to ensure the consistency of the discount rate.

---

[23] All extrapolations are never as empirically sound as interpolations. However, the results are intuitively appealing.

Adjustments to the Discount Rate

The discount rates in Table 5.4 represent the average rate of return for the average publicly held firm in each size (value) category. However, not all firms are average. If your firm is likely to differ in any material way from the average publicly held firm in your size category, you should make adjustments to the discount rate.

Note the following common situations that imply making adjustments to the discount rate:

- *Very high or very low financial leverage*. The use of debt as part of the financing of a business is called "financial leverage." The two most common quantitative measures of financial leverage are Debt-to-Total Assets ratio, which is interest-bearing debt divided by total assets, and the Debt-to-Equity ratio, which is interest-bearing debt divided by the book value of equity. Most publicly held firms have a middling level of leverage, which often varies by industry. If your firm has an unusually high or low level of debt, it is appropriate to increase or decrease the discount rate to reflect that. Most commonly, I add or subtract 1 to 2 percent for unusual leverage, although I might make a larger adjustment for extremes, e.g., for a firm that is 90 percent or more debt financed. However, if your firm has very high leverage, you will likely need to use Invested Capital Method to value the firm, which is much more complicated and beyond the scope of this book.
- *Depth of management,* One of the obvious changes that occur in comparing very large firms to medium and small firms is that the quantity and quality of management tends to decline with the reduction in firm size. Billion dollar firms have hordes of MBAs from the best business schools, while small firms are often managed by a founder with no specific education in business management. Nevertheless, you should have a sense for how strong the management is in your firm compared to other firms of your size. If a preliminary DCF shows a valuation of $1 million, you should compare your firm to

the average $1 million firm. If you happen to have three members of the management team with MBAs from the University of Chicago,[24] then your firm has an unusually high level of management for its size, and I would reduce the discount rate by 2 percent. Why 2 percent and not 1 or 3 percent? Since I'm not aware of any empirical research on the impact in this case of qualitative factors on returns or values, there is no right answer. It's strictly a professional judgment call. If you have no one at the helm with any great business education, training, or talent, I would add 1 to 3 percent to the discount rate.

- *Dependence on the owner(s).* Very small businesses are almost always extremely dependent on the owner. This dependence is a big risk. Large businesses tend to be less dependent on any one person or small number of people. If your business is substantially more (or less) dependent on you than the average business in your size category, then I would add to (or subtract from) the discount rate accordingly. Also note that this factor is usually a result of the previous one, i.e., less dependence on the owner is usually a consequence of greater depth of management, and it is important not to double count. However, there are exceptions, e.g., firms with depth of management that are still overly dependent on their owners, who fail to delegate authority appropriately.
- *Dependence on a small number of customers or suppliers.* If you have only one customer—who can stop buying from you at any time—your business is extremely vulnerable, and you should add to the discount rate for that.[25] Similarly, if your business is entirely dependent on one exclusive supplier relationship that is vulnerable to being cancelled, this is a material risk that belongs in the discount rate.

---

[24] My alma mater. Yes, I am a chauvinist.

[25] There may be a more sophisticated way for professionals to handle this by forecasting multiple scenarios and weighting them. That approach is beyond the scope of this book.

- *Unusual stability or volatility.* The finding that firm size is correlated with the volatility of earnings means that we should adjust the discount rate for businesses that do not fit the usual profile. If a small firm has extremely stable profit margins, then it makes sense to treat it as if it were a large business and lower the discount rate accordingly—as long as the stability is real and not artificially generated by creative accounting to smooth out income—and vice versa for a large business with very volatile profit margins.

The above list is not exhaustive. Any factor that makes your cash flow more or less risky than the average business of your size is a candidate for an adjustment to the discount rate.

Let's create an extreme example to illustrate adjustments to the discount rate. If the preliminary valuation of your firm comes to $5 million, Table 5.4 tells us the discount rate should be 21.2 percent, which I would round to 21 percent. (There is no point in conveying a false degree of accuracy. I try to be accurate and scientific, but I almost never work in discount rates of tenths of a percent.)

Let's say that your firm has no interest-bearing debt and that you have a five-star management team, but your sales are to one customer only and you have only one supplier, with no others available. In other words, if your customer stops buying from you, or your supplier stops selling to you, you're out of business. Also, let's say your earnings are extremely volatile.

I would subtract 1 or 2 percent for the lack of debt—let's say 2 percent. I would subtract another 2 percent for the all-star management team. I would add about 5 percent for the one customer, 5 percent for the one supplier, and perhaps 2 percent for the extreme volatility. The net adjustment would be $-2\% - 2\% + 5\% + 5\% + 2\% = 8\%$, which when added to 21 percent leads to a discount rate of 29 percent. If we change the facts a little bit and say that there is another potential supplier, I might add only 1 instead of 5 percent, which would reduce the adjustment to the discount rate to 4 percent instead of 8, with the new discount rate being 25 percent. There is no magic or science to these adjustments. These are estimates, based on judgment.

Using CAPM to Calculate the Discount Rate

If the buyer of your firm is likely to be a very large firm or a well-diversified, wealthy individual, you should consider using a different model for calculating your discount rate. The most well-known discount rate model for publicly held firms is the Capital Asset Pricing Model (abbreviated as CAPM, pronounced as "CAP-M"). CAPM produces much smaller discount rates than the size-based model; however, it presumes a degree of diversification that rarely exists for most small- to medium-size private firms and their owners.

Here's the formula for CAPM:

$$r = r_f + (\beta \times ERP)$$

Where r_f is the risk-free rate, usually taken to be the yield on Long-Term U.S. Treasury bills; β = beta, a measure of relative market risk;[26] and *ERP* is the equity risk premium, most commonly calculated as an historical number equal to the average market returns minus the current risk-free rate.

The technical nuances of using CAPM are far beyond the scope of this book, so we are going to keep this as simple as possible. Let's take the 30-year Treasury bond rate as of October 31, 2003, which was 5.5 percent.[27] The long-run equity premium is approximately 6 to 8 percent, although it was negative for 1998-2002.[28] Nevertheless, most practitioners use the long-run ERP for CAPM calculations. Let's use 8 percent.

Next we need to understand beta. It is a measure of the volatility of the stock we are trying to measure compared to the volatility of the market as a whole. As a proxy for ownership in your own personal firm, valuation analysts would use a sample of publicly held companies in your industry to calculate your beta. A beta of 1.00 means that your firm is, on average, equally as volatile as the stock market overall, usually measured by the S&P 500 index. A beta of 1.2 means that your firm is 20 percent more volatile than the market, and a beta of 0.8 means that your firm is 20 percent less volatile. Some industries are

---

[26] Technically, beta is the covariance of the returns on a particular stock divided by the variance of the returns on the market.

[27] http://www.federalreserve.gov/releases/H15/Current/.

[28] SBBI-2003, Ibbotson Associates, Chicago, 77, Table 5.5.

known to be volatile, and others are the opposite. Typically, agricultural commodities are less volatile, because people need to eat—whether the market and the economy are good or bad. Luxury items, such as caviar or expensive travel, tend to have high betas. Let's assume your firm has a beta of 1.2, and we will see the appropriate discount rate under CAPM.

Substituting our assumed values into the CAPM equation, we get: $r = 5.5 + (1.2 \times 8\%) = 15.1\%$, or 15 percent rounded. Note that a beta of 1.0 would have led to a discount rate of 13.5 percent. Both are very low for a small firm. The low interest rates now compared to their levels in the prior 20 years draw down the discount rate further. I would still consider adding at least some size-based premium to the discount rate, in addition to other firm-specific adjustments

Using the CAPM instead of the size-based discount rates can easily double or triple your valuation. However, I strongly caution you to be realistic about your likely buyer. Unless you have a firm worth at least $10 million, and perhaps many times that, your likely buyer is an undiversified individual or firm, and it's unrealistic to think that your buyer would require such a low Return on Investment in your small firm (which would result in your being paid a fabulously high PE multiple). If you have such a possibility and there is real potential for much money on the table, then it's time to bring in professional help.

I had a client in 1994 with net income after corporate taxes around $1.2 million that sold for close to $30 million. So the dream deals occasionally happen. For planning purposes, be very wary of the very expensive sin of self-deception. Relatively few small businesses ever make deals like this, and for most firms it is more realistic to use the much more conservative size-based discount rates in Table 5.4.

CONCLUSION

In this chapter you have learned:

- How to calculate Return on Investment (ROI, also known as Return on Equity, ROE) for publicly and privately held firms.

- The mathematics of how to calculate future values and present values.
- Volatility of Return on Investment is the way that we measure risk. The higher the risk, the higher the expected return must be to entice investors' money into a particular business or project.
- The discount rate is the appropriate rate of Return on Investment used to discount forecast cash flows to present value.
- Inserting the appropriate discount rate into Present Value equation will produce the present value of that year's cash flow.
- How to roughly select the correct discount rate from using the sized-based discount rates in Table 5-4.
- How to make adjustments to the discount rate.
- When to use the CAPM (Capital Asset Pricing Model) instead of the sizebased discount rates.

The present value factors are the necessary mathematical conversion of expected cash flow forecasts, which we covered in the last chapter, to present value today. Thus, we have almost completed the second step of the DCF Method.

There still remains one important component that we will need to address: how to calculate the present values of cash flows in neat and compact manner. It would be very messy if we had to project 30 or more years of cash flows, discount them to present value, and add them up to calculate FMV. Fortunately, there is a wonderful shortcut, called the Gordon Model, which we'll go into in the next chapter, that will enable us to forecast as little as one year—and probably no more than five years—of cash flows, discount those to present value using PVFs, and add them up. Then we can use the Gordon Model, which is a single mathematical formula, to value the rest of the cash flows.

Chapter 6

Valuation Using the Gordon Model

In the last chapter we covered discounting to present value, which is necessary in order to incorporate the risk of the business into the discount rate and to translate forecast future cash flows in value today. However, this only works for forecast cash flows year by year, and we definitely do not want to have to forecast and discount 30 to 100 years of cash flows. Life is too short! We will need a more powerful tool to make the mechanics of valuation easier: the Gordon Model.[1]

HOW THE MODEL WORKS

Present Value of a Perpetuity with Constant Growth

The Gordon Model multiple (GMM) is the present value of receiving \$1.00 at the end of next year, $\$(1.00 + g)$ at the end of two years, $\$(1.00 + g)^2$ in three years . . . forever, when discounted to present value at the discount rate, r, and where g is

1 The model was first developed in 1938 by J. B. Williams, then amplified in 1956 by M. J. Gordon, after whom it is named, and Eli Shapiro. M. J. Gordon. and E. Shapiro, "Capital Equipment Analysis: The Required Rate of Profit," *Management Science*, 3 (1956), 102–110. Thinking about this, maybe it's time for me to replace Williams' press agent with Gordon's and hire him to rename $E = mc^2$ as "The Abrams Equation"!

the perpetual growth rate of cash flows. For example, if $g = 5\%$ and $r = 25\%$, then the GMM is the present value of receiving \$1.00 at the end of Year One, \$1.05 at the end of Year Two, \$1.1025 at the end of Year Three, and so on, discounted to present value at a 25 percent discount rate.

While we will cover the formulas for the GMM later in the chapter, for now take it as truth that the correct GMM for this series of cash flows is equal to 4.00, which means that for every one dollar of forecast cash flow in Year One, you should be willing to pay \$4.00 now for the right to receive those specific cash flows. If you forecast the first year's cash flow to be \$10,000, then the forecast cash flows are \$10,000 at the end of Year One, \$10,500 at the end of Year Two, \$11,025 at the end of Year Three . . . and you should be willing to pay \$10,000 × 4.00 = \$40,000 for the right to receive those cash flows.

The Gordon Model will enable you to value a mature business—one for which we forecast cash flows that grow at a constant rate forever. If the business already is mature, all you will need to do is forecast one year of economic cash flows, multiply that by the GMM, and check to make sure that the answer is consistent with the assumptions in the GMM. We will work a numerical example of this later in the chapter. At the end of the chapter, we'll discuss how to handle the valuation of a firm that is not yet mature.

The Gordon Model works exactly only for a company whose cash flows grow at a constant rate forever. In practice, it is reasonably accurate for mature firms in relatively stable industries. Even if your own company is not in this category, this method is nevertheless very important. There are two reasons for this:

1. While startup firms typically experience rapid growth for a few years, that growth usually slows down to a steady state after some number of years. We will still need the Gordon Model formula to value all cash flows after that point in time.
2. Even for companies with more variable sales, beyond a certain point we lose our ability to forecast each year's unique high or low growth with any sort of accuracy. For example, let's say that after 10 years in your busi-

> ness it seems silly to presume that you can accurately forecast cash flows as growing 8 percent in Year 11, 5 percent in Year 12, 7 percent in Year 13, 6 percent in Year 14, etc. Nobody has a crystal ball that good. It makes sense to say that the best we can do is assume that cash flows will grow at some reasonable average—say 6 percent—forever, value the remaining forecast cash flows accordingly, and discount them to net present value.

I should warn you that the next few pages have some mathematical detail. Don't worry if you have some difficulty understanding the math. My valuation spreadsheet in Chapter 7, which you can download from my Web site, will do the difficult calculations for you. It's important, however, as I've stated before when we've encountered formulas and equations, that you develop an intuition of what these formulas are and why they work, which should empower you to use the valuation spreadsheet with more accuracy.

You'll find a rigorous mathematical derivation of the Gordon Model on my Web site, www.abramsvaluation.com. Once there, select "Articles," then "Articles in .pdf," then download "The Gordon Model: Derivation & Relation to PE Multiple." More mathematically inclined readers would benefit by reading that first before proceeding. The only skills required are algebra and the ability to work with exponents.

The Value of a Stagnant Perpetuity

As the Gordon Model is the present value of a perpetuity with constant growth, it is a helpful preliminary step to discuss the value of a stagnant perpetuity.

A perpetuity is a cash flow that will pay a certain amount to you (and your heirs) forever. A stagnant perpetuity is one with a constant cash flow forever, i.e., growth is zero. Let's say you are entitled to \$100 per year forever. The value of that perpetuity is the annual income divided by the appropriate market rate of return for that income. If the rate of return is 10 percent, the value of the perpetuity would be \$100/0.10 = \$1000.

We can check that by multiplying through the equation by 0.10, which would give us $1000 × 0.10 = $100. In other words, at a value of $1000, a 10 percent annual return would mean we should receive $100 interest each year.

If the market rate of return for such a perpetuity is 8 percent instead, then its fair market value is $100/.08 = $1250. Again, we can check that by noting that an asset worth $1250 with an 8 percent annual rate of return would generate $100 per year income, $1250 × .08 = $100.

Valuation Equations

In Equation 6.1 we make the mathematical statement that the value of the perpetuity is equal to the economic cash flow that we forecast it will produce in the coming year, divided by the discount rate:

$$FMV = \frac{CF_{t+1}}{r} \tag{6.1}$$

This equation is fine for valuing a completely stagnant business—for example, a firm with economic net income expected to stay at $100,000 forever and whose rate of return is, let's say, 25 percent. The value would be $100,000/0.25 = $100,000 × 4 = $400,000. Note that dividing by 0.25 is mathematically equivalent to multiplying by 4. Thus, a 25 percent discount rate when there is no growth translates to a Price-to-Cash Flow multiple of 4.

Now we must generalize the above formula in order to handle constant, perpetual growth (or decline), where g is the constant growth—usually in the zero to 6 percent range. If cash flow comes at the end of each year, then we use Equation 6.2, the End-of-Year Gordon Model formula, which is:

$$FMV = \frac{CF_{t+1}}{r - g} \tag{6.2}$$

Some observations on this formula:

- Notice the subscript $t + 1$ in the numerator. This means that we use *next* year's forecast cash flow, not the prior year's actual cash flow. This causes much confusion, even among professionals, since when using a Price Earnings multiple in a Guideline Companies Method (see the appendix to Chapter 2, Table 2.1), we use *last* year's earnings. In other words, with the Gordon Model, we use next year's earnings, and in a Guideline Company Method we use last year's.

- Equation 6.2 only makes sense when $g < r$, which is to say, when long-term constant growth is less than the rate of return (the discount rate). If $g \geq r$, the results are nonsense. This could only happen in a very high growth business, and even then, only for a few years at most. In such cases, it will be impossible to apply the Gordon Model multiple to the first year's cash flows. You will have to use a Discounted Cash Flow valuation approach with several years of annual forecasts before using the Gordon Model to value the subsequent lower growth cash flows. (We covered the multiyear Discounted Cash Flow in Chapter 5.)
- Equation 6.2 will produce a larger number than Equation 6.1 as long as the constant growth is positive, which is the most common case. Equation 6.2 will equal Equation 6.1 when growth is zero, and it will be less than Equation 6.1 when growth is negative, i.e., when you forecast the business to have a long-term, constant decline in cash flows.
- The normal rates of return, i.e., the usual range of reasonable values for r, are 12 to 20 percent for publicly traded firms. If a private firm is of the same size as a public firm, then it is reasonable to use a similar rate of return—unless the business has much higher financial risk due to high debt, or it has substantially different business risk. Most privately held firms are smaller than publicly held firms, and a normal range of discount rates for smaller private firms is 23 to 26 percent (see Table 5.4 in the previous chapter).[2]

[2] Again, some valuation authorities feel these discount rates are too high. There is room for legitimate difference of opinion.

- A normal range of growth rates for most mature private firms in the United States is 1 percent (which is a real 2 percent decline, assuming 3 percent inflation) to 6 percent, or 3 percent inflationary growth and 3 percent real growth.[3] It's true that startup firms have been known to grow at 100 to 500 percent per year—sometimes for several years. However, there are limits to that. Take a firm with cash flows of $100,000 last year—Year Zero—and project 100 percent growth for 10 years. Then Year 10 forecast cash flows will be over $100 million and Year 20 cash flows about $105 billion. As you can see, exponential growth at inappropriately high growth rates or appropriate rates for too long easily leads to ridiculous results. It's all too easy to make assumptions that a single firm will be larger than the U.S. economy by Year 20. Be careful in assuming realistic growth rates. It's also important to understand that growth rates in sales and growth rates in cash flows are not the same. It's possible to have a rapid increase in sales and to make less money. It's growth rates in cash flows that count in valuation, not just sales growth.

While Equation 6.2 is closer to reality than Equation 6.1 for valuing a business, we must make one more adjustment for the timing of the income. Most businesses produce cash flow

[3] The 55-year real (i.e., in constant 1996 dollars) growth rate in GDP from January 1, 1949 – January 1, 2004 was 3.45 percent (from my calculations of data in a downloadable file from the St. Louis Federal Reserve Bank, www.research.stlouisfed.org/fred2/series/GDPPOT.XLS). However, the long-term trend is toward slowing growth. The 25-year real growth rate was 3.0 percent, the 15-year rate was 1.8 percent, and the five-year rate was 1.2 percent. It is likely that the higher growth rates in the earlier years is because Europe and Japan had little productive capacity after World War II and needed time to become more competitive. Some of the real growth came from startup firms (net of the loss from bankruptcies and declining firms). Thus, it is likely that the average existing firm grows less than 3 percent in nominal dollars. For example, assuming 2 percent of the growth came from startup firms and using the 1.2 percent five-year growth rate as a starting point, it is reasonable to estimate growth of the average existing firm as 1.2 percent plus 3 percent inflation, minus 2 percent from net startups, equals 2.2 percent growth.

throughout the year more or less evenly, rather than producing nothing throughout the entire year and making everything on the last day. If the cash flow occurs evenly through the year, in a present value sense it is as if all income occurs in the middle of the year. Adjusting the valuation formula for midyear cash flows, we use the following Midyear Gordon Model formula:

$$FMV = \frac{\sqrt{1+r}}{r-g} \times CF_{t+1} \tag{6.3}$$

Again, as in Equation 6.2, we use our forecast of next year's economic cash flow. We can create an alternative formula for the value of the perpetuity by substituting the relationship that cash flow equals net income times the Payout Ratio, or $CF = Inc \times POR$, into Equation 6.3, which leads to an alternate Midyear Gordon Model formula:

$$FMV = \frac{\sqrt{1+r}}{r-g} \times Inc_{t+1} \times POR \tag{6.3a}$$

GORDON MODEL MULTIPLES

Table 6.1, below, contains the Gordon Model multiples (GMMs) for a wide range of discount and growth rates. Section 1 of the table is identical with Table 5.4 in Chapter 5. It is the results of my statistical analysis of stock market returns for 1938-2001.

Section 2 of the table contains the GMMs for growth rates from −2 percent (column D) to 8 percent (column N), and for discount rates of 13.7 percent in row 7 to 26.4 percent in row 22 (which relate to firm sizes of $10 billion down to $25,000, respectively).

You can see that as we move down any column, the discount rate rises and the GMM declines. As we move to the right across any row, as the growth rate rises, the GMM also rises. Thus, the GMM rises as we move northeast in the table, so to speak, and declines to the southwest.

Gordon Model Example

Let's do a simple example. Suppose economic net income was $119,048 last year, and we expect cash flows to grow by 5 percent a year. That means we expect economic net income to be $119,048 × 1.05 = $125,000 next year. We calculate (or estimate) the Payout Ratio to be 80 percent. Therefore, our forecast economic cash flow is $125,000 × 80% = $100,000 next year. The steps in the valuation process are as follows:

1. Let's make an initial guess—which will turn out to be incorrect—that the FMV of the business is $1 million, which implies the correct discount rate is 22.8 percent (Table 6.1, B16). The GMM is 6.2 (K16). We multiply $100,000 × 6.2 = $620,000.
2. We compare the value assumed of $1 million with the calculated value[4] of $620,000 and find that they are materially different. So we need to do another iteration of calculations.[5]
3. We use the $620,000 we just calculated as our next round's assumed value. The closest FMV in Table 6.1, Section 1, is $500,000 (A17), which has a GMM of 6.0 (K17). We multiply $100,000 × 6.0 = $600,000.
4. We compare the $600,000 calculated FMV with the assumed FMV of $500,000 and find that there is no other FMV in column A that is closer to $600,000. We can stop now. In nerd language, we have iterated to a steady state. (I'm sure you can breathe a lot easier knowing that.)
5. Just to show you that this model works regardless of your initial guess, if we had initially guessed the business had an FMV of $100,000, we would have used a GMM of 5.6 (K20). That would have led to a calculation of $100,000 × 5.6 = $560,000, which, in turn, would have lead us to the 6.0 multiple again for a $500,000 FMV firm. Thus, as long as you follow through with the iterations, you will get the same answer, regardless of your initial guess. In nerd language, the model is convergent.

---

[4] The spreadsheet has more decimal points than the table shows, so the actual result is different by an apparent but not real rounding error. The same is true of subsequent calculations. For simplicity, we use rounded numbers.

[5] An iteration is a round of calculations.

Congratulations! You have just performed your first business valuation! You could have stopped after the fourth step, so you could have done this in one or two minutes—once you have a forecast of economic net income and the Payout Ratio.

Shortcut Midyear Gordon Model Formula

As you have seen in Table 6.1, most small businesses should require rates of return of 23 to 26 percent. The square root of one plus those two numbers are 1.11 and 1.12, respectively. For mathematical ease, we can approximate the midyear correction for small business as being about 10 percent. We can then use Equation 6.4 as a "quick-and-dirty" Gordon Model formula approximation:

$$FMV \cong 1.1 \times \frac{1}{r-g} \times CF_{t+1} \tag{6.4}$$

In other words, this approximation formula for midyear cash flows is 10 percent larger than the End-of-Year GMM. The approximation works over a wide range of firms, with fairly little error. While we do not use Equation 6.4 in this chapter, we will make use of it later in the book.

VALUATION WHEN A FIRM IS NOT MATURE

The foregoing valuation is fine for an already mature firm. If it will take, let's say, five years to reach "maturity," first you will need to discount the first five years of cash flows to present value, as you learned in Chapter 5. Then you will forecast Year Six economic cash flow, determine the appropriate GMM—given your forecast of constant growth in cash flows and your best initial estimate of the value of the firm—and multiply your tentative GMM times Year Six economic cash flow. The result of that multiplication is the present value of the Years Six to infinity cash flows as of the end of Year Five. Then you will discount that back five years to present value as of time zero (now), and add the present value of Years One through Five cash flows.

This becomes a tentative FMV of your company. You will need to go through the iteration process to make sure that the

	A	B	C	D	E	F	G	H	I	J	K	L	M	N
1	**TABLE 6.1**													
2	Gordon Model Multiples													
3														
4	**Section 1 [1]**			**Section 2: GMMs (Midyear)**										
5		**Avg**		**Constant Growth Rate = *g***										
6	**Mkt Cap = FMV**	**Return**		**−2%**	**−1%**	**0%**	**1%**	**2%**	**3%**	**4%**	**5%**	**6%**	**7%**	**8%**
7	$10,000,000,000	13.7%		6.8	7.3	7.8	8.4	9.1	10.0	11.0	12.3	13.9	16.0	18.8
8	1,000,000,000	16.0%		6.0	6.4	6.8	7.2	7.7	8.3	9.0	9.8	10.8	12.0	13.5
9	100,000,000	18.2%		5.4	5.7	6.0	6.3	6.7	7.1	7.6	8.2	8.9	9.7	10.6
10	50,000,000	18.9%		5.2	5.5	5.8	6.1	6.4	6.9	7.3	7.8	8.4	9.2	10.0
11	25,000,000	19.6%		5.1	5.3	5.6	5.9	6.2	6.6	7.0	7.5	8.0	8.7	9.4
12	20,000,000	19.8%		5.0	5.3	5.5	5.8	6.1	6.5	6.9	7.4	7.9	8.5	9.3
13	10,000,000	20.5%		4.9	5.1	5.4	5.6	5.9	6.3	6.7	7.1	7.6	8.1	8.8
14	5,000,000	21.2%		4.7	5.0	5.2	5.5	5.7	6.1	6.4	6.8	7.3	7.8	8.4
15	3,000,000	21.7%		4.7	4.9	5.1	5.3	5.6	5.9	6.2	6.6	7.0	7.5	8.1
16	1,000,000	22.8%		4.5	4.7	4.9	5.1	5.3	5.6	5.9	6.2	6.6	7.0	7.5
17	500,000	23.5%		4.4	4.5	4.7	4.9	5.2	5.4	5.7	6.0	6.4	6.8	7.2
18	250,000	24.1%		4.3	4.4	4.6	4.8	5.0	5.3	5.5	5.8	6.1	6.5	6.9
19	125,000	24.8%		4.2	4.3	4.5	4.7	4.9	5.1	5.4	5.6	5.9	6.3	6.6
20	100,000	25.0%		4.1	4.3	4.5	4.7	4.9	5.1	5.3	5.6	5.9	6.2	6.6
21	50,000	25.7%		4.0	4.2	4.4	4.5	4.7	4.9	5.2	5.4	5.7	6.0	6.3
22	25,000	26.4%		4.0	4.1	4.3	4.4	4.6	4.8	5.0	5.3	5.5	5.8	6.1
23														
24	[1] Section 1 is the same as Table 5.4.													

value assumed and the value calculated are consistent. Don't worry too much about the iterations, because the valuation spreadsheet that you can download from my Web site automates this process for you. We will present and explain this software in Chapter 7.

For example, suppose your firm plans to retain all net income for the first five years of operations. The first year in which you forecast dividends (whether explicit dividends or implicit dividends in the form of excess compensation) is in Year Six, for $1 million. After that you expect 6 percent growth in cash flows forever. The valuation steps are as follows:

1. Assume a FMV of $1 million. The GMM is 6.6 (Table 6-1, L16).
2. Multiply $1 million × 6.6 = $6.6 million. That is the tentative FMV as of the end of Year Five for the forecast cash flows from Years Six to infinity.
3. Discount five years back to present value today. Note, here we do not use a midyear present value factor. We discount exactly five years. The present value factor at a discount rate of 22.8 percent (B16) is 0.36, i.e., $(1/1.228^5) = 0.36$. We multiply $6.6 million × 0.36 = $2.4 million (rounded).
4. The calculated value is closer to an FMV of $3 million than it is to the $1 million, so we need to do one more iteration. The GMM for $3 million is 7.0 (L15).[6] Then, $1 million × 7.0 = $7.0 million. Multiplying this by the present value factor of 0.36, the second iteration valuation is $2.5 million (rounded), which is consistent with the FMV that we assumed and the 7.0 GMM. Thus, we can stop with a valuation of $2.5 million.

---

[6] If you want to be sophisticated, you could choose a GMM of 6.9. This would be reasonable, since the GMM for a $2.4 million firm should be between the 6.6 GMM for $1 million firms and the 7.0 for $3 million firms, and closer to the GMM of 7.0 of the $3 million firms.

CONCLUSION

In these first six chapters I have laid the essential conceptual groundwork in business valuation. We have developed the Gordon Model formulas and performed two sample valuations using the Gordon Model. You have now learned most of the mathematics and theory that you will need to value a business. The rest should be relatively easy.

In the next chapter we will discuss how to use my valuation spreadsheet, which you can download from my Web site at www.abramsvaluation.com.

Chapter 7

Sample Discounted Cash Flow Valuation

Now that we've gone into the fundamentals of valuation, we're ready to discuss a basic Discounted Cash Flow valuation. This chapter will lead you through a spreadsheet presentation.[1] You can access a sample valuation spreadsheet from www.abramsvaluation.com. The Web site also has a blank version so you can perform a "quick and dirty" valuation of your business.

THE SAMPLE DCF

The numbers in this sample valuation are not based on any actual company; they are arbitrary. In Table 7.1, row 5, we call the future years simply One, Two, and Three (seen as numerals in the table, but spelled out in the text to avoid confusion with economic numbers).[2] Thus, if the current year is 2003, these years would correspond to 2004, 2005, and 2006.

---

[1] The author gratefully acknowledges the significant assistance by Chaim Borevitz in drafting this chapter.

[2] For simplicity, we assume all years are fiscal years following the valuation date, e.g., if the valuation date is 10/31/03, then Years One, Two, and Three are the 12 months ending 10/31/04, 10/31/05, and 10/31/06. If your projections are for calendar years but the valuation date is not the beginning of the year, there are complications in the present value factors, which professionals deal with regularly and are beyond the scope of this book.

	A	B	C	D
1	**TABLE 7.1**			
2	Sample Discounted Cash Flow Valuation			
3				
4				
5	**Future Years**	**1**	**2**	**3**
6	Forecast Economic Net Income	125,000	135,000	143,100
7	Payout Ratio (B19)	80%	80%	80%
8	**Forecast Economic Cash Flow**	**100,000**	**108,000**	**114,480**
9	Present Value Factor (Midyear Assumption)	0.9017	0.7331	0.5960
10	Present Value of Economic Cash Flow (Row 8 * Row 9)	90,167	79,171	68,229
11	**Total Present Value of Economic Cash Flow: Years 1-3**	**237,567**		
12	Forecast Economic Cash Flow Year 4 [D8 * (1 +B21)]	120,204		
13	Gordon Multiple	6,1614		
14	Economic Cash Flows Year 4 to Infinity: At End of Year 3	740,626		
15	Present Value Factor to Discount Year 4 to Infinity CF to Year O	0.5374		
16	Present Value of Economic Cash Flows Year 4 to Infinity	398,001		
17	**Total Present Value of Economic Cash Flows (B11+B16) [1]**	**635,567**		
18	*Assumptions*			
19	Payout Ratio	80%		
20	Discount Rate	23%		
21	Long-Term Cash Flow Growth Rate	5%		
22				
23	[1] Many business sales are structured in a way that the seller retains some of the working cap-			
24	ital items, usually cash, receivables, and payables. If you are thinking about making such a			
25	transaction, you will need to adjust FMV to purchase price by subtracting cash and receiv-			
26	ables and adding back payables that remain with the seller. See Chapter 10 for more details.			
27				
28	[2] In "The Equity Premium," Eugene Fama & Kenneth French, *Journal of Finance,* April 2002, 647-			
29	659, the authors forecast future returns will be lower than historical returns by approximately 4			
30	percent. In "The Supply of Stock Market Returns," Roger G. Ibbotson and Peng Chen, Yale ICF			
31	Working Paper 00-44, the authors forecast future returns will be lower than historical returns only			
32	by 1 percent. It will take a long time to sort through the arguments and come to some consen-			
33	sus, if there ever will be one. I use my professional judgment to choose Ibbotson's more con-			
34	servative 1 percent adjustment. In the meantime, obviously this creates a great deal of uncer-			
35	tainty about values.			

Looking at the table, you'll see that we assume forecast economic net income of $125,000 in B6 for the first forecast year. Net income grows by 8 percent in Year Two and 6 percent in Year Three (growth rates not shown in the table). In the last chapter you learned to use the Gordon Model multiple when growth in cash flow, in percentage terms, is constant. In our example we assume that in the fourth future year, cash flow will begin growing at a constant rate. Therefore, we forecast only three years of cash flow in detail and then use the Gordon Model multiple to forecast Years Four through infinity.

To transform net income to cash flow, we need to select a Payout Ratio. For simplicity, we assume a Payout Ratio of 80 percent (B19, transferred to row 7), which is the benchmark guesstimate from Chapter 4. To calculate cash flow in row 8, we multiply net income in row 6 by the Payout Ratio in row 7. Next, we calculate the present value factor, which I introduced in Chapter 5. We use a midyear present value factor, which assumes cash flows occur approximately evenly throughout the year. The formula for the midyear present value factor is $\frac{1}{(1 + r)^n}$, where r is the discount rate and n is the midpoint of the future year. The discount rate in this example is 23 percent (B20).[3] To discount the forecast cash flow to present value in row 10, we multiply the forecast cash flow in row 8 by the PVF in row 9. In B11 we sum the present value of forecast cash flow for the first three future years. Thus, the present value of forecast cash flow in future Years One to Three is $237,567.

We now use the Gordon Model multiple to calculate the present value of forecast cash flows from future Years Four to infinity.

First, we compute forecast cash flow for Year Four by multiplying forecast cash flow in Year Three, $114,480 (D8), by one plus the long-term cash flow growth rate, which we assume to be 5 percent (B21). Forecast cash flow in Year Four equals $120,204 (B12). We calculate a Gordon Model multiple of 6.1614 (B13) by inserting the 23 percent discount rate and the 5 per-

[3] I compute the discount rate using my log-size equation, updated for the years 1938-2001. See *Quantitative Business Valuation, ibid*, 117–169.

cent growth rate into the GMM formula: $GMM = \frac{\sqrt{1+r}}{r-g} = \frac{\sqrt{1.23}}{23\% - 5\%} = \frac{1.11}{0.18} = 6.1614$. Multiplying Year Four forecast cash flow by the Gordon Model multiple yields the value of cash flow from Year Four to infinity as of the end of Year Three, which is $740,626 (B14). Then we discount this value three years to arrive at the present value of forecast cash flow from Year Four to infinity. To do this, we calculate the present value factor for discounting three full years, which is $\frac{1}{(1 + 23\%)^3} = 0.5374$ (B15). This means that each dollar at the end of Year Three equals approximately 53¾ cents at time zero, when using a discount rate of 23 percent. Multiplying $740,626 by 0.5374, we calculate the present value of economic cash flows from Year Four to infinity of $398,001 (B16). We add cells B11 and B16 to produce the present value of all cash flows, $635,567 (B17).[4]

The total present value of cash flows in B17 is the Fair Market Value on a marketable minority basis, a concept I'll explain in the next chapter. This is so because the discount rate is based on returns for marketable minority interests, i.e., publicly traded stock. Normally the reader wants to know the value of control interests that are not publicly traded. In the majority of cases, the value of a 100 percent interest in a privately held firm will not be materially different than the marketable minority value. However, there are exceptions, which can be extreme, but they are not in the scope of this book. Adjustment for control and marketability are some of the most complex and controversial aspects of valuation. Therefore, I left them out of this sample valuation.

Sensitivity Analysis

To help give you a sense of how changes in the discount rate and long-term growth rate will change the valuation result, look at Table 7.1A, a sensitivity analysis.

---

[4] There is an apparent but not real $1.00 rounding error.

	E	F	G	H	I	J	K	L
58	**TABLE 7.1A**							
59	Sample Discounted Cash Flow Valuation							
60								
61			**Discount Rate**					
62			**15%**	**17%**	**19%**	**21%**	**23%**	**25%**
63	**Growth Rate**	**−1%**	$761,005	$680,337	$615,806	$563,008	$519,010	$481,780
64		**0%**	$799,684	$709,899	$639,013	$581,625	$534,213	$494,382
65		**1%**	$843,888	$743,156	$664,799	$602,104	$550,798	$508,035
66		**3%**	$954,398	$823,923	$726,041	$649,887	$588,944	$539,063
67		**5%**	$1,109,113	$931,612	$804,780	$709,617	**$635,567**	$576,297
68		**7%**	$1,341,185	$1,082,377	$909,765	$786,412	$693,846	$621,806

The final value calculated in the example in Table 7.1 appears in Table 7.1A, K67: $635,567. You'll notice, as you move to the right in the table, that the discount rate increases and the valuation decreases. Conversely, as you move to the left-hand side, the values rise with the lower discount rates. As you move down, the growth rate increases and so do the values. As you move up, the growth rate declines and the values decrease. Thus, the highest value ($1,341,185 at G68) is at the bottom left-hand corner, and the lowest value ($481,780 at L63) is at the top right-hand corner.

Valuation Spreadsheet

On the Web site www.abramsvaluation.com, click on the "Books" menu, then click on the menu for this book, and you will find a spreadsheet that looks like Table 7.2. It is a version of Table 7.1 waiting for your company's data. The spreadsheet requires the user to input the following items:

- Net income forecasts for three years in cells B6, C6, and D6
- A Payout Ratio assumption in B19
- A long-term cash flow growth rate assumption in B21

	A	B	C	D
1	**TABLE 7.2**			
2	Discounted Cash Flow Valuation			
3				
4				
5	**Future Years**	**1**	**2**	**3**
6	Forecast Economic Net Income			
7	Payout Ratio (B19)	80%	80%	80%
8	**Forecast Economic Cash Flow**	-	-	-
9	Present Value Factor (Midyear Assumption)	0.8980	0.7242	0.5840
10	Present Value of Economic Cash Flow (Row 8 * Row 9)	-	-	-
11	**Total Present Value of Economic Cash Flow: Years 1-3**	-		
12	Forecast Economic Cash Flow Year 4 [D8 * (1 +B21)]	-		
13	Gordon Multiple	(5.8608)		
14	Economic Cash Flows Year 4 to Infinity: At End of Year 3	-		
15	Present Value Factor to Discount Year 4 to Infinity CF to Year O	0.5245		
16	Present Value of Economic Cash Flows Year 4 to Infinity	-		
17	**Total Present Value of Economic Cash Flows (B11+B16) [1]**	-		
18	*Assumptions*			
19	Payout Ratio	80%		
20	Discount Rate	24%		
21	Long-Term Cash Flow Growth Rate	5%		
22				
23	[1] Many business sales are structured in a way that the seller retains some of the working cap-			
24	ital items, usually cash, receivables, and payables. If you are thinking about making such a			
25	transaction, you should adjust the value to purchase price by subtracting cash and receiv-			
26	ables and adding back payables that remain with the seller. See Chapter 10 for more details.			
27				
28	[2] In "The Equity Premium," Eugene Fama & Kenneth French, *Journal of Finance,* April 2002, 647-			
29	659, the authors forecast future returns will be lower than historical returns by approximately 4			
30	percent. In "The Supply of Stock Market Returns," Roger G. Ibbotson and Peng Chen, Yale ICF			
31	Working Paper 00-44, the authors forecast future returns will be lower than historical returns only			
32	by 1 percent. It will take a long time to sort through the arguments and come to some consen-			
33	sus, if there ever will be one. I use my professional judgment to choose Ibbotson's more con-			
34	servative 1 percent adjustment. In the meantime, obviously this creates a great deal of uncer-			
35	tainty about values.			

This spreadsheet will aid you in estimating a "ballpark" value for your business. It is not meant as a substitute for a professional business appraisal. When conducting your own appraisal with the spreadsheet, you have control over how much detail and sophistication you want. For example, if your company does not have formal financial forecasts, you can use last year's net income as a guide, average your company's net income over the last few years, or use the forecasting process I describe in Chapter 3.

I have set up the spreadsheet for simplicity and ease of use for the most readers. For those readers who want to use a more detailed method, there are additional spreadsheets on the Web site (also under the menu item for this book) to aid in calculating historical sales growth and forecasting future sales growth, transforming net income to economic net income, forecasting future economic net income, and calculating the Payout Ratio from historical balance sheet data. I will explain the additional spreadsheets in the Appendix to Chapter 7.

As discussed in Chapter 4, and as you can see in Table 7.2, row 7, you can use 80 percent as a benchmark Payout Ratio for a small to mid-size firm with 3 to 4 percent growth. On average, if your business is growing quickly, you should decrease the percentage, and if it's stagnant or in decline, you should increase the Payout Ratio.

For the long-term cash flow growth rate, we found in Chapter 6 that the average nonstartup firm grows about 2 percent per year in nominal terms (-0.5 to -1 percent in real terms, as long-term inflation forecasts have ranged between 2 and 3 percent for the last several years[5]). If your business is mature but growing quickly, you may choose a long-term growth rate of 4 to 7 percent.[6] If your business is contracting, you may choose a zero to 2 percent growth rate. In extreme cases of downhill (maybe over-the-hill) momentum, the long-term growth rate should be negative. Of course, the company's historical growth is normally a very important part of the forecast.

---

[5] See the *Survey of Professional Forecasters* published by the Federal Reserve Bank of Philadelphia, http://www.phil.frb.org/econ/spf/index.html.

[6] Of course, startup firms usually have much higher growth rates for the first several years.

The discount rate is automatically calculated based on my log-size equation and is accurate for firms worth up to $258 million. To use the spreadsheet, you will need to forecast three years of net income and input a reasonable Payout Ratio and long-term cash flow growth rate, and the spreadsheet will do the rest.

Like the example in Table 7.1, the spreadsheet does not adjust for control and marketability issues. You will have to read the next chapter to understand the issues of control and marketability. As we already discussed, in most cases the Fair Market Value of a 100 percent interest in a privately held company will not materially vary from the marketable minority interest FMV. For our "quick-and-dirty" valuation purposes, it was reasonable not to make the adjustment for control and marketability here.

There is one more important caveat to this spreadsheet. Many business sales are structured so the seller retains some of the working capital items, usually cash, receivables, and payables. If you're thinking about making such a transaction, you should adjust the value in B17—Total Present Value of Economic Cash Flows—by subtracting cash and receivables and adding back payables. In Chapter 10, I explain this in more detail.

Finally, just as Table 7.1A is the sensitivity analysis to Table 7.1, Table 7.2A is the sensitivity analysis to Table 7.2. While it currently appears to show zero percent everywhere in

	E	F	G	H	I	J	K	L
58	**TABLE 7.2A**							
59	Sample Discounted Cash Flow Valuation							
60								
61					Discount Rate			
62			15%	17%	19%	21%	23%	25%
63	Growth Rate	−1%	-	-	-	-	-	-
64		0%	-	-	-	-	-	-
65		1%	-	-	-	-	-	-
66		3%	-	-	-	-	-	-
67		5%	-	-	-	-	-	-
68		7%	-	-	-	-	-	-

the table, the numbers will automatically calculate when you input the data in Table 7.2.

CONCLUSION

In this chapter we have reviewed a sample discounted cash flow valuation spreadsheet and learned how to use the valuation spreadsheet to perform your own business valuation. I wish you great success using my spreadsheets!

Appendix to Chapter 7

To perform a DCF valuation, you must forecast cash flow, and in order to do this, you need to first forecast sales, economic net income, and the Payout Ratio. Chapter 7 presented various ways to make these forecasts. The simpler methods are less precise, but quicker and easier. This appendix is for readers who desire a greater degree of precision in their valuations, and the goal is to demonstrate how to use the spreadsheets available on www.abramsvaluation.com, which aid in forecasting sales, economic net income, and calculating the Payout Ratio in a more detailed fashion.[1]

Note that all of the tables in this appendix except for Table A7.3 will show apparent but not real error messages, which will disappear when you enter your data properly.

CALCULATING HISTORICAL SALES GROWTH

The first step in forecasting is to analyze the past. Table A7.1, is a spreadsheet that will allow you to quickly compute the average annual sales growth of your business.

[1] The author gratefully acknowledges the significant assistance by Chaim Borevitz in drafting this appendix.

	A	B	C	D	E	F	G
1	**TABLE A7.1**						
2	Spreadsheet to Calculate Historical Sales Growth						
3							
4							
5		**1999**	**2000**	**2001**	**2002**	**2003**	**Avg**
6	Total Sales						
7	Annual Sales Growth		#DIV/0!	#DIV/0!	#DIV/0!	#DIV/0!	**#DIV/0!**
8							
9		**2000**	**2001**	**2002**	**2003**	**Avg**	
10	Total Sales						
11	Annual Sales Growth		#DIV/0!	#DIV/0!	#DIV/0!	**#DIV/0!**	
12							
13		**2001**	**2002**	**2003**	**Avg**		
14	Total Sales						
15	Annual Sales Growth		#DIV/0!	#DIV/0!	**#DIV/0!**		
16							
17	First forecast year	**2004**					
18							
19	**Spreadsheet Formulas:**						
20	Cell C7: =(C6/B6)-1						

To begin using the spreadsheet, you must first determine the first forecast year of your valuation. Normally, that will be next year. For example, if today's date is sometime in 2003, then your first forecast year will be 2004. You need to input the first forecast year into cell B17 (Table A7.1). This will automatically set up the correct years in rows 5, 9, and 13 in the spreadsheet.

Next, you need to input the historical sales of your business into the spreadsheet. If you have five years of sales data, you should input the data in row 6. If you have four years of sales data, you should place the information in row 10, and if you have only three years of data, input it in row 14. After you input your sales data, the average annual sales growth will be automatically calculated in the last cell on the right.

HISTORICAL ECONOMIC PROFIT MARGIN

The purpose of Tables A7.2A, A7.2B, and A7.2C is to calculate the historical economic profit margin. By design, these tables

	A	B	C	D	E
1	**TABLE A7.2A**				
2	**Income Statements (3 Years) for Calculating Economic Net**				
3	**Income & Profit Margins**				
4					
5	**Year**	**2001**	**2002**	**2003**	**Avg or Total**
6	Total Sales				
7	Cost of Sales				
8	Gross Profit	-	-	-	
9	Total Expenses				
10	Net Income Before Taxes	-	-	-	
11	Adjustments to Net Income				
12	+ Owners' Actual Compensation				
13	− Owners' Arm's Length Compensation				
14	+ Optional Charitable Contributions				
15	+ Loss From Discontinued Operations				
16	+ Moving Expense				
17	− Allocated Moving Expense				
18	= Total Adjustments	-	-	-	
19	**Economic Net Income Before Taxes**	-	-	-	
20	Corporate Income Taxes	-	-	-	
21	**Economic Net Income After Corporate Taxes**	-	-	-	
22	**Economic Profit Margin**	**#DIV/0!**	**#DIV/0!**	**#DIV/0!**	**#DIV/0!**
23	Sum-of-the-Years' Digits	1	2	3	6
24	Sum-of-the-Years' Digits-%	16.7%	33.3%	50.0%	100.0%
25	**SYD Weighted Profit Margin**	**#DIV/0!**	**#DIV/0!**	**#DIV/0!**	**#DIV/0!**
26					
27	First forecast year	**2004**			
28	Combined Federal & State Corp. Inc Tax Rate [1]	**40.0%**			
29					
30	[1] This equals the federal corporate rate plus the state corporate rate minus the product of				
31	the two. For a nontax entity, this is normally zero. However, it is 1.5 percent in California.				

will also help you compute economic net income. The only difference among the three tables is the number of years of data used to calculate the average economic profit margin.

	A	B	C	D	E	F
1	**TABLE A7.2B**					
2	**Income Statements (4 Years) for Calculating Economic Net**					
3	**Income & Profit Margins**					
4						
5	**Year**	**2000**	**2001**	**2002**	**2003**	**Avg or Total**
6	Total Sales					
7	Cost of Sales					
8	Gross Profit	-	-	-	-	
9	Total Expenses					
10	Net Income Before Taxes	-	-	-	-	
11	Adjustments to Net Income					
12	+ Owners' Actual Compensation					
13	− Owners' Arm's Length Compensation					
14	+ Optional Charitable Contributions					
15	+ Loss From Discontinued Operations					
16	+ Moving Expense					
17	− Allocated Moving Expense					
18	= Total Adjustments	-	-	-	-	
19	**Economic Net Income Before Taxes**	-	-	-	-	
20	Corporate Income Taxes	-	-	-	-	
21	**Economic Net Income After Corporate Taxes**	-	-	-	-	
22	**Economic Profit Margin**	**#DIV/0!**	**#DIV/0!**	**#DIV/0!**	**#DIV/0!**	**#DIV/0!**
23	Sum-of-the-Years' Digits	1	2	3	4	10
24	Sum-of-the-Years' Digits- %	10.0%	20.0%	30.0%	40.0%	100.0%
25	**SYD Weighted Profit Margin**	**#DIV/0!**	**#DIV/0!**	**#DIV/0!**	**#DIV/0!**	**#DIV/0!**
26						
27	First forecast year	**2004**				
28	Combined Federal & State Corp. Inc Tax Rate [1]	**40.0%**				
29						
30	[1] This equals the federal corporate rate plus the state corporate rate minus the product of					
31	the two. For a nontax entity, this is normally zero. However, it is 1.5 percent in California.					

	A	B	C	D	E	F	G
1	**TABLE A7.2C**						
2	**Income Statements (5 Years) for Calculating Economic Net**						
3	**Income & Profit Margins**						
4							
5	**Year**	**1999**	**2000**	**2001**	**2002**	**2003**	**Avg or Total**
6	Total Sales						
7	Cost of Sales						
8	Gross Profit	-	-	-	-	-	
9	Total Expenses						
10	Net Income Before Taxes	-	-	-	-	-	
11	Adjustments to Net Income						
12	+ Owners' Actual Compensation						
13	− Owners' Arm's Length Compensation						
14	+ Optional Charitable Contributions						
15	+ Loss From Discontinued Operations						
16	+ Moving Expense						
17	− Allocated Moving Expense						
18	= Total Adjustments	-	-	-	-	-	
19	**Economic Net Income Before Taxes**	-	-	-	-	-	
20	Corporate Income Taxes	-	-	-	-	-	
21	**Economic Net Income After Corporate Taxes**	-	-	-	-	-	
22	**Economic Profit Margin**	**#DIV/0!**	**#DIV/0!**	**#DIV/0!**	**#DIV/0!**	**#DIV/0!**	**#DIV/0!**
23	Sum-of-the-Years' Digits	1	2	3	4	5	15
24	Sum-of-the-Years' Digits-%	6.7%	13.3%	20.0%	26.7%	33.3%	100.0%
25	**SYD Weighted Profit Margin**	**#DIV/0!**	**#DIV/0!**	**#DIV/0!**	**#DIV/0!**	**#DIV/0!**	**#DIV/0!**
26							
27	First forecast year	**2004**					
28	Combined Federal & State Corp. Inc Tax Rate [1]	**40.0%**					
29							
30	[1] This equals the federal corporate rate plus the state corporate rate minus the product of						
31	the two. For a nontax entity, this is normally zero. However, it is 1.5 percent in California.						

Table A7.2A is for three years of historical data. I will explain how to use it. Tables A7.2B and A7.2C function identically for four and five years of data, respectively.

As in Table A7.1, the first thing you need to do in Table A7.2A is input the first forecast year in cell B27. Next, if your company is a C corporation, input your combined federal and state corporate income tax rate in B28. That will be equal to the federal rate plus the state rate, minus the product of the two.

For example, if the relevant federal and state tax rates for your company's tax bracket are 35 and 5 percent, then the combined rate is $35\% + 5\% - (35\% \times 5\%) = 40\% - 1.75\% = 38.25\%$. If your business is a pass-through tax entity—an S corporation, LLC, or partnership—you should input zero.[2] However, in the supplementary chapter on the valuation effects of entity, also available on my Web site, you will discover that pass-through entity valuation is more complicated than this, and this may result in an overvaluation. However, for our "quick-and-dirty" valuation purposes, the magnitude of the error is not worth the complication of the additional calculations that would be necessary for greater accuracy.

Next, input the historical financial data for your business in rows 6, 7, and 9. Rows 8 and 10 calculate automatically.

The following step is a bit more difficult. Rows 12 to 17 are the adjustments to net income to calculate economic net income. You will need to add back owners' salaries in row 12. This should also include the total of all compensation to all employees that are not arm's length, as I explained in Chapter 3. If there are four family members in the company who are paid at more or less than an arm's length rate, then row 12 should be the total actual compensation for all four people. Then you need to subtract the arm's length compensation in row 13.

In row 14 you should include all optional charitable contributions. If you had any discontinued operations, add back losses (or subtract gains) from their being discontinued in row

---

[2] There are exceptions. California has a 1.5 percent S corporation tax rate. Also, if you are calculating the FMV of your firm and your relevant universe of buyers are C corporations (which would probably mean that you own a large company), then it is their tax rate, not your tax rate, that counts. If your firm is acquired by a C corporation, it will pay corporate taxes on your net income.

	A	B	C	D
1	**TABLE A7.3**			
2	Spreadsheet for			
3	Forecasting Economic Net Income			
4				
5	**Future Years**	1	2	3
6	Forecast Total Sales			
7	Forecast Profit Margin			
8	Economic Net Income After Corporate Taxes	-	-	-

15. This is true not only in the year of closure, but in prior years as well. We want to forecast only continuing operations in the future. If you had any moving expenses, you need to add them back in row 16, and subtract the annual allocation in row 17. As a reminder, the annual allocation equals the total amount of moving expenses divided by the number of years you estimate there will be between moves. Row 18 will automatically total the adjustments,[3] and row 19 will calculate economic net income before taxes. Row 21 will automatically subtract taxes to calculate economic net income. Row 22 will compute the economic profit margin, and the average economic profit margin of your business will appear in E22. Rows 23 through 25 will automatically calculate the sum-of-the-years' digits weighted average economic profit margin.

FORECASTING ECONOMIC NET INCOME

The spreadsheet for Table A7.3 calculates economic net income for you, which is the first input you need for the DCF spreadsheet in Table 7.2 in Chapter 7.

To use Table A7.3, you first need to forecast sales. This should be easy if you used Table A7.1. In cell B6, you need to

[3] You can insert rows in the spreadsheet, if you have additional adjustments that I have not considered in this standard format. However, be careful that the sum formula in the current row 18 includes all of the rows. If you inserted rows at either row 12 or row 18, Excel will not do that for you automatically. If you insert at rows 13 through 17, it should be automatically correct.

multiply your previous year's sales by one plus the average annual sales growth rate you calculated in Table A7.1:

$$\text{Sales}_{\text{last year}} \times (1 + \text{Average Annual Growth Rate}) = \text{Forecast Sales}_{\text{next year}}$$

Alternatively, if you have a specific sales growth forecast for each year, you can use that instead of the average growth rate. Cell C6 should equal B6 times one plus the average annual growth rate, and D6 should equal C6 times one plus the average annual growth rate.

In row 7, you need to input your forecast economic profit margin. You will take this from Table A7.2A (or Tables A7.2B or A7.2C). You need to decide which profit margin is more indicative of the future of your business—the simple annual average economic profit margin in E22 (F22 in Table A7.2B, or G22 in Table A7.2C) or the sum-of-years' digits weighted average economic profit margin. After choosing one of these, place it in row 7. The spreadsheet will then automatically calculate economic net income after corporate taxes, which you can input into Table 7.2, row 6.

Chapter 8

Adjusting for Control and Marketability

Adjusting for control and marketability is part of the fine-tuning of the valuation. For our "quick-and-dirty" valuation purposes, it's the icing on the cake. It is not the cake itself. In a professional valuation context, there can be much controversy over these valuation adjustments, and they can become a significant "slice of the cake." In a number of lawsuits, the arguments have been about the valuation discounts, not the Discounted Cash Flow Method calculations.

If my only goal were to teach you to value your own business as a whole, this chapter would not be in the book. However, there are two additional goals that I have in mind.

The Broader Context

My first goal in this chapter is to convey the broader context of valuation well enough so you can interface more effectively with a professional appraiser when you need that kind of help. Most business owners eventually need professional appraisals for tax reasons. Hopefully, you will not need a professional for litigation, but it does happen on occasion. And, of course, many of you might eventually want to sell your business, at which point it would be wise to engage professional help for greater accuracy.

It's helpful to understand how a professional business valuator defines a valuation assignment. Understanding it can help you eliminate sloppy thinking that might lead to the kind of large errors in valuation that occur when the assignment is specified incorrectly. Logically, this should have been included in Chapter 1, since it is a foundation of business valuation. But plunging into the finer points of valuation might well have been a distraction when we first began. Now, however, having read this far, you're ready for some of those fine points.

Partial Ownership

Some readers will own a partial interest in a business, and they'll want to know how to value that. Valuing a partial interest is always more complex than valuing a whole interest. A control interest in a business is any interest greater than 50 percent. A minority interest in a business is any interest under 50 percent. If there are many owners of a firm, it is possible that a large minority interest may effectively control the company.

My second goal in this chapter is to help you understand how to begin to accomplish this partial interest valuation. Ignorance of technical details like the levels of value can lead to incorrect valuation results. Probably the most important part of this chapter is advice that I give to protect the value of minority interests before you invest.

OVERVIEW OF THE PROCEDURE

Let's begin with an overview of the valuation procedure:

1. Define the valuation assignment. This involves specifying the business interest, the effective valuation date, the purpose of the valuation, and the standard of value.
   a. A valuation is only valid as of a certain date. As time changes, value changes.
   b. A valuation is only valid for a particular business interest, and values are not strictly proportional. Thus, for example, the value of one-half ownership in a firm usually will be less than one-half of the value of the entire company, because the attributes

of control and marketability are less desirable for the one-half interest than they are for the 100 percent ownership interest. We will discuss this in detail later in the chapter.

2. Perform the valuation using the Discounted Cash Flow Method and the Gordon Model, which we covered in Chapters 5 and 6.
3. Adjust the value to the appropriate level of control and marketability for the business interest you are valuing. This is the main focus of this chapter, and it requires a discussion of the "levels of value."

DEFINING THE ASSIGNMENT

The first step in performing any valuation is to define the valuation assignment. For professional business appraisers, this is mandatory, and we have to do this in our engagement letters with our clients and in our reports. To define the assignment, one must specify the following items:

1. The business interest being valued. This, in turn, will determine the level of value that is appropriate to that interest.
2. The effective date of the valuation.
3. The purpose(s) of the valuation.
4. The standard of value.

We will cover each of these points in detail.

Business Interests

A complete description of a business interest is a statement of the legal form of the business entity (corporation, LLC, etc.), the size of the interest, i.e., the percentage of the company owned, the class of ownership, and the state in which the company is legally formed. Examples of different business interests are:

- 25 percent common stock interest in a California C corporation
- 15 percent Class C preferred stock interest in a Delaware C corporation

- 100 percent stock interest in an Arizona S corporation
- 1 percent General Partnership interest in a Nevada Limited Partnership
- 25 percent Limited Partnership interest in a Colorado General Partnership
- 50 percent member interest in a Washington Limited Liability Company (LLC)
- 100 percent of the assets of a Virginia C corporation

Defining the valuation assignment enables us to be precise about what we're valuing. This is important since the legal form of the business, state law, the company's legal documents (e.g., Articles of Incorporation, Bylaws, Partnership Agreement, etc.), and the magnitude of the interest usually affects the degree of control and marketability of the business interest, and this in turn will affect its fair market value. Of course, it's simpler when all we're concerned about is a 100 percent interest in the company.

Effective Date

As stated earlier, a valuation is effective only as of a specific date. However, it often takes one month or more to receive the year-end financial statements that we need to value a company, and it takes time to perform the valuation. Thus, by the time the valuation is finished, it will be somewhat "stale."

The general rule of thumb is a valuation that is more than three months past its effective date is in danger of being considered effectively stale. In the absence of extraordinary events that materially impact value, it is usually reasonable to use a valuation, for example, with a December 31, 2002, effective date for a transaction that will take place on or before March 31, 2003.

An extreme example of a "value-altering," extraordinary event was the terrorist attacks on September 11, 2001. A more pleasant and perhaps routine example would be signing a contract with a major new customer that will double sales within two years. Even so, if a reasonable investor in our example would have attached a 99 percent probability on December 31, 2002, to signing the contract, then 99 percent of the value of the contract should be incorporated into the valuation as of that date, and the signing on January 31, 2003, would not be a material, value-altering event. If the probability had instead been only 25 percent, then signing the contract would be a value-altering event.

Purpose(s) of the Valuation

It is vital to state every purpose you have for performing your own valuation or hiring a professional to do it for you. There are many reasons why people hire professional appraisers: buying or selling a whole business or part of a business, establishing a buy-sell agreement, estate taxes, gift taxes, income taxes, financial statements, Employee Stock Ownership Plans (ESOPs), litigation, etc. In turn, there are multiple reasons for several items in that list. For instance, transactions that can lead to a valuation for income tax purposes include: a corporation spinning off a technology to its shareholders, transferring or selling assets to a related business entity, calculating Fair Market Value for the net unrealized built-in capital gains for a corporation electing S corporation status, and issuing incentive stock options.

More than once clients or their attorneys have informed me of one or two reasons why they needed a valuation and left out one valuation purpose. The purpose of the valuation dictates the scenario(s) that we need to consider. I can think of one instance where a last minute "Oh by the way" led to $20,000 of additional work—much of which could have been avoided had we known that valuation purpose from the beginning. Estate tax valuation, where there can be multiple trusts and entities, such as Family Limited Partnerships, is one area where it's particularly easy to be told to value the wrong asset—and not be told to value the right one. As the business owner engaging a professional appraiser, you will need to be careful to read the engagement letter and make sure you understand what your attorney has instructed the appraiser to value and what is not being valued—and agree with that.

Recently, I did a valuation for a corporation where the original purpose of the valuation was for income tax purposes for the new CEO, who was given stock in return for joining the firm. However, several weeks later he called me and told me the founder of the firm was dying and he needed to restructure the ownership of the company. The founder was personally liable for a percentage of the long-term debt, and he did not want to burden his family with that liability. The CEO needed to provide a valuation to the founder and his attorneys to show him the value of the latter's ownership of the company. Unlike the stock to the new CEO, these shares did not have limited liability, and they were worth less than the same percentage ownership owned by anyone else. This is an example of how two different valuation purposes dictate different valuation results—even of the same percentage ownership of the company.

I assume that the only reason the reader, as a business owner, would do his or her own valuation is for internal planning purposes. Be careful. Your appraisal of your own company—no matter how well done—will suffer from lack of independence, and the valuation will not be acceptable for most legal purposes. Also, when accuracy is important, at a minimum you should have your valuation reviewed by a professional appraiser.

Standard of Value

The concept of the standard of value is extremely important in valuation, and we covered that in Chapter 1. The standard of value usually determines whether discount for lack of control, discount for lack of marketability, and synergies belong in the valuation calculations.

LEVELS OF VALUE

It's vital to understand the concept of levels of value in business valuation. Over the years of my professional practice, it's been my experience that many of my clients are initially surprised, and a few are stunned, to discover that there is no such thing as "the value" of a firm. Value depends on the context and scenario of the valuation, as well as the nature of the business interest we are valuing.

FIGURE 8.1

4 × 2 levels of value chart

Public Company	Private Company
Strategic Value	Strategic Value
Control Value[1]	Control Value
Minority Interest (well treated) Value	Minority Interest (well treated) Value
Minority Interest (abused)[2] Value	Minority Interest (abused) Value

There are differences of opinion among professionals as to the appropriate levels-of-value chart. The nuances of this professional controversy are outside of the scope of this book. My own levels-of-value chart appears in Figure 8.1.[3]

The chart shows eight potential combinations of ownership characteristics in a firm. The columns show whether the firm is either publicly or privately held, and the rows show the degree of synergy, control, and well-being, all of which affect the value. One can value a strategic interest, a control interest, a well-

[1] This level of value probably exists only in theory. It is my opinion that acquisition premiums for public firms are not for control. They are for synergies. See *Quantitative Business Valuation*, Chapter 7. However, there are different opinions, and the nuances are beyond the scope of this book.

[2] In the United States, most minority shareholders of public companies are well-treated, and the relatively few who are not have remedies available to them, such as class-action law suits and SEC oversight, that private minority shareholders could only wish for. Thus, this category is close to nonexistent in the U.S., although it is a well-known phenomenon in other countries.

[3] Jay B. Abrams. *Quantitative Business Valuation, ibid.*, 230. This chart is an extension of the 2 × 2 chart proposed by Michael Bolotsky in "Adjustments for Differences in Ownership Rights, Liquidity, Information Access, and Information Reliability: An Assessment of 'Prevailing Wisdom' versus the 'Nath Hypothesis,'" *Business Valuation Review*, September 1991, 94–110. The traditional levels-of-value chart used in the profession is one column only, with "Strategic Value" on the top, "Control Value" next, "Marketable Minority Value" next, and "Private (or Illiquid) Minority Value" on the bottom. It is my opinion that this one-dimensional levels-of-value chart leads to errors in thinking and valuation, and therefore I do not discuss it any further in this book.

treated minority interest, or an abused minority interest in the firm.[4] Of course, there are gradations in between.

Since most financial models for calculating discount rates use stock market data, the public minority level of value is our usual beginning frame of reference in our Discounted Cash Flow/Gordon Model multiple calculations. Those shares are marketable, since they can be sold and converted to cash in three days, and they are minority interests, since buying 10 shares of IBM does not give you control of the corporation. Therefore, the above procedure yields a Public Minority interest, commonly known as a "marketable minority" interest Fair Market Value.

To value a privately held firm, we must subtract a discount for lack of marketability (DLOM). All things being equal, the lack of instant marketability of ownership in a private firm makes it less valuable than ownership in an otherwise identical public firm. After subtracting DLOM, the resulting level of value is called a well-treated Private Minority interest FMV, also known as the "illiquid minority interest" FMV.

If we want to value a control interest in a company, then we have to add a control premium, since control has value. The control premium is the value that people attach to the peace of mind that comes from being invulnerable to being fired and/or abused. Also, there is a positive aspect to control, which is the freedom to operate the business in an optimal fashion. I am aware of a restaurant owner who is having a lot of trouble due to lack of control. He has significant experience successfully running restaurants. He owns one of his restaurants with some partners who do not have a food-service background, and the restaurant is failing in large part because of the inexperienced partners' management decisions. Meanwhile, the expert is unable to make needed changes because he lacks control.

In *Quantitative Business Valuation* I estimated the control premium as 21 to 28 percent. In our examples in this chapter we will use the average of 25 percent. If one person has partial control or two or more people share control, the control premium will either diminish or disappear.

---

[4] Remember the story of Leonardo and the Snakeman in Chapter 2.

The levels of value are in descending order going down either column of Figure 8.1. Thus, a strategic control interest will have a greater value than a simple (i.e., nonstrategic) control interest. A control interest will have a greater value than a well-treated minority interest of the same kind, i.e., public versus private. In turn, that will be worth more than an abused interest of the same kind. There is no guarantee of the same sort of descending order of value when moving across columns. In moving from a well-treated Public Minority interest to a private control interest, the valuation increases because of the control premium and it decreases because of DLOM. There is no guarantee that for any particular firm either one always will dominate. For two different firms, it's possible that the control premium will dominate for one and DLOM will dominate for the other, and the private control FMV can be above, at, or below the Public Minority FMV.

Control and marketability have an interesting relationship. Control has value in itself, for the peace of mind it brings with freedom of action and freedom from abuse. Control also indirectly affects value through its effect on marketability. Control interests in private firms are much more marketable than minority interests.

For example, in a corporation owned by one 90 percent shareholder and one 10 percent shareholder, the control shareholder can decide today that he or she wants to sell the firm, and six to 18 months later the firm is likely to be sold. If the 10 percent shareholder wants to sell and the 90 percent shareholder does not, the former may have to wait 30 years to sell. There are many more potential buyers for the control interest. There is an organized market for buying whole interests in private businesses, while there is no organized market for buying minority interests in private businesses. Therefore, the minority shareholder in a private firm suffers from a double whammy in valuation—a discount for lack of control and a more severe discount for lack of marketability. It also is important to determine if there are any restrictions or enhancements of the legal rights of the interest being valued, since those affect the value of the interest.

Valuation of a Strategic Interest

A strategic buyer is one who has synergies with your company. Often, although not always, these are two firms in the same industry, who can share resources more efficiently than each one alone.[5] The combined entity can either sell more than the sum of the two as separate entities, achieve the same level of sales with lower expenses, or both. Therefore, a strategic buyer can afford to pay more than a control interest value, since the synergies of two firms with a very good fit can easily add another 35 to 65 percent of value above the control level. That is very important to understand in selling your business, but this level of value generally will not come into play in most valuations for tax or other legal purposes.[6]

Valuation of a Control Interest

Throughout this book we have been valuing a 100 percent ownership interest in a business. However, the Discounted Cash Flow Method produces a marketable minority—a public well-treated minority—interest. To be more precise in the valuation, we need to add a control premium and subtract a discount for lack of marketability (DLOM). Table 8.1 shows my calculations of DLOM, which range from 10 to 20 percent, depending on firm size.[7] It's important to note that using a different methodology[8] usually leads to larger DLOMs for small businesses. Consider Table 8.1 as the minimum DLOM. It will take further research to decide which methodology is more accurate.

Let's use the average of 15 percent. To convert the marketable minority interest FMV from the DCF Method to a pri-

---

[5] The other typical strategic scenario is a technological synergy, e.g., as in the acquisition of Lotus Development Corporation by IBM.

[6] The exception to this is acquisitions by publicly held firms necessitate SFAS 141 and 142 valuations, and synergies do count in measuring fair value for that purpose.

[7] This is based on my methodology in *Quantitative Business Valuation, ibid.*, Chapter 7, with calculations updated for the years 1938-2001.

[8] A Black-Scholes put option, a mathematical technique beyond the scope of this book.

	A	B	C
1	**TABLE 8.1**		
2	Discount for Lack of Marketability		
3	By Average Firm Size		
4			
5	FMV	DLOM [1]	
6	25,000	10.8%	
7	75,000	11.0%	
8	125,000	11.1%	
9	175,000	11.2%	
10	225,000	11.6%	
11	375,000	13.6%	
12	500,000	15.6%	
13	750,000	19.9%	
14	2,000,000	18.0%	
15	5,000,000	15.8%	
16	10,000,000	15.5%	
17			
18	[1] Source: Same methodology as Jay B. Abrams, *Quantitative Business*		
19	*Valuation: A Mathematical Approach to Today's Professionals*, New York:		
20	McGraw-Hill, 2001, 362, row 23. However, here author used the 1938-2001		
21	data for the regression, 1938-1986. Note: These DLOMs are averages for firms		
22	of that size. Specific businesses may vary in their DLOM calculations. Using		
23	the Black-Scholes put option often leads to a larger DLOM. That is beyond		
24	the scope of this book. Consider Table 8.1 as the minimum DLOM.		

vate control FMV, we would multiply the marketable minority FMV by $1.25 \times (1 - 15\%) = 1.0625$. Thus, the private control FMV is, on average, about 6.25 percent higher than the marketable minority FMV. Of course, that varies by firm size, at a minimum. Professionals would be interested in a host of other characteristics of the firm, but for our purposes in this book, this is as accurate as we need to be.

Valuation of a Minority Interest

Valuation of a minority interest in a business generally is not for amateurs. I will give you a general idea of how it is done, but this is a very detailed and controversial area of business valuation.

Suppose you have valued a 100 percent interest in your company at $1 million, i.e., on a private control level. The question is: "How should we value a 10 percent interest in the same company?" We start by calculating its net asset value, which is the proportional Fair Market Value of the company. In this case, it is $1 million × 10% = $100,000. If there were no adjustments for the levels of value, this would be our answer. However, we need to move from a private control level to a private minority level. We do not yet know how well-treated or how exploited this interest is, and we will discuss that further on.

I have seen enough situations in my career that the appropriate combined discounts for lack of control and lack of marketability—let's call this the "fractional interest discount"—can range anywhere from zero to 95 percent. However, a range that wide is not very helpful to you. The most common range for the fractional interest discount is 30 to 45 percent. So, for a "quick-and-dirty" estimate, the most likely range for the valuation is one minus the discounts times $100,000, or $55,000 to $70,000.[9]

Just to give you one idea of the many complicating factors that professional business valuators need to consider, in California a coalition of one-third of the shares of a corporation has the power to initiate a shareholder dissolution suit, while less than a one-third interest does not have this power. Therefore, if we were valuing a 40 percent interest in the company (assuming it is a corporation) instead of 10 percent, the fractional interest discount logically would be less, since the discounts for lack of control and marketability should be smaller, even though it is still not a control interest. Perhaps 25 to 40 percent would be a more reasonable average range for the most likely combined discounts for a 40 percent interest, which would then lead us to calculate the most probable range of FMV to be $1 million × 40% × [(1 − (25% to 40%)] = $240,000 to $300,000.

---

[9] (1 − 0.45) × $100,000 = $55,000, and (1 − 0.30) × $100,000 = $70,000.

If you are an exploited minority interest, you should increase the discount significantly, depending on the severity of the exploitation and the extent of your legal rights.

Again, I have to state a big disclaimer. Calculating the discount for lack of marketability is one of the most difficult, controversial, and technical areas of valuation. An amateur cannot possibly understand all the complexities and nuances of valuing a minority interest, so do not place much confidence in your estimates. Your own valuation may be fine for a "quick-and-dirty" estimate for planning purposes, but if there are many dollars at stake, you'll need professional help for a transaction, or for tax, litigation, or most other purposes.

How Minority Shareholders Can Protect Themselves

If you are considering investing in a private firm, it's vital that you protect the value of your investment before you sign your contracts. There are certain rights that will protect your investment. They are:

- Limit the compensation to the control shareholder for management of the firm. Otherwise, the control shareholder can render your stock worthless or close to it by sucking all the value out by paying him- or herself enough compensation to eliminate all or most of the net income.
- Drag-along right of sale. This is a right that gives the minority shareholder the right to sell at the same price as the control shareholder. Otherwise, the latter can sell his or her stock, leaving the minority shareholder still illiquid.
- Provide a mandatory buyout at Fair Market Value, assuming arm's length compensation to the control owner.
- Make sure you have the right to register stock in the event of the company making an initial public offering (IPO). This is a right that would primarily come to play in the event of good news. The first three items are to protect against disaster, while this one is intended to maximize your value for an exit via an IPO.

CONCLUSION

This chapter has presented most of the conceptual groundwork in business valuation. We covered:

1. How to define the valuation assignment, which involves:
   - **a.** Defining the business interest
   - **b.** Specifying the effective date of the valuation
   - **c.** Specifying the purpose(s) of the valuation
   - **d.** Specifying the standard of value
2. The levels of value
   - **a.** How to value control interests
   - **b.** How to value minority interests
3. How a prospective minority investor in a business can protect him or herself

In the next chapter we will cover how to value a business as of a future date, and how to manage your business to maximize its value in the future.

Chapter 9

Increasing the Value of Your Business

To this point, we have examined how to value a business as of a current date. Now we'll discuss what creates value. Understanding the philosophy of value, you can manage your business to maximize the price for which you can sell it at some time in the future—whether one year or 30 years from now. Obviously, this chapter will be more useful to those who have more time to manage their businesses in order to maximize value before the sale, but it's still valuable for those with only one year to retirement and sale.

If you plan on selling or giving your business to your children, it is vital that both you and they understand the principles involved in increasing the value of your business. For this reason, most readers should find this the most important chapter in this book.

ANNUAL GROWTH RATE

Let's go back to Billabong Boomerangs and assume that economic net income last year was $1,190,476. Connie Billabong forecasts a Payout Ratio of 80 percent and constant growth in cash flows of 5 percent. Forecast economic cash flow next year is $1,190,476 × 1.05 × 80% = $1 million. Referring to Table 6.1 in Chapter 6, for an assumed Fair Market Value of $5 million

(A14), the discount rate would be 21.2 percent (B14), and the Gordon Model multiple (GMM) would be 6.8 (K14).[1] We can calculate the FMV as \$1 million × 6.8 = \$6.8 million. The calculated FMV is reasonably consistent with the assumed FMV, so we will stick with that as our valuation as of today.

Now let's ask what we think Billabong Boomerangs will be worth five years from now with the information we have today. Assuming we are at time zero now, we have already forecast economic cash flows for Year One as \$1 million. Therefore, we need to "roll forward" our forecast to Year Six, since we want our valuation to be effective as of the end of Year Five—even though our information about the firm is only current as of now, i.e., time zero.

Assuming the 5 percent per year growth is correct, Connie should forecast economic cash flow in Year Six of $\$1{,}000{,}000 \times 1.05^5 = \$1{,}276{,}000$ (rounded to the nearest thousand). The 27.6 percent increase in cash flow after five years will push up the valuation of the firm by at least that much. In fact, it pushes it up a little more, since the valuation will be closer to \$10 million (Table 6.1, A13) than \$5 million (A14). Thus, the appropriate discount rate is lower, and the GMM is higher. We use a GMM of 7.1 (K13). Our valuation as of the end of Year Five will be \$1.276 million × 7.1 = \$9.0 million.

The compound annual growth rate ("compound growth," or CAGR) in Fair Market Value over the five years is 5.86 percent, which is higher than the 5 percent forecast growth in economic cash flows. This means that \$6.8 million × 1.0586^5 = \$9.0 million. The CAGR is higher than the forecast growth in economic cash flows because the growth of the company will put it in a new size category, which should give it additional stability and less risk—hence the lower discount rate and the higher GMM.

FUTURE VALUATION OF STARTUPS

This observation gives us a clue to the answer to a problem that puzzled me in the early 1980s, when I was fairly new in the val-

[1] We use column K, because K6 shows this is the column for 5 percent growth.

uation profession. I noticed that when I valued a high-growth, high-tech firm as of the then current date and rolled the valuation forward to future dates, the value of the firm increased approximately by the discount rate each year, which seems logical. I could not understand how a firm with forecast sales in Year One of $1 million and in Year 10 of $500 million could ever come to be worth the billions of dollars that large, publicly held firms were. The value simply did not increase fast enough.

Finally, the answer dawned on me. When we are standing at time zero and forecasting for all of eternity, the firm is a high-risk startup. There is a substantial probability that it will fail, and that probability is captured by the high discount rates that business valuators and venture capitalists use in the Discounted Cash Flow valuations. It is typical to use a discount rate of 30 percent when fully accounting for the probabilities of failure and less-than-full success, and it's common to use a discount rate in the 50 to 75 percent range when discounting the cash flows forecast by the ever-optimistic entrepreneur.[2]

But when a company survives for five years and makes its forecasts, it is no longer a high-risk startup, and its discount rate comes down to normal business levels. Often, businesses backed by venture capital are on the Initial Public Offering track, and the discount rate can come down from 30 percent to as little as 12 to 16 percent. This has an enormous impact on the valuation of the company.

Now that you understand the fundamental mechanics of future valuation, let's go to the big payoff: understanding how to manage your business to maximize its value over time. We will begin that by reviewing Equation 6.4 from Chapter 6, the shortcut Gordon Model formula, which we repeat below as Equation 9.1. For our analytic purposes, it has the benefit of eliminating the square root term in the numerator of the exact midyear Gordon Model formula. Thus, it is a simpler formula to analyze.

---

[2] For an extensive discussion of the topic, see Chapter 12 of *Quantitative Business Valuation, ibid.*

VALUATION IN THE FUTURE

In this section I will:

1. Make a slight modification to the shortcut Gordon Model equation, discussed in Chapter 6, to use as our future valuation formula
2. Analyze the meaning of the future valuation formula
3. Make strategic statements about how you need to manage your business to maximize value

There will be a moderate amount of mathematics to deal with. It is not important that you understand the algebra. Follow it as best as you can. What is important is to understand the implications of the final future valuation equation and what it means to you in managing your business.

Future Valuation Formula

There was a fair amount of mathematics to develop our shortcut valuation formula in Chapter 6, which I reproduce below as Equation 9.1. The equation says that the value of a mature business with constant growth in its forecast economic cash flows is approximately equal to 1.10 times forecast economic net income times the Payout Ratio times the end-of-year Gordon Model multiple, which equals one divided by the discount rate minus the constant growth rate.[3] The equation:

$$FMV_0 \cong 1.10 \times Inc_1 \times Payout\ Ratio_1 \times \frac{1}{r_0 - g_0} \tag{9.1}$$

One difference between this formula and Equation 6.4 is a subscript zero under the FMV, discount, and growth rates, to signify that this is our valuation as of now, which I call "time zero." Also, I added a subscript 1 under the economic net income forecast for Year One and the Payout Ratio to indicate that it

[3] For simplicity in this discussion, we are ignoring the discount for lack of marketability and the control premium. Adding those factors would likely raise the valuation by about 6 percent.

is the forecast (Year One) economic net income and Payout Ratio that we use in the formula.

Now let's modify the formula to produce the FMV of the firm n years from now. In other words, with now being Year Zero, imagine yourself standing at the end of year n. You will forecast economic net income and the Payout Ratio for Year $n + 1$, as well as the discount rate (r) and the constant growth rate (g) that will apply at that time, i.e., the end of Year n. The valuation formula for the FMV of the firm as of the end of Year n is Equation 9.2.

$$FMV_n \cong 1.10 \times Inc_{n+1} \times Payout\ Ratio_{n+1} \times \frac{1}{r_n - g_n} \quad (9.2)$$

This equation says that the Fair Market Value of the firm as of the end of Year n is approximately equal to 1.10 times economic net income forecast for Year $n + 1$ times the Payout Ratio for Year $n + 1$ times the end-of-year Gordon Model multiple, using the discount rate that we expect to prevail at the end of Year n and the average growth rates that we expect to prevail from the end of Year n to infinity. So, if you want to know the valuation of the company 10 years from now, then $n = 10$, and it is the forecast of economic net income and Payout Ratio for Year 11 that we use in the formula, and the discount and growth rates for the end of Year 10.

However, Equation 9.2 is not a final equation for our analysis, as it has some "hidden variables" that we need to bring to light and explicitly incorporate into the future value equation. So let's look at each variable to see what lies underneath it.

The factor 1.10 is not a variable, so we do not have to worry about it. Let's look at the second term on the right-hand side, forecast economic net income in Year $n + 1$. That equals actual economic net income last year times one plus the compound average growth rate for the n years to the nth power, which we show in Equation 9.3:

$$Inc_{n+1} = Inc_0(1 + g)^n \quad (9.3)$$

The next term in Equation 9.2 is the Payout Ratio, the formula for which comes from Chapter 4 and is expressed in Equation 9.4:

$$POR = 1 - \frac{(Capital\ Expenditures - Depreciation) + Increase\ in\ NWC}{Net\ Income} \tag{9.4}$$

Note that the net income in the denominator is for Year $n + 1$, the first forecast year, which is defined by Equation 9.3.

The final terms in Equation 9.2 are the discount rate and the growth rate that we expect to prevail at the end of Year n, which we will leave as is for now. Substituting Equations 9.3 and 9.4 into Equation 9.2, our future valuation date equation becomes Equation 9.5:

$$FMV_n \cong 1.10 \times Inc_0(1 + g)^n \times \left[1 - \frac{(Cap\ Expend - Depr) + Incr\ NWC}{Inc_0(1 + g)^n}\right] \times \frac{1}{r_n - g_n} \tag{9.5}$$

Analysis of the Equation

Let's work to understand the meaning of Equation 9.5. The 1.10 is not a variable and certainly is not under your control. Inc_0—last year's economic net income—is an historical number over which you have no control. Nor will you have any significant control over depreciation expense in Year n, since that is a relatively mechanical calculation that results from your capital expenditures.[4] Thus, the only variables over which you have any control that determine the value of your business—whether now or at a future date—are the following:

- Growth rate for the first n years (g).
- Management of fixed assets (*Capital Expenditures – Depreciation*).
- Management of net working capital (*NWC*).
- Discount rate (r), which measures the risk of your business.

[4] It is true that your depreciation policy, such as your choices of using accelerated depreciation and depreciable lives, may have some impact. However, that should be immaterial.

- Long-term growth rate after year n (g_n). We can combine this term with growth in the first n years as long-term growth, as both terms increase the value of the firm—one in the numerator of Equation 9.5 and one in the denominator.

That's it. This is the bird's-eye view of the value of your business in the future, and nothing else will affect the value. However, as we "drill down" into the meaning of these five variables, you will discover some surprising insights into how to manage your business to maximize its value over time.

MAXIMIZING BUSINESS VALUE

The purpose of the previous section was to identify the variables over which you have control, which can affect the valuation of your business. Now we'll discuss in detail what you can do to maximize the value of your business over time. In order, we will cover each of the above four[5] items in the future valuation equation, from the growth rate to the discount rate, with some interactions between items that might otherwise appear unrelated.

Growth Rate

There are two things you can do to maximize the growth rate of your cash flows. The first, a broad category, is to manage your business efficiently and effectively.

In a Peter Drucker book[6] I read almost 30 years ago, he said that being efficient means doing things right, being effective means doing the right things, and the latter is more important. Every action you take that increases your sales more than your expenses, or decreases your sales less than it decreases your expenses, increases net income and, hence, the growth rate of net income. As to how to achieve that, you can begin by

---

[5] With the two growth terms counted as one term.

[6] Peter F. Drucker, *Management: Tasks, Responsibilities, Practices.* New York: HarperBusiness, 1993. Thirty years ago I read the original hard cover edition, published in 1973 by Harper & Row.

reading Linda Feinholz's supplemental chapter on management on my Web site. Also, I suggest you read literature on marketing, sales, and management, and consider hiring professionals in those fields to help you.

The second thing you can do to maximize the growth rate is to stop playing tax games of pocketing cash income and not reporting it, and charging personal expenses to the business. Minimally, you should do this for at least three and preferably five years before you plan to sell the business. You will report more income, pay more taxes, and have less personal cash flow for those three to five years, but by "going legit," you should be able to sell the business for many times the additional taxes you will pay.

The faster you (and others) forecast that you will able to increase your cash flows, the more valuable your business will be. Usually, though not always, this will depend on your having demonstrated the ability to produce and manage high growth in the past. As with the other variables, there is a tradeoff. Fast growth means sales will be higher, which requires more net working capital. Thus, fast growth increases net income, which adds to cash flow but also requires more net working capital, which decreases cash flow. The worst combination is fast growth in sales, which decreases cash flow through its effect on net working capital, combined with a declining profit margin, which decreases net income and cash flow. This occurs when the business owner is managing growth poorly.

Fast growth creates excitement for a business, but also strain. It requires a greater degree of structure and organization at each new size level, and it requires greater professionalism. This ties into the ideas in the previous section on reducing risk.

It is appropriate to point out the effect of growth on risk. There is a big bonus for those who can manage high growth rates for many years. Reiterating a point made in Chapter 5, if your firm grows to a size large enough to be attractive in the Mergers & Acquisitions market or for purchase by a public company, then the likely buyers will be well-diversified investors, those who are able to diversify away the risk of the smaller size of the business by including it in a larger portfolio. Such investors may be using the Capital Asset Pricing Model to calculate the discount rate, which typically results in much smaller discount rates, and therefore much higher values and selling prices.

In such cases, there is a lower value ("the floor") of the business as a stand-alone entity or as one sold to an undiversified buyer—where its size risk cannot be diversified away—and a higher value ("the ceiling") of the business to the fully diversified buyer. The transaction could then take place at either end or anywhere in between, depending on the negotiating skills and staying power of the parties. In such a case, there is no such thing as "the right price." There is an entire range of possible prices—all of which are reasonable.

Management of Fixed Assets

Maximizing value through management of fixed asset purchasing is a matter of spending wisely for Property, Plant & Equipment and balancing the costs of buying too much with the costs of buying too little. It is a good idea to begin by comparing your Return on Assets (equal to net income divided by total assets) with industry statistics to see how you stack up against your competition. If your ROA is lower than your industry, it means that others are using fewer assets to make the same income, or they're making more income with the same assets—or some combination of the two. That would be an indicator that you need to be more efficient in your use of assets.

Extending the average life of your equipment adds to value by reducing the Retention Ratio, thus increasing the Payout Ratio. The logic behind this is that if you buy equipment less often without affecting income—a trade-off I will discuss next—you can take the money home and spend it there.

This does not necessarily mean that spending more money on equipment each time you buy, but buying less often, will increase the business value. It might, but that is an analytic exercise. I invented an equation that I call the "Period Perpetuity Factor," which I believe is the most efficient method existent for evaluating large capital expenditures and determining which strategies will maximize your value. However, that is somewhat quantitative. Those who are interested can pursue it in my first book.[7]

As in almost all decisions in life, usually there is a trade-off. Perhaps using that old computer instead of buying something faster is costing you more in lost income than you're gaining by increasing the Payout Ratio. If so, the value will decrease by stretching out capital expenditures, because you will multiply a lower forecast net income by a higher Payout Ratio, with the final valuation being lower. The economic approach always is to equalize the costs of both alternatives to achieve equilibrium. This can be done quantitatively with fairly high precision to maximize firm value. If there are enough dollars at stake, it can make sense to seek professional help to assist in making the right decisions.

Managing Net Working Capital

Management of net working capital is often an overlooked area of maximizing value. Paying close attention to, and management of, credit policy may help a business lose its "flab." Loose credit policy leads to high accounts receivable, which increases net working capital, lowers the Payout Ratio, and lowers value. Of course, an overly tight credit policy loses sales and net income. So, ultimately there has to be balance.

Again, as an economist, I will tell you to equalize the costs of both extremes, which means being in balance. Because management of cash flow and net working capital is so important, I asked Jim Ward to write about management of cash flow from a more operational point of view than I did in Chapter 4. To learn more about managing cash, read his entertaining chapter in the supplementary chapters on my Web site.

The Discount Rate: Managing Risk

Risk, which appears in Equation 9.5 as the discount rate that you forecast will be applicable in Year n, is the variable about

---

[7] *Quantitative Business Valuation, ibid*, 78–84. Also see the *CFO* magazine article about the Period Perpetuity Factor, April 2002, 18.

which I will have the most to say. It is the least understood way that an owner can increase value. There are many actions you can take to reduce risk, and the impact of reducing the discount rate even by as little as 1 or 2 percent can be huge—much larger than managing cash effectively.

Let's begin with the huge impact of the size of the discount rate. Mechanically, in Equation 9.5, the discount rate is a nonlinear variable, as it appears in the denominator. Let's look at Table 9.1 to see how small changes can have such a large impact on the valuation.

Section 1 shows the Gordon Model multiples for combinations of discount rates (r) from 15 to 25 percent and constant growth rates (g) from zero to 8 percent. Section 2 shows how the GMM changes in percentage terms for each 1 percent drop in the discount rate. For example, cell B22 equals the 4.2 GMM in B7 divided by the 4.0 GMM in B6, minus one, or $(4.2/4.0) - 1 = 4.2\%$.[8] While Section 1 resembles Tables 5.4 and 6.1 earlier in the book, it differs in two ways: (1) The previous tables use the midyear Gordon Model formula, while this uses the end-of-year formula; and (2) the previous tables are organized by firm size, while Table 9.1 is organized by discount rate, with only whole numbers.

You can see that 4.2 percent is the smallest increase in all of Section 2. The amount increases going down each column and across each row, which means that the less risky the firm is to begin with, the greater the impact of reducing the discount rate by an additional 1 percent. As a practical matter, it means that the valuation impact of reducing risk and dropping the discount rate by 1 percent has a greater impact on large firms than on small firms. Remember, large firms have lower discount rates.[9] This is the case even though the impact of lowering the discount rate on small firms is still large. We saw above that dropping the discount rate from 25 to 24 percent, only a 1 percent re-

---

[8] There is an apparent but not real rounding error, since the table only shows one decimal point, but the spreadsheet actually carries out the calculations to 16 decimal points.

[9] For a more detailed, mathematical treatment of this topic, see *Quantitative Business Valuation*, *ibid*, 390–404.

	A	B	C	D	E	F	G	H	I	J
1	**TABLE 9.1**									
2	**Section 1: Gordon Model Multiples-End of Year [1]**									
3										
4		**Constant Growth Rate = *g***								
5	*r*	**0%**	**1%**	**2%**	**3%**	**4%**	**5%**	**6%**	**7%**	**8%**
6	25%	4.0	4.2	4.3	4.5	4.8	5.0	5.3	5.6	5.9
7	24%	4.2	4.3	4.5	4.8	5.0	5.3	5.6	5.9	6.3
8	23%	4.3	4.5	4.8	5.0	5.3	5.6	5.9	6.3	6.7
9	22%	4.5	4.8	5.0	5.3	5.6	5.9	6.3	6.7	7.1
10	21%	4.8	5.0	5.3	5.6	5.9	6.3	6.7	7.1	7.7
11	20%	5.0	5.3	5.6	5.9	6.3	6.7	7.1	7.7	8.3
12	19%	5.3	5.6	5.9	6.3	6.7	7.1	7.7	8.3	9.1
13	18%	5.6	5.9	6.3	6.7	7.1	7.7	8.3	9.1	10.0
14	17%	5.9	6.3	6.7	7.1	7.7	8.3	9.1	10.0	11.1
15	16%	6.3	6.7	7.1	7.7	8.3	9.1	10.0	11.1	12.5
16	15%	6.7	7.1	7.7	8.3	9.1	10.0	11.1	12.5	14.3
17										
18	**Section 2: Percentage Change in GMMs [2]**									
19										
20	*r*	**0%**	**1%**	**2%**	**3%**	**4%**	**5%**	**6%**	**7%**	**8%**
21	25%	NA	NA	NA	NA	NA	NA	NA	NA	NA
22	24%	4.2%	4.3%	4.5%	4.8%	5.0%	5.3%	5.6%	5.9%	6.3%
23	23%	4.3%	4.5%	4.8%	5.0%	5.3%	5.6%	5.9%	6.3%	6.7%
24	22%	4.5%	4.8%	5.0%	5.3%	5.6%	5.9%	6.3%	6.7%	7.1%
25	21%	4.8%	5.0%	5.3%	5.6%	5.9%	6.3%	6.7%	7.1%	7.7%
26	20%	5.0%	5.3%	5.6%	5.9%	6.3%	6.7%	7.1%	7.7%	8.3%
27	19%	5.3%	5.6%	5.9%	6.3%	6.7%	7.1%	7.7%	8.3%	9.1%
28	18%	5.6%	5.9%	6.3%	6.7%	7.1%	7.7%	8.3%	9.1%	10.0%
29	17%	5.9%	6.3%	6.7%	7.1%	7.7%	8.3%	9.1%	10.0%	11.1%
30	16%	6.3%	6.7%	7.1%	7.7%	8.3%	9.1%	10.0%	11.1%	12.5%
31	15%	6.7%	7.1%	7.7%	8.3%	9.1%	10.0%	11.1%	12.5%	14.3%
32										
33	[1] The formula is GMM-End of Year = 1/(r−g)									
34										
35	[2] For example, cell B22 = (B7/B6)−1									

duction, increases the valuation by 4.2 percent, which is 420 percent larger than the drop in the discount rate.

The numbers are larger in Section 2 as we move to the right across the columns because the larger the constant growth rate, the greater the impact of dropping the discount rate by each 1 percent. This means that large, high-growth firms have a huge "valuation leverage," and even small changes in a company's risk cause enormous changes in its valuation—for the good or the bad. Thus, dropping the discount rate from 16 to 15 percent for a firm with 8 percent constant expected growth will increase the valuation by 14.3 percent (J31).

The previous discussion established the very large impact of the discount rate on the valuation. It is important to mention that the long-term growth rate (g_n) in Equation 9.5 has essentially the same impact on value as the discount rate—but in the opposite direction.[10] You can see this by noticing that the denominator depends on $r - g$, so increasing g by 1 percent has the same impact as decreasing r by 1 percent.

We'll proceed to discuss risk: what, exactly, it is; how business valuators measure it; and how you can reduce the risk of your business.

RISK: WHAT IS IT AND HOW DO WE REDUCE IT?

Increasing the growth rate of cash flows and reducing risk are the two most powerful ways you can increase the value of your business—much more so than the other factors. Increasing the growth of cash flows is mainly a matter of being able to increase net income. How to accomplish this is, again, the subject of hundreds of thousands of pages of management literature.

This book's main contribution to your understanding of how to increase the value of your business is primarily focused on reducing risk. Thus, it behooves us to discuss what risk is, what factors contribute to it, and how to reduce it.

---

[10] In fact it is even slightly larger, because in the exact Gordon Model equation, the numerator has the square root of $1 + r$ in it.

What Is Risk?

Academic financial economists define risk as the volatility of stock returns and measure it with the statistical measure known as the *standard deviation of stock returns*. It is not necessary for us to dive into the statistical formulas to understand the concept. However, one question arises. There is a fundamental difference between public and private firms. The public firms have an objectively determined stock price, which private firms do not. So, since volatility in stock returns has no direct equivalent in private firms,[11] we need to look at the volatility of other financial measures that exist in both public and private firms to find a measure of risk that is meaningful to both.

It is logical that volatility in income—as measured by operating margin (operating income divided by sales)—underlies the volatility in returns, and indeed that is the case.[12] This is also true of volatility in the accounting return on equity, which itself is dependent on volatility of income.

Therefore, we can say that whatever makes your business volatile reduces its value compared to the otherwise identical business with less volatility. In this sense, a cyclical business will tend to have more risk than a noncyclical business—and here I mean multiyear cycles.

Sources of Risk

There are two types of risk: risk inherent in the business and risk to the buyer of being able to ascertain the honesty of the seller

---

[11] This is also the reason why it's necessary to do iterations in the valuations discussed in Chapters 5 and 6. To value a private firm using my log-size model ("log" is short for logarithms), we need assume a value of the firm to select a discount rate, which we use to value the firm! This is circular reasoning and is valid only as long as the value assumed equals the value calculated.

[12] Roger Grabowski and David King, "New Evidence on Size Effects and Rates of Return," *Business Valuation Review*, September 1999, 112–130. The writers used operating margin as their measure of profitability. More technically, they used the operating margin and the logarithms of the coefficient of variation of operating margin and Return on Equity. While the mathematical transformations are important mechanically, for our purposes they are not important conceptually.

and the financial information. We will focus on the risk in the business first and deal with the risk to the buyer later in the chapter.

There are two broad categories of sources of risk/volatility in a business: operational risk and financial risk. Operational risk factors are those risks that exist in the nature of the business. They include the business cycles of the industry, fixed costs, and dependence on the owner. Financial risk arises from the presence of debt financing. An all equity firm has no financial risk. It has only operational risk.

We will discuss these various risk factors in the following several pages, with dependence on the owner as the last item, since this is the most important source of risk to your business. I call it the "Big Banana."

Industry Business Cycles

The U.S. economy has business cycles of booms, normal growth, recessions, and depressions. Some industries have their own cycles. Agricultural staples such as grains and vegetables tend not to be cyclical. They are affected by the weather, but people have to eat these staples whether their income is high or low. In contrast, people don't have to eat caviar, so luxuries are more dependent on national income. Construction and heavy equipment industries are more dependent on the overall economy. So, business cycles affect different industries differently, and these are an operational risk inherent in each business.

Does that mean you should diversify if your business is cyclical? No. A potential buyer of your company can diversify his or her assets more easily than you can diversify your company's operations. Academic finance literature tells us that diversification within the firm tends to destroy value, not enhance it.

For example, researchers found that focus-decreasing (diversifying) mergers decreased stockholder wealth by 18 percent, and mergers that preserve business focus or enhance it do not decrease shareholder wealth.[13] So, if the nature of your busi-

---

[13] William L. Megginson, Angela Morgan, and Lance Nail, "The Determinants of Positive Long-term Performance in Strategic Mergers: Corporate Focus and Cash," a working paper, June 2002.

ness is cyclical, make sure you are very profitable, in order to outweigh the negative effects on value of being cyclical—but don't diversify to try to solve the problem. On the other hand, any portion of the cyclical nature of the business that you can control and "smooth out" should enhance your company value—as long as you are not unintentionally reducing net income by "bending into a pretzel" to artificially smooth out your net income.

Fixed Costs

Fixed costs are those the business will incur even when there are no sales. Depreciation on equipment, rent on the building, and salaries of high administrative personnel are examples. Variable costs are those that vary directly with sales, and are typically expressed as a percentage of sales.

If variable costs are 60 percent, then for every $1.00 increase in sales, they should increase by 60 cents. Your break-even volume should be approximately your fixed costs divided by one minus variable costs. If fixed costs are $2 million and variable costs are 60 percent, then your break-even volume is $2 million divided by 40 percent, or $5 million. To check the accuracy of this calculation, we can work it back in the other direction. At sales of $5 million, variable costs will be $5 million × 60% = $3 million, and fixed costs are $2 million, for a total of $5 million, leaving a zero net profit. For every dollar of sales above $5 million, your net income will be 40 percent times sales above $5 million.

Let's create an extreme example to illustrate the principle that high fixed costs exaggerate the effect of cycles. If you spend, for example, $5 million on a high-tech piece of equipment that makes production go very quickly and requires virtually no personnel to manufacture your product, your variable production cost is zero percent. If the equipment has a five-year life, your fixed cost is $1 million per year of depreciation expense. If your sales are $100 million, you will make $99 million net income. If your sales are $500,000, you'll lose $500,000 ($500,000 sales − $1 million depreciation).

If instead you had a low-tech machine that requires personnel to operate it, in the good years your net income will be high, but not as high as with the high-tech machine, and in bad years you can lay off personnel and keep your costs low. You can't lay off your high-tech machine. Therefore, a high fixed cost operation has additional risk that a low fixed cost operation does not have. Taking on high fixed costs is a two-edged sword: You gain higher expected profitability, but it comes with higher volatility of income.

That does not mean you should not automate. Just understand that undertaking high fixed costs is a business risk and a valuation risk, and you need to receive enough of a return on it to justify the risk. In a valuation sense, it means that your increase in forecast income from the high-tech equipment should more than compensate for the higher discount rate that comes with the higher volatility of earnings. Before buying such extremely expensive equipment, it would be wise to do a valuation of the company, as well as a valuation after the hypothetical purchase, using a higher discount rate—probably by 1 to 3 percent, depending on the cost of the equipment—for the after-the-purchase scenario.

Financial Risk

Financial risk is the effect on returns of a firm having debt, rather than equity, providing some of its financing. Let's use the valuation format of a balance sheet, where we subtract current liabilities—except the current portion of interest-bearing debt, which we will lump together with long-term debt—from current assets to get new working capital. Thus, the left-hand side of the balance sheet is net working capital, plus fixed assets, plus other assets, the latter of which are usually small and can be ignored, to add to total assets. The right-hand side of the balance sheet will be interest-bearing debt plus equity (again ignoring miscellaneous items).

The term "financial leverage" means the amount of financing of the right-hand side of the balance sheet that comes from interest-bearing debt. There are two common ways of measuring financial leverage. The first measure is the percentage of the right-hand side of the balance sheet coming from interest-bearing debt, which is the debt divided by debt plus equity. If debt equals $2 million and equity equals $8 million, then debt represents 20 percent of the right-hand side of the balance sheet, and equity represents 80 percent. The second measure of financial leverage is the debt-to-equity ratio, which in this example would be $2 million divided by $8 million, or 0.25.

Financial leverage usually causes average returns to increase and always causes volatility to increase. Let's look at Table 9.2 to see how this happens.

We begin with rows 5 through 7. Firm A and Firm B both have $10 million of financing. Firm A is 100 percent equity financed, while Firm B is only 20 percent equity financed, i.e., equity equals $2 million (C6) and debt equals $8 million (C5).

We now skip to cells B12 through B15 and C12 through C15. This shows four different possible levels of sales for four assumed scenarios, with their associated probabilities. Firms A and B have a 25 percent probability each (C12 through C15) that sales will be $10 million (B12) in the Best Case Scenario, $8 million (B13) in the Second Best Case, $6 million (B14) in the Third Best, and $4 million (B15) in the Worst Case Scenario.

Next we will construct income statements for both firms in the four scenarios.

We assume both firms have the same operating income and expenses, and the only difference between their income statements will be in the interest expense (row 23). Sales appears in row 20, according to the scenarios above. We assume variable expenses of 75 percent (B32, carried forward to row 21), which leaves net income before interest expense of 25 percent of sales, which is $2.5 million (B22, C22) in the Best Case Scenario, $2 million (D22, E22) in the Second Best Case Scenario, $1.5 million in the Third Best, etc.

Row 23, as noted above, is interest expense. We assume interest at 8 percent (B33) of interest-bearing debt of zero (B5) and $8 million (C5) for Firms A and B, respectively. Thus, Firm A has zero interest expense, and Firm B has $640,000—regardless of scenario.

Net income in row 24 equals row 22 minus row 23. In the Best Case Scenario, net income equals $2.5 million − 0 = $2.5 million (B22 − B23 = B24) for Firm A, and $2.5 million − $640,000 = $1.86 million (C22 − C23 = C24) for Firm B.

Return on Equity (ROE), also known as Return on Investment (ROI), equals net income divided by equity. For Firm A, that is \$2.5 million divided by \$10 million = 25.0% (B24/B6 = B25). For Firm B, that is \$1.86 million divided by \$2 million = 93.0% (C24/C6 = C25). So far, it looks like debt is a great deal. Bring it on!

Well, not so fast. In the Second Best Scenario net income is \$2 million (D24) and \$1.36 million (E24) for Firms A and B, respectively, and their ROEs are 20 percent (D25) and 68 percent (E25). In the Worst Case Scenario the ROEs are 10 percent (H25) and 18 percent (I25) for Firms A and B, respectively. The gap in ROE narrows as the scenario gets worse. However, under these assumptions, Firm B always seems to win.

Let's calculate the weighted average return on equity and the standard deviation of returns. We copy the ROE from row 25 back to rows 12 through 15 in column D for Firm A and column G for Firm B. Thus, cells B25, D25, F25, and H25 copy to D12 through D15, and cells C25, E25, G25, and I25 copy to G12 through G15. We multiply the ROEs in columns D and G by their probability of occurrence, which we have assumed for simplicity at 25 percent each (C12 through C15) to calculate the weighted ROEs in columns E and H. The sum of E12 through E15 is 17.50 percent (E16), which is the weighted average return for Firm A. The sum of H12 through H15 is 55.50 percent (H16), which is the weighted average return for Firm B. The standard deviation of ROE for Firm A is 5.59 percent (F16), and for Firm B it is 27.95 percent (I16).[14]

We transfer the results from row 16 to a summary section in rows 28 and 29. In D28 we show the relationship ratio of weighted average ROE of Firm B to Firm A: the 55.50 percent (C28) ROE for Firm B divided by the 17.50 percent (B28) ROE for Firm A. Firm B's weighted average ROE is 3.2 (D28) times higher than Firm A's. However, Firm B's standard deviation (which is our measure of volatility) is 5.0 (D29) times higher than Firm A's. Thus, the effect of financial leverage in this table is to raise both expected returns and risk, as measured by the standard deviation of returns. (By the way, it is important to

[14] I do not show the details of the calculations of standard deviation to avoid straining the patience of the nonmathematical reader. The Excel formula in cell F16 is stdevp(D12: D15). Note: the *p* indicates a population rather than sample standard deviation.

TABLE 9.2

Effect of Financial Leverage on Returns & Volatility—75% Variable Expense

	A	B	C	D	E	F	G	H	I
1	TABLE 9.2								
2	Effect of Financial Leverage on Returns & Volatility—75% Variable Expense								
3									
4	**Skeleton RHS of Balance Sheet [1]**	**Firm A**	**Firm B**						
5	Interest-Bearing Debt	$0	$8,000,000						
6	Equity	$10,000,000	$2,000,000						
7	Total Debt & Equity = Total Assets	**$10,000,000**	**$10,000,000**						
8									
9				**Firm A**			**Firm B**		
10				**ROE**	**Weighted**	**Standard**	**ROE**	**Weighted**	**Standard**
11	**Scenario**	**Sales**	**Probability**	**(Row 25)**	**ROE**	**Deviation**	**(Row 25)**	**ROE**	**Deviation**
12	Best Case	$10,000,000	25%	25.0%	6.25%		93.0%	23.25%	
13	2nd Best Case	$8,000,000	25%	20.0%	5.00%		68.0%	17.00%	
14	3rd Best Case	$6,000,000	25%	15.0%	3.75%		43.0%	10.75%	
15	Worst Case	$4,000,000	25%	10.0%	2.50%		18.0%	4.50%	
16	Total		**100%**		**17.50%**	**5.59%**		**55.50%**	**27.95%**
17									

	A	B	C	D	E	F	G	H	I
18	**Scenario**	**Best Case**		**2nd Best Case**		**3rd Best Case**		**Worst Case**	
19	**Income Statements**	**Firm A**	**Firm B**	**Firm A**	**Firm B**	**Firm A**	**Firm B**	**Firm A**	**Firm B**
20	Sales	$10,000,000	$10,000,000	$8,000,000	$8,000,000	$6,000,000	$6,000,000	$4,000,000	$4,000,000
21	Variable Expenses @ 75%	(7,500,000)	(7,500,000)	(6,000,000)	(6,000,000)	(4,500,000)	(4,500,000)	(3,000,000)	(3,000,000)
22	Net Income Before Interest Exp	**2,500,000**	**2,500,000**	**2,000,000**	**2,000,000**	**1,500,000**	**1,500,000**	**1,000,000**	**1,000,000**
23	Interest Expenses @ 8%	0	(640,000)	0	(640,000)	0	(640,000)	0	(640,000)
24	Net Income	**2,500,000**	**1,860,000**	**2,000,000**	**1,360,000**	**1,500,000**	**860,000**	**1,000,000**	**360,000**
25	**Return on Equity (ROE) [2]**	**25.0%**	**93.0%**	**20.0%**	**68.0%**	**15.0%**	**43.0%**	**10.0%**	**18.0%**
26									
27	**Summary of Results**	**Firm A**	**Firm B**	**B/A**					
28	Weighted Average Return on Equity	**17.50%**	**55.50%**	**3.2**					
29	Standard Deviation	**5.59%**	**27.95%**	**5.0**					
30									
31	**Assumptions**								
32	Variable Exp	75%							
33	Interest Exp	8%							
34									
35	[1] RHS = Right-Hand Side								
36	[2] Return on Equity (ROE) = Net Income/Equity								

note that these are accounting-based measures of return and volatility, which is all we can do with a privately held firm. The returns and standard deviation of returns described in Chapter 5 are for publicly held firms, and those returns are cash returns—dividends and capital gains—on stock prices. Those are not accounting-based returns and volatilities.)

Table 9.3, below, is identical to Table 9.2, with one assumption changed. Variable expenses are 85 percent (B32) instead of 75 percent. Note that in the Worst Case Scenario, Firm B has a $40,000 loss (I24), and its return is −2.0 percent (I25), while Firm A has net income of $600,000 (H24) and an ROE of 6.0 percent (H25). Therefore, the presence of debt lowers ROE below that of the debt-free firm (Firm A) if the scenario is bad enough.

In Table 9.4, below, we raise variable expenses to 90 percent (B32) of sales, and the ROEs are identical in the Second Best Case (D25, E25), while Firm A has superior results in the bottom two scenarios (F25 > G25 and H25 > I25). Note in the summary sections of Tables 9.3 and 9.4 that Firm B's standard deviation (volatility) of returns is still 5.0 (D29) times that of Firm A, but the ratio of their ROEs declines to 2.0 and 0.4 (D28), respectively. Thus, the high leverage in Table 9.4 is obviously a bad choice, as expected return for the leveraged Firm B is only 40 percent (D28) that of the debt-free Firm A, while its volatility is five times as much. In Tables 9.2 and 9.3, the trade-offs are less obvious. The optimal amount of debt is a subject of academic research and is beyond the scope of this book. A professional valuator should be helpful in making your choice.

It is important to note that for simplicity, we did not consider the tax savings of paying interest expense. That would have increased the return from leverage, since the government is essentially subsidizing part of the cost of the debt, which it does not do for capital. A little bit of debt does lower the cost of capital and raise returns, as long as you are able to make productive use of the money. At some point, though, the benefits of debt diminish and the cost of debt rises.

Summarizing this discussion, the presence of debt, also known as financial leverage, usually causes expected returns to rise, unless there is "too much debt," in which it case it causes expected returns to decline. The presence of debt always causes volatility to rise. Since volatility is risk, the more debt, the more risk. Thus, debt increases the risk of your firm.

As an aside, if you are comparing publicly traded firms, it's important to remember the effect of financial leverage on volatility. The volatility of earnings and returns are the sum of business and financial risk. Those readers who invest in the stock market are familiar with beta, from the Capital Asset Pricing Model (CAPM), which we discussed earlier in the book. Beta is a measure of the volatility of a particular stock relative to the volatility of the market. The presence of debt raises the beta of the stock, which is known as the equity beta. Some researchers will also provide an asset beta of the stock, which is the beta of the stock with the effect of debt removed, i.e., assuming the firm is debt-free. Comparing asset betas of two firms in the same industry is much more of an apples-to-apples comparison than comparing two equity betas.

REDUCING RISKS TO THE BUYER

The previous section deals with risks inherent in the business. These are risks that the current owner lives with. This section deals with risks that are unique to the buyer. There are two main categories of risks that are unique to the buyer: (1) The risk that the seller is dishonest; and (2) The risk that the business is highly dependent on the seller and will fall apart after he or she leaves. Both risks are significant, but I call the latter, "The Big Banana," because it is usually the largest impediment to creating value.

Reducing the Fear of Seller Dishonesty

The most important step the seller can take to reduce a buyer's fear of being taken to the cleaners is to get audited financial statements for at least three and preferably five years before selling the business.

Since audits are expensive, obviously this applies only to businesses of some substance, as the cost of the audits must be

	A	B	C	D	E	F	G	H	I
1	**TABLE 9.3**								
2	Effect of Financial Leverage on Returns & Volatility—85% Variable Expense								
3									
4	**Skeleton RHS of Balance Sheet [1]**	**Firm A**	**Firm B**						
5	Interest-Bearing Debt	$0	$8,000,000						
6	Equity	$10,000,000	$2,000,000						
7	Total Debt & Equity = Total Assets	**$10,000,000**	**$10,000,000**						
8									
9				**Firm A**			**Firm B**		
10				**ROE**	**Weighted**	**Standard**	**ROE**	**Weighted**	**Standard**
11	**Scenario**	**Sales**	**Probability**	**(Row 25)**	**ROE**	**Deviation**	**(Row 25)**	**ROE**	**Deviation**
12	Best Case	$10,000,000	25%	15.0%	3.75%		43.0%	10.75%	
13	2nd Best Case	$8,000,000	25%	12.0%	3.00%		28.0%	7.00%	
14	3rd Best Case	$6,000,000	25%	9.0%	2.25%		13.0%	3.25%	
15	Worst Case	$4,000,000	25%	6.0%	1.50%		−2.0%	−0.50%	
16	Total		**100%**		**10.50%**	**3.35%**		**20.50%**	**16.77%**
17									

	A	B	C	D	E	F	G	H	I
18	**Scenario**	**Best Case**		**2nd Best Case**		**3rd Best Case**		**Worst Case**	
19	**Income Statements**	**Firm A**	**Firm B**	**Firm A**	**Firm B**	**Firm A**	**Firm B**	**Firm A**	**Firm B**
20	Sales	$10,000,000	$10,000,000	$8,000,000	$8,000,000	$6,000,000	$6,000,000	$4,000,000	$4,000,000
21	Variable Expenses @ 85%	(8,500,000)	(8,500,000)	(6,800,000)	(6,800,000)	(5,100,000)	(5,100,000)	(3,400,000)	(3,400,000)
22	Net Income Before Interest Exp	**1,500,000**	**1,500,000**	**1,200,000**	**1,200,000**	**900,000**	**900,000**	**600,000**	**600,000**
23	Interest Expenses @ 8%	0	(640,000)	0	(640,000)	0	(640,000)	0	(640,000)
24	Net Income	**1,500,000**	**860,000**	**1,200,000**	**560,000**	**900,000**	**260,000**	**600,000**	**−40,000**
25	**Return on Equity (ROE) [2]**	**15.0%**	**43.0%**	**12.0%**	**28.0%**	**9.0%**	**13.0%**	**6.0%**	**−2.0%**
26									
27	**Summary of Results**	**Firm A**	**Firm B**	**B/A**					
28	Weighted Average Return on Equity	**10.50%**	**20.50%**	**2.0**					
29	Standard Deviation	**3.35%**	**16.77%**	**5.0**					
30									
31	**Assumptions**								
32	Variable Exp	85%							
33	Interest Exp	8%							
34									
35	[1] RHS = Right-Hand Side								
36	[2] Return on Equity (ROE) = Net Income/Equity								

	A	B	C	D	E	F	G	H	I
1	**TABLE 9.4**								
2	Effect of Financial Leverage on Returns & Volatility—90% Variable Expense								
3									
4	**Skeleton RHS of Balance Sheet [1]**	**Firm A**	**Firm B**						
5	Interest-Bearing Debt	$0	$8,000,000						
6	Equity	$10,000,000	$2,000,000						
7	Total Debt & Equity = Total Assets	**$10,000,000**	**$10,000,000**						
8									
9				**Firm A**			**Firm B**		
10				**ROE**	**Weighted**	**Standard**	**ROE**	**Weighted**	**Standard**
11	**Scenario**	**Sales**	**Probability**	**(Row 25)**	**ROE**	**Deviation**	**(Row 25)**	**ROE**	**Deviation**
12	Best Case	$10,000,000	25%	10.0%	2.50%		18.0%	4.50%	
13	2nd Best Case	$8,000,000	25%	8.0%	2.00%		8.0%	2.00%	
14	3rd Best Case	$6,000,000	25%	6.0%	1.50%		−2.0%	−0.50%	
15	Worst Case	$4,000,000	25%	4.0%	1.00%		−12.0%	−3.00%	
16	Total		**100%**		**7.00%**	**2.24%**		**3.00%**	**11.18%**
17									

	A	B	C	D	E	F	G	H	I
18	**Scenario**	**Best Case**		**2nd Best Case**		**3rd Best Case**		**Worst Case**	
19	**Income Statements**	**Firm A**	**Firm B**	**Firm A**	**Firm B**	**Firm A**	**Firm B**	**Firm A**	**Firm B**
20	Sales	$10,000,000	$10,000,000	$8,000,000	$8,000,000	$6,000,000	$6,000,000	$4,000,000	$4,000,000
21	Variable Expenses @90%	(9,000,000)	(9,000,000)	(7,200,000)	(5,400,000)	(5,400,000)	(5,400,000)	(3,600,000)	(3,600,000)
22	Net Income Before Interest Exp	**1,000,000**	**1,000,000**	**800,000**	**800,000**	**600,000**	**600,000**	**400,000**	**400,000**
23	Interest Expenses @ 8%	0	(640,000)	0	(640,000)	0	(640,000)	0	(640,000)
24	Net Income	**1,000,000**	**360,000**	**800,000**	**160,000**	**600,000**	**−40,000**	**400,000**	**−240,000**
25	**Return on Equity (ROE) [2]**	**10.0%**	**18.0%**	**8.0%**	**8.0%**	**6.0%**	**−2.0%**	**4.0%**	**−12.0%**
26									
27	**Summary of Results**	**Firm A**	**Firm B**	**B/A**					
28	Weighted Average Return on Equity	**7.00%**	**3.00%**	**0.4**					
29	Standard Deviation	**2.24%**	**11.18%**	**5.0**					
30									
31	**Assumptions**								
32	Variable Exp	90%							
33	Interest Exp	8%							
34									
35	[1] RHS = Right-Hand Side								
36	[2] Return on Equity (ROE) = Net Income/Equity								

economically justified by the ability to sell for a higher price. If you cannot afford an audit, then get reviewed financial statements. Compiled financial statements contain no analytical work by your accountant, and your potential buyers should be skeptical of the accuracy and honesty of your financial statements. In equation 9.5, this means sacrificing a small amount of future growth, g, by paying for the audit in return for reducing the discount rate, m. It is highly likely that the tradeoff will be favorable for any business with a FMV over $500,000, and perhaps less. Implicit in the audit process is eliminating unreported income and personal expenses from the business. Any attempt to add back unreported income and personal expenses to calculate economic net income will tend to raise the buyer's fear of your honesty, and your gains from playing tax games are very likely to disappear in selling your company.

The "Big Banana"

However, the foregoing is still not the largest component of risk in privately held businesses. As I have stated in several places earlier in this book, and as Linda Feinholz states in the downloadable Web site chapter, the largest single risk to most privately held businesses is overdependence on the business owner.

If you want to make your business valuable, you need to wean your employees away from dependence on you. How? By hiring and training excellent employees, creating a logical system of organization with good structure and procedures, being computerized (with an impeccable backup system) and very professional—just like big business, but hopefully without the cumbersome bureaucracy.

Many people think of their business as "their baby." A child is a good metaphor for a business. Babies need near constant attention or they won't survive. As children grow, a responsible parent will make sure to give them life skills and responsibilities, so they learn to be independent. Eventually, they will need to live their own lives. A parent who does everything for an older child is crippling the child. The same is true of a business. Your young business may be "your baby," but if you want to sell your business for a lot of money someday, make sure it becomes "your big boy or girl"—wean it off of dependence on you.

The more "turnkey" you can make your business, the more you can enjoy life, and the more you receive when you sell it. I remember valuing a business in 1987 that was so turnkey, the president was preparing to leave for a one-year fishing trip on his own ship. He was leaving his various generals, captains, and lieutenants in charge and going off for the time of his life—and he had the chutzpah not to invite me to join him! While you may or may not like fish, that degree of independence from the owner is the model for any private business to become valuable.

CONCLUSION

In this chapter you have learned the methodology to value your business as of a future date. Additionally, we have analyzed the future valuation equation to understand how you can maximize your company's value over time. Here are the actions you can take to maximize value, in descending order:

1. Reduce the risk of your business.
   a. Reduce its dependence on you. Make it a turnkey operation, to the extent possible. Become well-organized, systematic, and professional.
   b. Strike the proper balance in fixed versus variable costs. Only take on high fixed costs when your expected gain from higher income outweighs the additional risk of the higher volatility of income that goes along with high fixed costs.
   c. Use debt wisely, remembering that relatively smaller amounts will increase your expected return and decrease your risk, while large amounts of debt decrease expected return while increasing risk. All other things being equal, the higher the operational risk of your business, the lower should be your financial risk. Thus, startups, cyclical businesses, and businesses with high fixed assets should use little or no debt.

2. Create the highest possible sustainable growth in cash flows. This includes weaning yourself away from hiding income and charging personal expenses.
3. Manage net working capital carefully. This includes managing your credit policy.
4. Manage fixed asset purchasing carefully. Strike the right balance between buying too much, which lowers the Payout Ratio, and buying too little, which at some point will reduce net income.

This is the final chapter in Part One. The chapters in the next part will discuss valuation and the sale of a business from the viewpoint of an appraiser (myself), as well as the points of view of a business broker, an investment banker, and a venture capitalist. There is also a chapter on the taxation of a business—including the sale of a business—and a chapter on valuation controversy written by the Internal Revenue Service's top valuation official.

Part Two

THE SALE AND FINANCING OF A BUSINESS

This part of the book encompasses Chapters 10 through 15 and covers the sale, financing, and taxation of a business. The sale is a relatively straightforward concept, although the details of buying or selling a business are extremely important.

The financing of a business is less simple. There are two common situations in which the financing is an issue.

The first situation is finding the debt financing that will permit the sale of a business to go through. This is common in the sale of small businesses, where it is usual for the seller to take a note, which is a loan from the seller to the buyer, for a portion of the purchase price of a business. This is part and parcel of the sale of 100 percent of a whole business, and for the remainder of Part Two that is not what I mean by the financing of a business unless I specifically note as much.

The second situation is the true financing of a business, which is to say, raising additional capital to enable the business to expand. This type of financing is a partial sale of equity, i.e., the buyer contributes capital—usually cash, but occasionally property, which can be intellectual property—and in return receives a partial equity interest in the company.

VALUATION FOR A SALE

Chapters 10 through 12 are on valuation for purposes of a sale by an appraiser (myself), a business broker, and an investment banker, respectively. In Chapter 10, I focus on valuation issues specific to the sale of a business. I also discuss how the valuations of an appraiser and a business broker and investment banker may differ, since their environment, clients, technical skills, understanding of the market, and motivations are different.

VENTURE CAPITAL FINANCING

Chapter 13 is a must read for anyone who seeks venture capital (VC) financing. Bruce Taragin is an information technology venture capitalist in San Francisco, and he does an excellent job of communicating how to work with a VC—what to expect, what to do and not to do, etc.

I would like to add an important insight to the VC process that Bruce does not cover in his chapter, from the perspective of a business valuator. It is important to understand that entrepreneurs who make deals with VCs are consciously—or more often unconsciously—valuing their businesses. If the VC commits to provide $1 million of financing to you and you give him or her 40 percent of the firm, you have just implicitly valued your firm at $1 million ÷ 40% = $2.5 million. If all you did was to cut the best deal you knew how to without having valued your business, then you've just harmed yourself if the true Fair Market Value—as best we can measure it—is, let's say, $10 million. If that's the case, then you should have given up only 10 percent of your company to the VC ($1 million investment ÷ $10 million FMV = 10%). So, do your homework!

TAX CONSIDERATIONS AND STRATEGIES

Chapter 14 is a "must read" for two categories of business owners: (1) Those who are about to start a business and have not yet chosen the form of the entity, and (2) those who are contemplating the sale of their business within the foreseeable future, say within five years. So, if you have already selected your entity form and do not contemplate the sale of your business within five years, you can consider skipping this chapter.

This chapter is not easy or light reading, although for most nonmathematical readers, it still will be easier than Part One of this book. It contains a lot of information, and the frustrating, but understandable, aspect of it, given the complexity of the tax code, is that you will not come through this chapter with a detailed knowledge of tax law that will enable you to be your own tax attorney. But you should develop a healthy respect for the need for the right professional help when you begin a business or are in the process of selling one.

However, knowledge and wisdom is power. In Chapter 14, David Boatwright spends considerable time presenting the tax law that serves as the foundation for making wise choices in structuring the sale of a business. More significant, he gives quite a number of important strategies that are gold nuggets, if not diamonds. Look for the sections entitled "Strategies." Additionally, look for strategic statements set off in italics.

Business owners may not fully absorb the entire body of tax law in this chapter, but that is not the point. As an owner contemplating a sale, you should read the entire chapter and spot the issues that seem relevant to you, in order to discuss them with your tax attorney and accountant. Not all professionals operate at the same level, and the more knowledge you have at your disposal, the more likely you are to ensure the best outcome for yourself. If you choose to use an attorney whose practice is more general and who may have relatively light experience in the tax intricacies involved in the sale of a business that is a risk. I would suggest that the larger the business, the less you can afford that risk.

In any case, you can reduce this risk by making sure your attorney (and accountant) is familiar with the contents of this chapter. You should ask him or her questions that you feel are relevant to your sale, and if your attorney appears less than fully knowledgeable, you should insist that he or she associate with a tax attorney who is specialized in transactional work, or replace your attorney with a tax specialist.

Chapter 15 is about valuation controversy and how to reduce it. Howard Lewis is the new Engineering Program Manager at the Internal Revenue Service. That means he is the top IRS employee in charge of valuation issues. This chapter is another must read for the business owner, as well as for the professionals who serve you—your accountant, attorney, and succession planning insurance agent.

Eventually we all need to deal with Uncle Sam, and the wisdom in this chapter can help you have a more successful outcome. Valuation controversy can drag on for a long time, cause enormous stress to business owners, and interfere with their ability to run their companies. Mistakes made in the process may not only be stressful, but very costly. The maximum estate and gift tax rate varies by year and is as large as 55 percent, so it is vital to manage the process well. As a bonus, Chapter 15 is well written, clear, concise, and interesting.

Chapter 10

An Appraiser's Perspective on Valuation for Sale

In this chapter we will deal with the following topics:

- Adjusting the nominal selling price of a business to the real selling price.
- How appraisers, business brokers, and investment bankers work differently.
- The dangers of seller ignorance, self-deception, and greed.
- Investment Value versus Fair Market Value.

ADJUSTING THE NOMINAL PRICE TO THE REAL PRICE

Seller financing and earn-outs often make the apparent (i.e., the nominal) selling price of a business appear larger than the real selling price. We will discuss each of these elements.

Seller Financing

In the next chapter Jim Levy will tell us that the typical financing structure for the sale of a small business is 40 to 60 percent cash down, with the seller taking a note from the buyer for the rest. Let's use the midpoint of 50 percent for our calculations.

Suppose Constance Billabong finally wants out of the business and decides to sell. The sales price is $1 million. If she's paid all of that in cash, then that is also the real selling price of the company. However, if she gets $500,000 in cash and takes a note from the buyer secured by the business for the other $500,000, then $1 million is only the nominal selling price of Billabong Boomerangs. If the note requires payment of an arm's length interest rate that a bank would charge for a loan of the same risk, then the Fair Market Value of the note is equal to its face (nominal) amount, and the nominal selling price of the business equals its real selling price.

However, that arrangement is unusual. In most circumstances, sellers take notes with interest rates that are below the rate a bank would charge for a fairly high-risk loan. Let's go through a numerical example to illustrate how to calculate the real selling price of a business.

Calculating the Real Selling Price

In *Quantitative Business Valuation: A Mathematical Approach for Today's Professionals*, I derived the equation to adjust the nominal selling price of a business to its real selling price.[1] It is the real annuity discount factor divided by the nominal ADF.[2] Annuity discount factors are available as an appendix in many standard finance texts.

Let's assume the seller finances the 50 percent (Table 10.1, B11) balance for seven years, which is 84 months (B8, C8) at 8 percent (B5), and the bank charges a market rate of 14 percent (C5).

---

[1] *Quantitative Business Valuation, ibid*, 85, equation (3-23).

[2] The formula is $ADF = \dfrac{1 - \dfrac{1}{(1+r)^n}}{r}$, where r is the discount rate and n is the number of time periods (usually months in a business loan) from the valuation date. The only difference between the nominal and the real ADF is that in the former, we use the nominal interest rate of the loan, which is fixed for the entire life of the loan, while in the latter, we use the current market rate that a bank would charge on this loan, which varies almost constantly.

	A	B	C
1	**TABLE 10.1**		
2	Calculation of FMV of Loan		
3			
4		Nominal	Market
5	r	8%	14%
6	i = r/12	0.6667%	1.1667%
7	Yrs	7	7
8	n = Yrs *12	84	84
9	ADF @14%, 84 Mos.	64.15926114	53.36175991
10	Discount on Total Prin	16.8%	
11	% Financed	50%	
12	Discount on % Financed	**8.4%**	

If the discount rate were zero, then the present value of the loan would be equal to the total payments of \$1.00 per month × 84 months = \$84.00. The real annuity discount factor discounts the 84 monthly payments of \$1.00 at the real interest rate, which we assume here is 14 percent. The real ADF is 53.3618 (C9), which means that an investor who requires a 14 percent rate of return—presumably a bank in this example—would pay \$53.36, rounded, for the right to receive the \$84 over seven years. At the nominal 8 percent rate of interest, the ADF is 64.1593 (B9), which means that an investor who requires an 8 percent rate of return for a loan of this risk would be willing to pay \$64.16 for the right to receive the \$1.00 per month for 84 months.

We can now calculate the ratio of the real selling price to the nominal selling price, and thereby the percentage discount. If the loan were 100 percent financed, the real present value of the loan is only $\frac{\$53.3618}{\$64.1593} = 83.2\%$ of the nominal present value of the loan. Thus, the real selling price would bear a discount of 1 − 83.2% = 16.8% (B10) from the nominal selling price. We multiply this by the 50 percent financed (B11) to calculate the average discount to cash equivalent value of 8.4 percent (B12).

The 8.4 percent is a fairly realistic discount for many business sales. This means that the selling price in an average business sale is "inflated," and appears larger than it really is. Connie Billabong, the seller, is receiving less than she thinks that she is; in the above example, 8.4 percent less.

The percentage discount depends only on the length of the loan, the nominal interest rate, and the real interest rate. It does not depend on the amount of the loan. Of course, the market rate of interest on the loan depends on the collateral. If the business itself is the only collateral, the loan is high-risk, because if the buyer turns out to be incompetent at running the business, he will destroy the collateral, and the business will boomerang right back to Connie (sorry, that pun was just too irresistible). But if so, it won't be the healthy business that she sold—it will be a troubled company.

On the other hand, if the buyer secures the note of the sale of the business with a piece of commercial real estate worth $5 million net of its mortgage, then the risk of the loan goes down significantly. Perhaps a bank would be willing to make such a loan at 7 percent, in which case the Fair Market Value of an 8 percent note actually would be above the face value. This is unusual, but does occur rarely.

Earn-outs

An "earn-out" is that portion of the selling price of a business that is conditional. Usually it is conditional on achieving some level of sales or profitability. Buyers like earn-outs to protect themselves against the business disappearing or falling apart after the seller leaves the company. The earn-out is not a sure thing, and therefore that portion of the selling price must be reduced to its expected value in order to calculate the real selling price.

Suppose Constance Billabong sells the company to Sir Harvard Cucumber for $5 million cash, plus another $1 million if sales are at least $12 million in the third year after sale. Thus, it appears that the selling price of the company is $6 million. Suppose sales are now $10 million, and Connie assesses the probability of Sir Harvard reaching sales of $12 million as two-thirds. It might appear that the FMV of the $1 million earn-out is $1 million $\times$ 2/3 = $666,667. However, there is still the time value of money to be accounted for.

Since we have already reduced the earn-out down to its expected value as of the end of Year Three, we need to discount it to present value at a business rate.[3] Assuming 20 percent is the appropriate rate, the present value factor (review Chapter 5 if you're feeling rusty at this) is 0.5787. Therefore, the FMV of the earn-out is $666,667 × 0.5787 = $385,803, and the real selling price of the business is then $5,385,803. Thus, what might have looked like an additional $1 million to the seller in the form of the earn-out was only less than 40 percent of its nominal amount.

Earn-outs can get much more complicated than this. If so, the level of mathematics and statistics necessary to quantify them rises.

The Strategic Bottom Line

The importance of the foregoing discussion is that you need to be careful in buying or selling a business, and understand the real value of what you are buying or selling. If you're the seller, make sure to charge an interest rate that is a market rate; if you cannot do that, you should negotiate a higher nominal selling price to make up for your loss in Fair Market Value from a below-market loan. If you're the buyer, then you want to push for the lowest possible interest rate on the loan.

Similarly, if you are a buyer, you would want to push for an earn-out to protect you. Sellers would want to avoid earn-outs, or at least be compensated—in the form of a higher price—for providing them.

HOW APPRAISERS, BROKERS, AND BANKERS DIFFER

It is important to understand how appraisers, business brokers, and investment bankers work differently, because if you do not, it may cost you a lot of money when you buy or sell a business.

---

[3] We would not use a risk-free discount rate just because the earn-out is already reduced to its expected value, since it is still an uncertain cash flow, subject to risk.

Assumptions of What Transfers in a Sale

This is a critical section, and failure to understand it can be disastrous. There are different customs about which assets transfer in a sale. Business brokers normally sell businesses under $10 million, while investment bankers normally sell businesses over $10 million. The border is not absolute, and there are occasional crossovers.

Appraisers normally assume that all of the assets of the seller pass over to the buyer. If there is excess cash in the company, Fair Market Value presumes that it still goes to the buyer, but the FMV of the firm should increase dollar for dollar, since that excess cash is available for immediate distribution as a dividend.

In businesses sold by business brokers, normally the seller keeps the cash, accounts receivable, and accounts payable from the sale. According to Michael Keane, whom you'll hear from in Chapter 12, when investment bankers facilitate the sale of a company, the buyer keeps the receivables and payables, which is the same assumption appraisers make. When the buyer is a public company, the cash usually goes to the buyer. When the buyer is a private firm, the seller usually keeps some or all of the cash.

Business brokers only sell 100 percent interests in businesses, which makes life simpler for them. Investment bankers sell whole businesses, but also arrange financing transactions wherein the investors buy a minority interest in the firm. In effect, they are selling fractional interests in businesses too. Business appraisers value both whole businesses and fractional interests in them. Furthermore, clients often commission professional appraisals for purposes other than actual transactions, e.g., for tax purposes, Employee Stock Ownership Plans, litigation, and many other purposes.

Therefore, the values these three categories of professionals are calculating are all different:

- *Business brokers* are calculating the purchase price of the business, not Fair Market Value. Furthermore, their purchase price assumes the seller keeps cash, receivables, and payables.

- *Business appraisers* normally calculate Fair Market Value, unless the assignment calls for a different standard of value. FMV presumes there are no synergies, which is equivalent to assuming a financial buyer.[4] They assume that cash, receivables, and payables go to the buyer. Therefore, if the sale calls for them to remain with the seller, then business appraisers make an adjustment to subtract the net amount of those items from FMV to calculate the purchase price. (Note that cash, receivables, and payables are the main components of net working capital—current assets minus current liabilities. The only other common components of net working capital are accounts receivable, the current portion of long-term debt, and accrued liabilities. While inventory is also part of net working capital, it obviously stays with the buyer, unless it is obsolete.)
- *Investment bankers* may be calculating Fair Market Value, Investment Value, or anything in between. They normally calculate their value assuming the buyer retains all cash, receivables, and payables, and if some or all of the cash remains with the seller, they reduce the purchase price accordingly.

Therefore, when it comes time for you to sell your business (or for someone to do it for you), it is imperative that you or your professional make an adjustment to reduce FMV or Investment Value down to the purchase price for these components of net working capital that we normally assume transfer to the buyer, but in fact will not. Thus, all other things being equal, the valuations of a business appraiser and investment banker before this adjustment to the purchase price will be higher than that of the business broker.

For example, suppose Constance will sell Billabong Boomerangs, and, to make some simple assumptions so the adjustment calculation will be simpler, let's say her sales are $12

[4] The exception is when synergistic buyers constitute the relevant market for a particular firm, in which case Investment Value becomes Fair Market Value. This normally only applies to firms large enough to be candidates for the M&A market serviced by investment bankers.

million per year, which is \$1 million per month. Let's also assume she gives 30 days credit to her customers and receives the same from her suppliers, and that her gross profit margin is 60 percent. Her receivables will be approximately \$1 million for one month of sales, and her payables should be (1 – 60%) × \$1 million = \$400,000.[5] And finally let's assume there is \$250,000 cash.

We would have assumed that when the buyer takes over the business, the net working capital in the company would include the \$1 million in receivables – \$400,000 of payables + \$250,000 cash = \$850,000. Since these items will remain with the seller, the buyer will have to invest \$850,000 to bring the balance sheet of the company in line with the correct amount of net working capital that it takes to produce the economic net income and cash flow we forecast in the Discounted Cash Flow method, and this \$850,000 investment should be subtracted from the purchase price as we have calculated it. If, magically, the business broker otherwise would have valued the company the same as the appraiser in all other respects, that valuation theoretically should be \$850,000 less than the appraiser's valuation before the adjustment to the purchase price.

Advantages, Disadvantages, and Costs

For most small and midsize businesses, investment bankers function in a similar way to business brokers.[6] So, for the purposes of this section, the term "business brokers" will include both. Most business brokers and investment bankers are seller oriented. Thus, if you are a buyer, do not expect a business broker or an investment banker to watch out for your best interests. Get a professional appraiser to help you.

---

[5] It is actually more complex than this, as I assumed she bought the boomerangs. A manufacturer does not simply buy finished product. It adds labor and capital to transform raw materials into a finished product. The additional complexity of this calculation for a manufacturer is outside of the scope of this book.

[6] The large investment banking houses offer much more sophisticated services for very large businesses, but that is largely outside of the scope of this discussion.

Appraisers usually have superior mathematical skills—which is not surprising, since it's what they do full-time—while brokers have a superior knowledge of the market. Also, an appraiser normally will not find a buyer for you. Thus, if you want someone to sell your business, you'll need a business broker. If you can afford both, it is best to have both skills working in your favor, each one "keeping the other honest" and supporting and sometimes challenging the other.

Business brokers normally will do the valuation for you for free, or it should be included in their representation fees. Usually, you'll save appraisal fees if you use only a broker. The broker earns his or her living by earning a commission on the sale. Their customary fee is 10 percent of the selling price for the first $1 million, and a lower percentage thereafter.

Appraisals can cost a few thousand dollars for small businesses, to several million dollars for giant mergers. Most valuations of small- and medium-size businesses cost from $5000 to $25,000 in 2004, but there can be much variation, depending on the complexity of your business, the reason you need a valuation, your risk of a poor result arising from not paying for enough work, the appraiser and firm doing the work, and a host of other factors.

Appraisal fees also partly or largely depend on the skill level of the business valuator you hire, and the size of the firm for whom he or she works. There is a wide range of skill levels in business valuation, from the uneducated and untrained, who do shoddy work; through CPAs, who do valuation part-time; to full-time valuation professionals—about half of whom are CPAs who specialize in valuation, and half are usually MBAs; and, finally, to a small number of world-class leaders in the profession. Generally, you get what you pay for. Usually the higher the skill level and the bigger the firm, the more expensive it is, with firm size probably the more important factor when it comes to cost.

There are inexpensive automated valuation services that produce appraisals. Those that I have seen rely on shortcuts, analyze only one year of data, and would not even qualify as an appraisal under the Uniform Standards of Professional Appraisal Practice. I do not recommend "cookie cutter" valuation, despite their claims of using sophisticated methods.

THE DANGER OF IGNORANCE, SELF-DECEPTION, AND GREED

While there are some sellers who get lucky and "sell high"—and I certainly have seen that—the majority of sellers need to be realistic. Seller ignorance, self-deception, and greed lead to disaster more often than they lead to a windfall. Of course, everyone wants to sell high, but the question is: "What value have you created that others will pay for?" If you've created a turnkey business that is profitable, has demonstrated strong growth, has a strong management team, and can function well with someone else filling your shoes, then you have created value, and maybe you might sell for a PE multiple[7] in the 6 to 12 range.[8]

Michael Keane, investment banker and author of Chapter 12, told me that his clients typically sell in the range of four to six times EBITDA (Earnings Before Interest, Taxes, Depreciation & Amortization). EBITDA is equal to net income before taxes plus interest expense, depreciation, and amortization. For most midsize businesses, EBITDA is much higher than net income after taxes, which is the basis for the PE multiple. EBITDA easily could be twice net income after taxes, which means if the Price-to-EBITDA multiple is 4 to 6, that easily could translate into a PE multiple of 8 to 12. In fact, the latter range should be somewhat wider, because the components of EBITDA—net income before taxes, interest expense, tax rates, depreciation, and amortization—can vary widely across firms. Additionally, Keane stated that the EBITDA multiple might be higher in an "up market" for a large firm with excellent historical and expected growth. For reference, his smallest clients have $10 million in Fair Market Value, and his absolute, all-time smallest client was at $5 million FMV. Thus, his clients are not in the same size range as the clients of business brokers.

While publicly traded firms often sell for PE multiples of 15 to 30, these are usually companies that are much larger, bet-

---

[7] Price Earnings multiple. For review, see Chapter 2 and its appendix.

[8] I have had one client with net income over $1 million sell to a Fortune 500 strategic buyer for a PE multiple of approximately 28, so the "dream deals" do happen on rare occasions. Even so, this was a large client with an exciting product and a very strong management team that stayed on long-term with the company, including the CEO.

ter financed, well-managed, and with higher expected growth and lower risk than privately held firms. If your company is large enough to sell to a public firm or a very large private firm—which probably means a "bricks-and-mortar" business with actual sales of at least $8 million or intellectual property with forecast sales of more— then these multiples may be realistic in the M&A market. If your company does not fit this description, then have realistic expectations of its value. Most small businesses sell for PE ratios in the 2 to 4 range. Generally, the PE ratio rises with the size of the business and its growth prospects.

There are some sharks out there who pander to and prey upon seller greed, and there are others who will attempt to cater to it, waste your time, and possibly endanger the value of your business. The former can be dangerous because they're callous and clever, while the latter, though well-intentioned, can be dangerous due to their ignorance and clumsiness. I would recommend that you be cautious with people who promise the sky. If it sounds too good to be true, it probably is.

If you want to sell your business, you need to find a professional with competence and integrity. With so many dollars at stake, the wrong choice can be ruinous. The right business broker or investment banker can be critical to your success, and the wrong one can lead you down a garden path that may lead to the destruction of your business value. Unfortunately, you cannot tell who they are by merely looking at them. It is critical to get referrals from competent people you know and can trust. In addition, you should interview past clients, who might give you a glimpse into how the broker you're considering operates and whether their experiences match the results you need.

Brokers face tremendous pressure from their clients to list the business at very high selling prices. Sellers often have unrealistic expectations of the value of "their baby," unsubstantiated by any appraisal, fueled by ignorance, wishful thinking, and sometimes greed. Furthermore, sellers are confronted by a ready supply of poorly trained business brokers who compete with the good ones, will do anything to get the listing and worry later about how to sell it. Interviews I've done with business brokers indicate that 80 to 85 percent of business listings never sell, and many sellers will not listen to reason.

After reading this book, you should have a more realistic viewpoint when it comes to business valuation. That understanding can support your decision as to whether you wish to sell your business. However, I do not recommend that a business owner rely on his or her own valuation for a sale—at least not without consulting a professional. Appraisers, who are fee-based, have no reason to slant the valuation to cater to your ego.

War Stories

I have a recent "war story" on this point. A pharmacist client of mine was working with a business broker on the possible buy of a pharmacy. When we spoke to the broker, I was stunned by his apparent ignorance. He was offering a pharmacy for $1 million that had lost about $400,000 two years in a row. I asked him what justified his positive price for a business that was losing any money, let alone one that was losing so much money. I expected him to come back with some explanation of either hidden income in cash sales that were never reported, huge amounts of personal expenses being charged to the business, which made a profitable company look like a loser, or some other explanation that at least we could investigate and analyze. He had no explanation to justify a zero price, let alone $1 million.

I still find it a wonder how he wasted his time, mine, and that of my client with such a ridiculous offer. Either he was wet behind the ears and was on the steep part of the learning curve where new brokers make no money, or there really are people who are so ignorant that they will buy such garbage, and brokers who are so unethical that they will sell it.

The idealistic chamber of my heart hopes the first explanation is right, but my head is telling me the second explanation is the more likely one—especially in light of the estimate that 80 percent of listings do not sell. Probably, the worst deals never sell, the best ones always sell, and some of the marginal ones also sell. Woe to the buyers of the marginal ones! The bottom line is that you should understand valuation before you buy or sell a business, because it is very hard for a first-time seller to tell the difference between a competent and an incompetent broker and between an ethical and an unethical one. The International Business Brokers Association (IBBA) is trying to upgrade the level of the profession, but the profession has a long way to go.

Jim Levy (of the next chapter) shared a recent war story of his. He met with a potential client and gave him his opinion of the expected selling price. The client felt it was worth more than that and listed with a large brokerage firm for a much higher price. One year later the business had not sold and had not even received any offers; on the contrary, it fell on hard times. Now, the owner wanted Jim to sell it for him, but Jim said that the liquidation value was higher than its value on an income basis, since income had dropped so much. Greed and wishful thinking may have cost this seller hundreds of thousands of dollars.

I have a similar war story. I valued a client about 12 years ago for a legal purpose. Three years earlier he had turned down an offer for his firm for $14 million—over $20 million in 2004 dollars. When I valued his firm three years later, it was worthless. Technological change eliminated over 95 percent of his business. We might be able to write that off as bad luck—and perhaps it was—but I have two thoughts that run contrary to that interpretation. For one thing, I wonder whether the original valuation—which I was unable to obtain and was irrelevant for my purposes at the time—was optimistic. Another and more serious objection to ascribing his losses purely to bad luck is that he'd left himself completely undiversified and exposed to very high risk, being in a fast changing, high technology industry. It would have been much better had he diversified his assets, heeding the warning of King Solomon, who wrote, "Divide your wealth into seven, even eight parts, for you cannot know what misfortune may occur on earth."[9]

How many mistakes of hundreds of thousands of dollars can one afford in life, let alone $20 million mistakes? Greed and

---

[9] Ecclesiastes, 11:2.

ignorance are expensive, and so is bad luck. The morale of these war stories is to become informed and get the best advice you can pay for when a lot of money is at stake.

My Advice

My advice is:

1. Know the value of your business before you try to sell it.
2. Do not engage in self-deception.
3. Try to sell when your earnings are high and your growth prospects are strong.
4. Try to sell in an "up market."
5. Try to sell high, but be willing to sell for a fair, realistic price.
6. Understand the risk of waiting to sell for a higher price. If you wait, you may run the risk of your company and/or the entire market declining, or find yourself running a company long after you wanted out!

INVESTMENT VALUE VS. FAIR MARKET VALUE

Our last major topic in this chapter is Investment Value versus Fair Market Value. FMV essentially is the price that any buyer would pay for your company. In practical terms, think of this buyer as being a financial buyer, with no particular synergies with your firm. Investment Value is the value of your firm to a particular buyer. For Investment Value to exceed FMV, synergies, by definition, must be positive. The synergies of each potential buyer with your firm will be different, and the one with the highest synergies should theoretically be willing to pay the most for your company.

Synergies arise when two firms merge and the combined entity increases sales or decreases costs. Examples of each are:

- The buyer has distribution that can enable the seller's products and services to be sold easily and inexpen-

sively. This is increasing the sales of the combined entity with little or no extra cost.
- The combined entity can eliminate duplicated staff. For example, the buyer has an accounting staff of 10 people, the seller has two, and the buyer will not need the staff of the seller. This is an example of lowering the costs of accomplishing the same tasks.

Purex Corporation: A War Story

Here's a war story of a real synergy.[10] In 1985, I valued the acquisition of Purex Corporation by Armour-Dial, Inc., then a subsidiary of Greyhound since 1970, which was a large conglomerate.[11] The Armour-Dial people told me they were excited about the acquisition, because of specific synergies that they felt Purex would bring to them. Purex made a limited line of inexpensive detergents, bleaches, and cleaners and shipped its products in carload quantities (i.e., by rail), while Armour-Dial made a wide range of high-end, specialty cleaning products and shipped by truck. Since Purex had a similar customer list, Armour-Dial expected to be able to piggyback its own shipments by rail onto the Purex shipments, thus lowering its own transportation costs considerably.

At the time, Armour-Dial expected to add 1 percent to its own net income after taxes by that acquisition. Assuming a Price Earnings multiple of, say 20,[12] the synergies from buying Purex

---

[10] I give my profound thanks to Conrad A. Conrad, Executive Vice President and Chief Financial Officer, and David Riddiford, the Senior Vice President and Treasurer, of The Dial Corporation, for their permission to publish this and their help with some of the financial details in this real story.

[11] Since then, Greyhound itself was spun off and split into three pieces. The first piece is Greyhound Lines, Inc., the bus company that we all know. In 1996, Greyhound spun off the Consumer Products Division, which included Armour-Dial, and it took on the name by which it is now known, The Dial Corporation. The third piece, which was mostly leasing and financing, was Viad.

[12] Armour-Dial, a subsidiary of Greyhound at the time, was not publicly traded. We would therefore look to Greyhound's PE multiple back then, which was unavailable.

should have been worth 20 percent of Armour-Dial's own sales—a very hefty number. Armour-Dial's sales were close to $1 billion before the acquisition, which means the synergies were $200 million from the acquisition itself.[13] Suppose Purex was worth $120 million as a stand-alone entity, i.e., its Fair Market Value.[14] Then Purex's Investment Value to Armour-Dial specifically would be $120 million plus $200 million = $320 million. The synergies were 167 percent of Purex's stand-alone value! Even if any other bidder might have been interested in Purex at the time—and to my knowledge there were none—you can see why Armour-Dial should have been willing to outbid them all.

At which price should the acquisition have taken place? With these assumptions, all we can say is that FMV is the "floor value," i.e., the minimum value below which the shareholders of Purex should not have sold the company, and $320 million is the "ceiling" value, i.e., the maximum amount that Armour-Dial should consider paying. The actual transaction price would represent the negotiating position and skill of the two parties.[15] They could share the $200 million in any way, including none at all.

Conrad A. Conrad and David Riddiford shared with me The Dial Corporation's subsequent experience with Purex. They said it is Dial's largest business. As of the end of 2002, they experienced two years of record sales growth. They said that Purex is the number two selling laundry detergent (behind Tide) in the United States, with sales of close to $500 million. That represents 6.2 percent compound average growth in sales since 1986. So, Purex is a tremendous success story—one that has created great value for many people.

---

[13] There probably were other sources of synergies in the operating efficiencies of combining the two firms, but rather than speculating, we will leave it at this.

[14] In 1985, Purex's sales were $180 million. Assuming a 5 percent after-tax return would mean net income of $9 million. Since Purex was a smaller business than Armour-Dial, which itself was smaller than Greyhound, it is reasonable to estimate a PE multiple of 12 to 15, which would lead to a valuation of $108 to $135 million. The figure $120 million is a reasonable average.

[15] The actual price was unavailable.

I have a poignant memory juxtaposed to this. When I visited the Purex offices in the Los Angeles area in 1985, the place was a ghost yard, since management of the company was transferring to Armour-Dial in Phoenix, and many positions were eliminated in the acquisition. Only a skeleton accounting crew was left. The atmosphere among the few who remained was gloomy. At one point in making my rounds to speak with various people, I saw a poster on the wall. It was one of Purex's old advertisements, done in a 1950s style, in the days before politically correct gender consciousness. It was a cartoon of a happy-go-lucky salesman carrying a briefcase. The caption read, "Your Purex Salesman—The Man on the Go." Some sardonic in-house political commentator had scribbled next to the caption: "Yeah, all of them."

This story reminds me of the difference between a recession and a depression. A recession is when you are out of work, and a depression is when I am out of work. Obviously, the subsequent success of the Armour-Dial acquisition of Purex was an acquisition that created much value and a lot of good for many people over a very long period of time. The cost of that was the stress of those who lost their jobs at the time—nothing to be minimized. Yet it was and still is a great success.

The Lazy Way vs. the Diligent Way

In my first book I demonstrated that the typical 35 to 50-plus percent "average control premiums" that occur in mergers and acquisitions are really premiums for synergies. Thus, if you want to sell your business for Investment Value the "lazy way," just slap on a 35 to 50 percent premium over FMV for synergies, and there you have it. In fact, the most recent average acquisition premiums are higher yet—in the 50 to 60 percent range, a magnitude we have not seen before. Of course, that requires a lot of cooperation from the buyer. Normally, this can only be accomplished after presenting an initial valuation with the lazy way acquisition premium. If the buyer accepts that, great, you're done. If not, then you may work with the buyer to quantify the synergies, which requires the buyer to reveal its financial information to you.

But the lazy way is less likely to impress a buyer to invest the additional money to buy your company at Investment Value. Like everyone else, it's likely that you'll have to "sing for your supper" and be diligent. That means identifying the individual synergies with your buyer and quantifying them. Of course, that requires a lot of cooperation from the buyer. Normally, this can only be accomplished after presenting an initial valuation with the lazy way acquisition premium. If the buyer accepts that, great, you're done. If not, then you may work with the buyer to quantify the synergies, which requires the buyer to reveal its financial information to you.

CONCLUSION

In this chapter we have covered how to calculate the real selling price of the sale of a business when part of the sale is financed or when there is an earn-out; the strengths and weaknesses of business appraisers, business brokers, and investment bankers; and Investment Value versus Fair Market Value.

This is my last chapter in the book. The rest of the book, as noted earlier, is written by several different contributors. I invited these experts to write about their areas of expertise, which in various ways are related to business valuation. I recommend that you read them wearing your "valuation lenses." For example, in David Boatwright's chapter on taxation, think of how each different tax affects the cash flows and how you would modify a Discounted Cash Flow valuation of your firm as a C corporation, an S corporation, LLC, etc.

Chapter 11

A Business Intermediary's Perspective

By Jim Levy

Retirement, divorce, partnership problems, burnout, illness, relocation, and company growth beyond the owner's capability or financial resources are typical situations motivating owners to sell their businesses. Commonly, businesses are sold to other family members, competitors, suppliers, or customers familiar with the business, as well as proactively marketed to entrepreneurs and corporate acquirers.

If you have received an offer to sell your business, how do you know what the price should be? Are there confidentiality issues that would compromise your business if you disclose proprietary information but do not close on the sale? These are some of the issues that should be considered before deciding how to proceed when presented with an offer.

There is a common misconception among business owners that the possibility of a sale occurs only when a buyer expresses interest in purchasing the business. That buyer is often a competitor, and competitors rarely pay premium prices. The reason that entrepreneur buyers will usually pay more than industry buyers is because of their need for its operating infrastructure, established accounts, ongoing cash flow, etc. On the other hand, competitors already have the infrastructure in place, and many facets of the business are likely to be redundant. They often believe they can recreate your business quite easily. It becomes difficult for them to justify even a reasonable purchase price. That being said, there are instances where competitors pay premium prices for strategic and/or synergistic opportunities. Also, there are certain industries in which industry buyers are almost always the best buyers.

Do not dismiss the option of proactively marketing your business simply out of fear of the unknown. It has been done successfully for decades by large and small businesses, covering virtually every industry. Proactively marketing your business is not only a realistic exit strategy, it is a deliberate process designed to find the best buyer and achieve the best price and terms.

VALUATION

Just as earnings fuel the value of most public companies, earnings usually determine the valuation of small businesses. In concept, most businesses sell in the range of 1.5 to 3.5 times earnings, expressed as “discretionary earnings,” which is defined below. In return for paying that sales price, the buyer receives all of the assets of the business, except for cash and accounts receivable. The seller keeps accounts payable and other liabilities. Inventory is a separate topic that I will discuss later.

While some types of businesses are valued on revenue, revenue-based rules of thumb are not as common as many sellers and their advisers believe. Generally, earnings, or discretionary earnings, is the most reliable method for determining value. It is my personal experience that buyers usually expect around a 30 percent return on their investment after subtracting a fair salary and debt service. However, that won’t apply to smaller businesses in which a reasonable salary represents a big chunk of the earnings. This return compensates one for the risk associated with a small business.

Discretionary Earnings vs. EBITDA

When discussing Fair Market Value, it is important to understand the definition of earnings. For small business sales, discretionary earnings are the relevant measure of earnings. Discretionary earnings are adjusted EBITDA (earnings before interest, taxes, depreciation, and amortization), plus owner's salary and appropriate add-backs. Add-backs are those nonessential expenses in the income statement that are credited toward discretionary earnings. Common add-backs include charitable contributions and personal expenses charged to the business.

Investment bankers, who sell larger firms, also use adjusted EBITDA. However, their adjusted EBITDA is different than the one described above. Theirs would add back only that portion of the owner's salary and related costs that are more than an arm's length salary. Thus, if an arm's length owner's salary is $100,000 and the owner actually took $300,000 salary, the add-back to discretionary earnings would be all $300,000, while the investment banker would add back only $200,000 to calculate his or her version of adjusted EBITDA. The difference between the two is the owner's arm's length compensation, which can make a significant difference between the two measures. In any case, the two terms are not interchangeable for valuation purposes.

EBITDA is *not* an acceptable basis for determining value of a small business. Methodologies for determining value are discussed at length in other chapters. The value basis represents the foundation of the sale, and an experienced Business Intermediary will have a solid understanding of business valuation to effectively communicate with sellers and negotiate with buyers. In general, the better the sales, earnings, profit margins, and trend, the higher the valuation multiple tends to be.

Understanding Value-Generating Characteristics

Understanding the factors that impact the valuation of your business can and should influence your business model and plan. Businesses that attract the most interest and highest valuations tend to have high customer retention and predictable cash flow.

For example, a contractor whose revenues are primarily generated by winning bids on public works projects has neither long-term customers nor a customer base to transfer to a buyer. The multiple for a business like this may be so low that its liquidation value may be its best value. (I gave this example to illustrate that how a company derives its earnings is important. It is possible that the company in this illustration can still have value drivers, such as consistent profitability, that support a high valuation.) On the other hand, a commercial insurance brokerage firm might have an exceedingly attractive valuation because of its high customer retention rate and annual premiums.

Similarly, an owner who dominates sales and management adversely affects the integrity of a business transfer, and in extreme cases the firm may not be salable at any price. In contrast, a business with management and sales responsibilities spread evenly among its employees is likely to achieve a better valuation. Precisely, the perceived stability of customers, employees, and vendors following the acquisition directly impacts the integrity of a business transfer. This is reflected in its transaction structure and ultimate valuation.

Capital Investments Prior to a Sale

Investing in new equipment or moving to another location one or two years prior to selling your company may not contribute to the value of your firm. The costs of these investments probably won't increase your valuation unless they've generated a corresponding increase in earnings on your year-end income statement(s). It is best to avoid making these sorts of unintentional charitable contributions.

The Mystery of Potential

I find it interesting that the more "profit challenged" a business is, the more the owner tends to tout its spectacular growth potential. In any event, one of the most common areas of misunderstanding is overestimating the value of growth potential. This is a complex subject that can be summed up as follows: If your historical sales and earnings have been rising and the trend is continuing, then your firm has proven growth potential, and it will probably command a premium valuation multiple. If not, buyers consider future growth a result of their own efforts and generally do not think it is fair to reward sellers for the buyer's work. If a seller insists that growth will be greater in the future than in the past, a buyer may be equally optimistic, but the valuation multiple will likely reflect the aggressive forecast. Pricing in unrealized potential by planning future expense saving and/or company building moves should lead a buyer to discount the valuation multiple to account for a risky growth forecast.

Using Equation 6.4, $FMV = 1.1 \times (1/r - g)$, the shortcut valuation from Chapter 6, if the seller insists on raising g by 3 percent above historical growth, the buyer may reasonably insist on raising r by 2 or 3 percent to compensate for the optimistic forecast of unproven growth. If we increase g and r both by 3 percent, there is no change in the valuation.

Mistaken Value Assumptions

There are objective and subjective methods of determining value, some of which were discussed above. However, Business Intermediaries and valuation experts consistently agree on a reasonable range of value. On the other hand, sellers and their advisers who do not have firsthand transaction or valuation experience often come up with values that are off the charts. This is unfortunate in that it can significantly skew the seller's retirement plans, estate planning, etc., as well as preclude the seller from selling when he or she should sell.

While small business owners often have demonstrated remarkable wisdom by guiding their firms through decades of challenging industry and economic cycles, they usually do not begin learning about the true value of their business or its value-generating characteristics until they decide to sell it. I am constantly amazed by the level of misunderstanding that business owners have in this regard.

Typical Transaction Structures

Most small business sales involve the sale of assets, not stock. Stock sales are the least preferred by buyers and are only done when necessary to minimize tax consequences for sellers. This is typically an issue when the company is a C corporation, which can lead to a seller being double-taxed on the gain. A primary reason stock sales are not popular among buyers is because of the transfer of potential liabilities after the sale. There are ways to mitigate the risk for buyers through the use of insurance for product and employee liabilities, but the sale of stock is usually done only as a last resort.

In an asset sale, the seller typically keeps the balance sheet items such as accounts receivables, accounts payables, notes, etc. Inventory can be included in or added to the selling price, depending on the type of business and value of inventory. As discussed below in "Preparing for the Sale," if the value of inventory is so high that it represents a significant portion of the price, it will likely be heavily discounted. It is best to sell obsolete inventory by any means available prior to marketing the business, because buyers are unlikely to pay you for it.

The most common transaction structures include a down payment of 40 to 60 percent, with seller financing secured by the business, and may or may not include the buyer's collateral for some or all of the note. This structure seems to provide the best balance in meeting the concerns of sellers and buyers. Sellers want a secure exit, and buyers want some security in the event of unforeseen problems following the acquisition. Buyers frequently prefer that sellers maintain a vested interest in the business to ensure its integrity and that the sellers are accessible for ongoing assistance as needed. Earn-outs involving a fixed percentage of revenues for a certain period of time are occasionally used in lieu of or in addition to seller notes. All-cash purchases may be discounted 20 to 30 percent or more, depending on the nature of the business. With all-cash purchases, both the time value of money and the added risk for the buyer exert downward pressure on the price. The Small Business Adminstration's (SBA) loan guarantee program provides an excellent avenue for sellers to cash out.

INTEGRITY OF FINANCIAL STATEMENTS

In any event, it is important to create a structure that will make it to the finish line. Transactions that fall apart before closing are frequently the result of unrealistic price and/or financing expectations and, generally, poorly planned transaction structures. Furthermore, I believe many of the horror stories of business sales gone bad resulted from inadequate down payments and excessive financing, with the buyers having very little invested in the businesses. That being said, for some types of businesses a low down payment may be necessary to accommodate certain risky business transfer issues. This would include, for instance, companies with a high risk of client or staff defections after a change in ownership. In this case, it should be a strong buyer with industry expertise and substantial resources.

A key facet in most business transfers is the quality of the Profit & Loss statement. From the buyer's perspective, accurate and consistent financial statements reduce an element of uncertainty in the process of ascertaining the continuity of profits. While the value of most businesses is fueled by historical earnings, financial statements of privately held companies usually reflect the lowest possible net profit, in order to minimize taxes. However, there is often an inverse relationship between tax savings and achieving the highest value when selling a business. The degree of impact depends on how tax aggressive you are. Let's use the following two tables to explain the potential impact.

Table 11.1 computes a valuation of discretionary income for a relatively conservative tax strategy. In the Tax Aggressive Scenario of Table 11.2 , the seller has been charging personal expenses to the business to reduce taxes and now wants to add these back to discretionary earnings to increase the valuation. The first four add-backs are normal add-backs and are the same ones from Table 11.1 that total $145,000. The next four add-backs total $83,000 (amount not shown) and are very aggressive. These expenses include $40,000 for public relations for the owner's son, who is in college, along with other miscellaneous personal expenses. The "add-backs" create a potential problem of credibility. The crafty seller wants to eat his cake and have it too (the original form of the old saying). While technically there is nothing wrong with this, it will make some or many buyers nervous and possibly drive up their discount rate. The amount of the extra $83,000 in add-backs that is credited toward the purchase in Table 11.2 will ultimately depend on the decision of the buyer and his or her advisers after reviewing related documentation. Referring to Table 11.2, if this company is selling for a multiple of 2.5 times discretionary earnings, this seller stands to lose up to $207,500, or 25 percent of the purchase price as a result of questionable add-backs.

TABLE 11.1

Wonderful Company

	Year End
Sales	$3,000,000
Cost of Sales	1,980,000
Gross Profit	1,020,000
Expenses	870,000
Net Profit	**$150,000**
Add-Backs	
Depreciation	15,000
Interest	19,000
Officer Salaries	100,000
Officer Payroll Tax	11,000
Total Add-Backs	145,000
Discretionary Earnings	**$295,000**

TABLE 11.2

Wonderful Company: Tax-Aggressive Scenario

	Year End
Sales	$3,000,000
Cost of Sales	1,980,000
Gross Profit	1,020,000
Expenses	913,000
Net Profit	**$107,000**
Add-Backs	
Depreciation	15,000
Interest	19,000
Officer Salaries	100,000
Officer Payroll Tax	11,000
Public Relations	40,000
Insurance	17,000
Auto	12,000
Entertainment	8,000
Phone	6,000
Total Add-Backs	228,000
Discretionary Earnings	**$335,000**

Also, the SBA does not allow add-backs for most personal expenses, which we'll get to below. Recognize the accuracy of your P&L is an important decision that can potentially impact the value of your assets. Understanding the potential consequences will allow you to make an informed decision that is best for your particular circumstances.

While we're on the subject of taxes, let's touch upon unreported income. For some types of businesses, particularly those involving cash transactions, it is not a matter of whether or not it exists, but how much. There are buyers willing to recognize unreported income in their valuations, but most buyers won't. Since the practice of underreporting income is illegal, it puts the seller at risk of being reported to the IRS by a disgruntled buyer during negotiations, or even after completing a transaction. It is best to avoid unreported income to achieve an optimum valuation and sleep soundly at night.

And Be Aware of . . .

Personal Expenses and Add-Backs

The Small Business Administration provides a source of liquidity for business owners. Its guaranteed cash flow–based loan programs through banks and financial institutions allow buyers to purchase businesses with as little as a 10 percent down payment. The lender's analysis for debt service capacity is usually based on the tax returns of the business over the past two to three years. Standard add-backs, such as interest, depreciation, and owner's salary are allowed, *but most personal expense add-backs are not.* The buyer's credit, collateral, living expenses, and business background are also factors impacting SBA lending parameters.

Funny Business

If you have employees who are overpaid, it's not easy to undo your act of generosity. It is unlikely that the new buyer would succeed at reducing their salaries. If you view your business from the standpoint of a prospective buyer, you may gain insight into matters that should be addressed early enough to prepare for a successful sale.

Excessive Inventory

Another important area impacting value is the inventory amount. If the inventory level is too high in proportion to the expected selling price, the excess amount may not be captured. Thus, mismanagement of inventory can have disastrous consequences on the sale proceeds. Since it can take months, if not years, to optimize inventory, it is an area that needs attention long before the sale of your business.

The Tax Consequences of a Sale

This can be a deal breaker and is an area that should be thoroughly assessed with your accountant as long as 10 years before a sale. (David Boatwright discusses this at length in Chapter 14.)

THE PROACTIVE SALE PROCESS

Sellers occasionally engage Business Intermediaries to initiate negotiations with one or more buyers designated by a seller. However, Business Intermediaries are usually brought in to proactively market businesses and find buyers, with the mandate of achieving the best possible price and terms.

It is almost always a seller's market, with good quality firms in short supply. Client companies usually have a clear history of sales and profitability. Most people view starting a business as an impossible and high-risk task. Thus, the prospect of acquiring a proven business model with cash flow from day one is very enticing. When you add the availability of cash flow–based financing for ongoing businesses, there are compelling reasons to purchase rather than start a business.

The First Steps

The Business Intermediary strives to identify the best buyers for your business. The process typically starts with a valuation followed by a discussion and agreement on a price range. Then the intermediary prepares an offering memorandum to profile the business and its industry.

The memo is a tangible tool used to document intangible assets and create a professional presentation that can inspire confidence, enhance the image of your firm, and entice buyers to act within a short period of time. In preparing the offering memorandum, it should effectively communicate the firm's profit-generating characteristics and highlight the value-generating characteristics that position the company for an optimum valuation. It should emphasize future profit-generating characteristics and the impact of industry and economic trends. The offering memorandum can range from one page to a comprehensive report, depending on the type and size of company and the quality of Business Intermediary services.

Locating Prospective Buyers

The next step involves advertising the business for sale without identifying it. Classified ads in local newspapers and on Web sites of businesses for sale are the most common forms of advertising. Some Business Intermediaries use mailings and networking for added exposure. The screening of prospective buyers varies dramatically. The Business Intermediary may screen prospective buyers verbally and require a financial statement and/or résumé.

Your business will be identified to selected candidates after they sign a Confidentiality Agreement. The first question prospective buyers usually ask me is why is he or she selling. Seemingly, the answer reveals the likelihood of hidden problems. Typically, at this stage buyers who continue to be interested will meet with the owner at the business after business hours. An experienced intermediary will have an intensive screening process to avoid parading numerous buyers in front of the seller. During this process, it is paramount for sellers to remain focused on running their business and continuing the best possible growth trend.

More on Confidentiality

Unlike the sale of real estate, the sale of a business is done confidentially. Most business owners are acutely aware of the importance of confidentiality, and it is probably the biggest reason that many owners do not consider proactively marketing their businesses. However, businesses can be sold discreetly and confidentially. The risks of dealing with prospective buyers are managed by carefully selecting and screening prospects. The business does not need to be widely "shopped." It can be shown only to carefully selected prospects.

There may be a decision not to include certain prospects, though they appear promising, due to the risks associated with providing those companies with confidential information. The identity of your business should only be disclosed to selected candidates after obtaining a signed Confidentiality Agreement. While you can expect to provide financial statements for recent years, along with other detailed information, proprietary information such as customer lists, vendor names, manufacturing processes, and so on, can be provided as one of the last steps before closing.

Some Business Intermediaries arrange buyer and seller meetings only after obtaining an acceptable offer indication. This offer is nonbinding, but it demonstrates more commitment on the part of the buyer and helps to identify unacceptable offers before additional information is divulged in a meeting with the seller. Maintaining confidentiality also requires controlling internal leaks. If you have partners, make sure you're all in agreement on who may be informed about the sale. During negotiations with a corporate buyer, be sure they have internal controls in place as well.

From Offer to Conclusion

If there is an offer presented, there will probably be a round of negotiations until both sides accept it. A deposit may or may not be required, depending on the size of the transaction and the sophistication of the buyer. Then the buyer, with the assistance of his or her advisers, starts due diligence to verify the accuracy of the books and records. The due diligence process can take two to four weeks or longer, depending on the business and the buyer. An on-site visit may be scheduled after business hours toward the end of due diligence. Depending on the nature of the business, the buyer may require interviews with key employees, sales reps, customers, etc. These interviews should be the last remaining contingency.

When the buyer completes due diligence, escrow is opened to manage the bulk sale requirements and other settlement items in the event of an asset sale. A bulk sale is the purchase and sale of a business or a major portion of the assets of a business. A bulk sale escrow provides a seller and buyer with an efficient process to ensure clean title transfer of the business ownership.

Escrow is primarily designed to protect the buyer from unknown liabilities, and it usually takes about 30 days. While escrow is common, it is not always used in every state or every situation. Some buyers are not concerned about unknown liabilities, and to save time and money, choose not to go through the escrow process. However, if real estate is involved and your state uses escrows, escrow should be used.

After the closing, the seller should expect to train the buyer for two to four weeks, depending on the nature of the business and agreement with the buyer. Free training is common for the first month or so,[1] and consulting fees are typically paid for longer periods of time.

WHY EMPLOY AN INTERMEDIARY?

Understandably, there can be a lot of trepidation on the part of the seller anticipating the sale of his or her firm. In a seller's mind, an offer from a familiar buyer beats the uncertainty of putting the firm on the block and paying the corresponding fees. But this convenient, reactive approach can result in leaving money on the table. Be sure to carefully evaluate your options.

The Business of Business Intermediaries

Let's begin with a brief explanation of titles employed by Business Intermediaries. Those selling main-street type businesses such as laundromats, dry cleaners, gas stations, liquor stores, small retail stores, etc., are almost universally known as Business Brokers. Many in the industry serving larger and more sophisticated companies and offering a higher level of services prefer to be known as Business Intermediaries or mergers and acquisitions (M&A) professionals. A skilled and conscientious

Business Intermediary will launch a selling process designed to achieve the best possible price and terms, and maintain confidentiality. (But, of course, the quality of service and the degree of confidentiality provided by Business Brokers and Business Intermediaries varies, as in any profession.)

Business Intermediaries are set up to optimally service the small business client. While some intermediaries handle transactions of $10 to $20 million in value, the majority of transactions are under $1 million. Transactions valued at $10 million and higher are generally handled by investment banking firms (see Chapter 12 for an in-depth discussion of investment bankers).

Intermediaries are usually paid by sellers, and, in turn, represent the sellers' best interests. The intermediary should give full disclosure to prospective buyers of any misrepresentations about the business and advise them to retain an accountant and attorney.

Fees

A success fee of 10 percent is common for transactions up to $1 million or so. There is a growing trend toward initial fees ranging from $500 to $10,000, depending on the size and complexity of the business. These fees may or may not be credited toward the commission. The commission and fee structure is usually such that the seller's and the Business Intermediary's interests are aligned in achieving a successful sale.

Be aware that there are firms, even major ones, that lure unsophisticated small business owners into paying obscenely high initial fees by selling them on the prospects of achieving sky-high valuations. Business Intermediaries can enhance the value of your business, but they cannot do magic. If you have toiled for decades building your business, you might have an understandable, deep emotional attachment to your "baby," which means your perception of value could be unrealistic. Like any other investment decision, if it sounds too good to be true, it probably is too good to be true. Check with trusted advisers first.

Experienced Business Intermediaries understand small company valuations and are accustomed to dealing with imperfect financials. They must also qualify buyers based on their financial ability to perform, and they must assess a buyer's motivation and fortitude to close. There is a long road ahead of every first-time buyer who may be putting his or her life savings at risk. Initial enthusiasm can often turn into fear of impending failure as the finish line gets closer.

Selecting a Business Intermediary

The Business Intermediary can influence the ultimate results of a sale, so your selection is an important decision. Begin by assessing the intermediary's professional qualifications, including experience and technical knowledge. Many states require Business Intermediaries to have real estate licenses. While the overall reputation of the firm is certainly important, the firm experience is relatively irrelevant. There is a high turnover in the business, so look for someone with at least two years of experience, and make sure you know who will be handling the sale of your business. Understand how confidentiality will be incorporated into the sale process, and contact references. This tends to be a local business. Unless there is an industry expertise that the intermediary brings to the process, it's usually best to work with a local firm.

A directory of Certified Business Intermediaries, a designation developed by the International Business Brokers Association, can be found at www.ibba.org. The *CBI* or *Certified Business Intermediary* designation is a convenient starting point for finding quality Business Brokers and Business Intermediaries. Alternatively, your accountant or attorney may be able to provide references.

CONCLUSION

The goal of selling a business for optimum value and terms is best realized when planned well in advance. Planning your exit strategy five years out will affect many of your strategic decisions today. Here are some questions to consider:

1. Can your business model be slightly changed to achieve a higher multiple?
2. Can you convert purchase orders into long-term contracts?
3. Is there an attractive acquisition opportunity that will increase your earnings?
4. Are you considering exit strategies in addition to tax strategies when preparing your tax returns?
5. Is your inventory at its optimal level?
6. Are you delegating management responsibilities?
7. Is your entity tax structure a potential impediment to realizing maximum proceeds from a sale?

Thoughtfully addressing these and other issues will help you achieve the best possible value for your business. Knowing the true value of your business will help you make informed decisions on matters ranging from determining the merit of capital investments to planning your retirement. Planning for a successful exit strategy can lead to improving the performance of your business and securing and building the value of your assets. Properly planning the sale of your business to attain the best valuation is one of the most important management decisions you will make.[1]

[1] I thank Jack Sanders, Spectrum Corporate Group, for editing my chapter. Jack is a highly respected colleague and business intermediary.

Chapter 12

An Investment Banker's Perspective

By Michael Keane

The term "investment bank" encompasses a broad range of international, regional, and boutique financial services firms. An international investment bank has offices around the globe and provides services that include sales and trading of international securities, research on publicly traded debt and equity, advising municipalities and underwriting municipal bonds, raising capital for corporations, and advising on mergers and acquisitions. Many large investment banks also house private equity operations, carry on arbitrage activities, and make loans. A small boutique firm, on the other hand, may have only a handful of employees focused on providing one particular service. A number of commercial banks have recently acquired investment banking firms in an attempt to cross-market products and services to the same client base. In addition, several large accounting firms currently provide some investment banking service, and others have announced plans to do so in the future.

DOING BUSINESS WITH INVESTMENT BANKERS

There are several aspects of doing business with an investment banker that we'll discuss:

- Identifying the primary investment banking services you require.
- Deciding between hiring an investment banker or a business broker.
- Who should sell your business?
- How to find the right financial adviser.
- The process and time involved to complete a transaction.
- The cost of investment banking services.

Primary Investment Banking Services

Essentially, investment banks provide two primary services: raising capital and/or advising on corporate finance transactions. Specifically, these transactions include private placements of debt and equity, public offerings of debt and equity, mergers and acquisitions, leveraged buyouts, fairness opinions, and providing valuations of businesses and securities.

While valuations can be a separate and distinct assignment, there is probably no investment banking service that does not require an implicit or explicit valuation to be performed. For example, an Initial Public Offering requires a valuation of the company before its shares can be sold to the public; a corporation buying a competitor will make some determination of its value before negotiating a purchase price; a private placement of stock requires a calculation of the current value and estimated future value of the investment, and a fairness opinion requires an estimation of value or value range. Valuation analytics, therefore, permeate almost every conceivable investment banking assignment.

Investment Banks vs. Business Brokers

Investment banks typically differ from business brokers in several significant respects. First, they usually provide a broader range of services, including raising capital. Secondly, investment banks are usually larger and may have more firm-wide resources to devote to a transaction. Finally, investment banks tend to have personnel with specialized knowledge in various areas, such as industry and transactional expertise. As a result, investment banks tend to handle larger transactions that may require a higher degree of sophistication.

Who Should Sell Your Business?

How should you decide whether to hire an investment banker, a business broker, or to sell your business yourself?

First, the size of a transaction will largely dictate which advisers will be interested in handling a transaction. Most investment banks will be reluctant to handle an assignment for a company where the enterprise value is less than $20 million. (Enterprise value is defined as the value of a company's interest-bearing debt plus the value of its equity less the amount of cash it has.) You may also want a knowledgeable adviser who is familiar with the particulars of your industry, to appropriately value the company. Also, you should realize that financial advisory services are highly personal, and that ultimately you are usually paying for the advice and attention of a single individual. You should make sure that you are comfortable with that individual's experience and knowledge.

Some larger investment banking firms are accused of pulling a "bait-and-switch" regarding advisers, particularly with their smaller clients. For example, a more senior adviser might be presented to the prospective client before they sign up, but once the firm is engaged, it's assigned a more junior, less experienced associate to work on the deal. You should make sure that the firm is willing to commit the right individual and appropriate resources to your company. Remember, your company might well be the most important thing in the world to you, but your adviser may have many other pending assignments, and the larger deal (with the larger fee!) will usually get their attention.

Often, company owners or managers are tempted not to hire an adviser, and instead will try to execute the prospective transaction themselves. Sometimes this approach is employed to preserve confidentiality by limiting the number of parties that know about a transaction, but usually it's a misguided attempt to save fees. And just as often, this is a "penny wise, pound foolish" approach.

The best reason to hire an adviser is that time required by the transaction will be a large drain on management's time. It is difficult to overestimate the time and resources necessary to properly execute corporate finance transactions. It is more than a full-time job, and management already has a full-time job—running the company! In fact, by distracting your attention away from the day-to-day operations of the business, you run the risk of impairing the valuation of the company.

A second compelling reason for not undertaking the assignment yourself is because these transactions are highly specialized and require a level of knowledge and experience that even the most seasoned manager may not have.

And finally, managers and business owners may be too emotionally attached to their businesses to appropriately negotiate a transaction. This is also why lawyers are advised not to handle their own cases and doctors may not treat family members. The advice of a dispassionate adviser can be critically valuable to maintaining the proper perspective on a transaction. As a result, a competent investment banker should more than compensate for his or her fee—not only with the savings in your time, but also in the increased valuation negotiated for your company.

How to Find an Investment Banker

As with most professionals, the best source can be referrals from professional advisers whom you already know and trust, such as your lawyer and accountant. Another source can be referrals from other company managers, even "friendly" competitors. If you're planning to sell your business, call on colleagues and business contacts who have gone through the same process. Ask them to share their experiences, what they would do differently, and to suggest an adviser.

You should interview several investment bankers or financial advisers and select one based on the following factors:

- If industry expertise is particularly important, determine how knowledgeable the adviser is with your business and your company's competition. Industry knowledge is typically critical when the industry is highly regulated (e.g., utilities) or has unique accounting methods (e.g., oil and gas) or has highly specific valuation metrics (e.g., cable television).[1]

- Often, knowledge of the industry is not nearly as important as a sophisticated understanding of the intricacies of the transaction you are trying to execute and/or a knowledge of the capital sources you want to access. Request a list of relevant prior transactions the investment bank has completed, and feel free to ask for references from the firm you consider hiring—and validate those references.
- Perhaps most important, you should know how your deal will be staffed and by whom, and request appropriate biographical information concerning those personnel.

I also recommend that you feel some personal chemistry with the person most responsible for working on your transaction. You're likely to spend a significant amount of time with them, much of which may be stressful and difficult, so it's important that you share a mutual respect and good communication.

The Process and the Time Involved

The time needed to complete a typical corporate finance transaction is usually a minimum of three months, with many sale or merger transactions taking six months or more. A rough timeline would include one month for your advisory firm to complete its due diligence and prepare an informational memorandum to be distributed to prospective investors or buyers, an additional month to contact prospective investors or buyers, another month for the selected party to complete its due diligence, and a final month for both parties' lawyers to document the transaction.

---

[1] Author's note: This is not generally true in the valuation, where industry expertise usually is not important. JBA.

The process can be delayed for a number of reasons, such as regulatory approvals, protracted negotiations, and complications discovered in due diligence and changes in market conditions. It is the investment banker's job to coordinate the process by acting as the "deal quarterback," keeping all parties focused on completing the deal on a timely basis. The investment banker should be responsible for shepherding all advisers, including lawyers and accountants, as well as the principal parties to the transaction, such as the buyer and seller.

The Cost of Investment Banking Services

Investment banking fees are fairly standardized, although they may be subject to some negotiation and adjustment depending on the particular circumstances of the assignment and the size of the transaction. Fees for raising capital are typically set as a percentage of the amount of funds raised and vary with the type of security being placed. Here are some examples:

- The senior secured debt placement fee is usually 1.0 to 1.5 percent; the subordinated debt fee is typically 4 percent; and the placement fee for equity ranges from 5 to 7 percent. Investment bankers also typically require warrants as compensation for placing subordinated debt and equity.
- Merger advisory fees typically are calculated as a percentage of the size of the company being sold. Larger deals are usually charged at 1.0 to 1.5 percent. Smaller deals require a larger percentage, typically from 3 to 5 percent.
- Fairness opinions provided to stockholders in public companies usually cost a minimum of $150,000.
- The price for stand-alone valuations can range from $25,000 to $100,000 or more, depending on the complexity of the assignment.

VALUATION

In this section we will discuss several aspects of valuation as it relates to an investment banking assignment.

Fundamentals

The primary determinants of corporate value were probably best identified by Harvard professor Michael Porter in his book *Competitive Strategy*. Porter's "Five Forces" that drive value are (1) rivalry among competitor firms, (2) availability of substitute products, (3) barriers to entry preventing new competitors from entering the market, (4) bargaining power of suppliers, and (5) the bargaining power of buyers. These are the primary determinants of a company's ability to maximize profitability, cash flow, and equity value. A well-prepared information memorandum should highlight a company's comparative advantages in each of these areas.

Gathering Data to Determine Value

Valuation is not determined in a vacuum. A proper valuation requires that an adviser review a significant amount of data regarding a company. This data can be drawn from numerous sources.

Documents

Information, data, and documents that are usually reviewed and analyzed by an investment banker in making a determination of value include:

- Legal documents describing the proposed terms of the transaction, such as a term sheet or letter of intent
- Financial and operating information with respect to the business, operations, and prospects of the relevant company
- Information concerning the future financial performance of the relevant company
- If the company is public, the trading history of the company's common stock and a comparison of that trading history with those of other companies that are deemed relevant
- Comparison of the historical financial results and present financial condition of the company with those of other relevant companies

- Comparison of the financial terms of the transaction with the financial terms of other relevant transactions

Management Information

The investment banker will interview the management of your company to discuss its business, operations, assets, financial condition, and prospects.

Concerning Accuracy

In arriving at a valuation, the investment banker typically relies upon the accuracy and completeness of the data reviewed, including historical and projected financial information. He or she also relies upon the assurances of the company's management that they are not aware of any facts or circumstances that would make the information relied upon by the investment bank inaccurate or misleading.

But it should be noted that the investment banker does not seek independent verification beyond the information he or she has gathered. Similarly, the investment banker typically does not make an independent appraisal of the specific properties or assets of the company.

Valuation Estimates

Depending upon the specifics of the assignment, the valuation determination may be a range of values or may be a specific point estimate. In either case, the client should be made aware that the valuation of a company or of its securities, although rigorous and complicated, can probably more accurately be described as an art rather than as a science, and that it is accordingly unrealistic to expect absolute precision from any such exercise.[2]

---

[2] Author's note: In my opinion, valuation is an art that sits on top of a science. JBA.

Other Factors

In arriving at a valuation, it is critical that an investment banker understand the perspective of the party for whom the valuation is being prepared. The value of a security or company can vary dramatically for different parties due to differing tax positions or because one party may be able to realize cost savings that another party may not.

Values will also differ depending on the liquidity of a stock, whether it is publicly traded or privately held, the size of the stock position, the size of the company, and whether there are any restrictions on the transferability of the stock.

Valuation Methodologies

The preparation of a valuation analysis involves a determination of the most appropriate and relevant methods of financial and comparative analysis, and the application of those methods to the particular facts and circumstances of the subject company or security. The most common and widely accepted methods include the comparable company, comparable transaction, Discounted Cash Flow, leveraged buyout, and market trading analyses described below. An investment banker typically draws no specific conclusions from any of these individual analyses, but he or she subjectively factors observations from each of these analyses into the qualitative assessments of the relevant facts and circumstances.

The following summarizes the most commonly employed methods used by investment bankers in performing valuations:

Comparable Company Analysis

Using publicly available information, an investment banker will compare select financial data of companies engaged in businesses considered comparable to your company. The investment banker will determine the current market value of each company in terms of its enterprise value (defined as equity market value plus interest-bearing debt less cash), and then calculate its enterprise value as a multiple of trailing 12 months' sales

TABLE 12.1

Sample Comparable Company Analysis

Company	Enterprise Value*	*Enterprise Value Multiples* LTM Sales	LTM EBITDA	LTM EBIT
Indigo N.V.	$395,990	2.2x	8.9x	7.2x
Imation Corporation	$344,055	0.3x	4.6x	3.8x
Schawh, Inc.	$283,869	1.4x	12.7x	12.5x
Xeikon N.V.	$85,421	2.0x	11.2x	9.5x
Baldwin Technology	$24,656	0.1x	3.7x	13.3x
High		**2.2x**	**12.7x**	**13.3x**
Median		**1.4x**	**8.9x**	**9.5x**
Mean		**1.2x**	**8.2x**	**9.3x**
Low		**0.1x**	**3.7x**	**3.8x**

*Dollars in thousands

(LTM Sales); trailing 12 months' earnings before interest, taxes, depreciation, and amortization (LTM EBITDA); and of trailing 12 months' earnings before interest and taxes (LTM EBIT). These values are then compared to any value proposed in a transaction, such as a proposed purchase price. In Table 12.1, five comparable companies are evaluated relative to these multiples.

Comparable Transaction Analysis

The investment banker will also analyze publicly available information on comparable deals and review the multiples paid in these transactions. These values are then compared to the multiples proposed by the transaction under consideration. The most popular multiples focus on the LTM Sales, EBITDA, and EBIT multiples. The range of high and low values is analyzed as well as the mean and median values. Table 12.2 is an example.

Discounted Cash Flow Analysis

The investment banker may also perform a Discounted Cash Flow analysis, which requires financial projections. These are

TABLE 12.2

Sample Comparable M&A Transactions

Date	Target	Acquirer	Enterprise Value*	Enterprise Value Multiples LTM Sales	LTM EBITDA	LTM EBIT
7/31/01	Fargo Elect.	Zebra Tech.	$86.0	1.4x	9.3x	11.2x
10/1/99	Multigraphics	Paragon Group	$11.8	0.1x	3.3x	7.7x
2/18/99	PTI Inc.	MacDermind	$449.3	2.0x	8.2x	10.6x
1/7/99	Trident Int'l	Illinois Tool	$102.9	3.1x	8.5x	9.4x
6/16/95	Imtran Ind.	Foilmark Inc.	$4.9	1.2x	5.9x	6.3x
		High		**3.1x**	**9.3x**	**11.2x**
		Median		**1.4x**	**8.2x**	**9.4x**
		Mean		**1.6x**	**7.0x**	**9.0x**
		Low		**0.1x**	**3.3x**	**6.3x**

*Dollars in millions

prepared by management or others, such as equity research analysts. The projections of EBITDA or free cash flow are then discounted to their present value. Most commonly, five-year projections are used, but they may be longer or shorter. Terminal values are then calculated by applying multiples of EBITDA in the final projected year. Ranges of 4.0 to 8.0 times are common. The cash flow streams and terminal values are then discounted to present values using ranges of appropriate discount rates, usually 10 to 20 percent.

For example, Table 12.3 presents a terminal value's net present value where the EBITDA cash flow stream is projected to be $1 million in five years. The EBITDA is multiplied here by a number ranging from 6.0 to 10.0 to determine the terminal value. The terminal value is then discounted back to the present at discount rates ranging from 15 to 20 percent. The resulting number is the net present value of the terminal value.

Premium Analysis

For mergers and acquisitions, one should analyze the takeover premium paid (in percentage terms) relative to the price the ac-

TABLE 12.3

Sample Present Value of Terminal Value

Discount Rate	Year Five EBITDA Multiples 6.0x	7.0x	8.0x	9.0x	10.0x
15.0%	$2,983,060	$3,480,237	$3,977,414	$4,474,591	$4,971,767
16.0%	$2,856,678	$3,332,791	$3,808,904	$4,285,017	$4,761,130
17.0%	$2,736,667	$3,192,778	$3,648,889	$4,105,000	$4,561,112
18.0%	$2,622,655	$3,059,765	$3,496,874	$3,933,983	$4,371,092
19.0%	$2,514,296	$2,933,346	$3,352,395	$3,771,444	$4,190,494
20.0%	$2,411,265	$2,813,143	$3,215,021	$3,616,898	$4,018,776

quired company's stock was trading at prior to the announcement of the deal. Attention must be paid to what is a comparable transaction and what time period may be relevant. Comparable transactions may be constrained by industry, size, or the form of consideration paid. Relevant time periods may range from the most recent six months to the past five years or longer. Premiums paid relative to the stock price one week, four weeks, three months, and six months prior to the announcement are typically analyzed. Table 12.4 is an example of a sample market premium analysis.

TABLE 12.4

Sample Market Premium Analysis

				Premium Paid		
Date	Target	Acquirer	Transaction Value*	One Day Prior	One Week Prior	Four Weeks Prior
8/22/01	Homeservice	MidAmerican	$32.9	38.8%	40.5%	56.5%
8/14/01	Medialink	United Bus.	$29.2	49.3%	39.3%	44.9%
7/19/01	Data Critical	GE Medical	$46.7	70.5%	89.4%	77.7%
7/16/01	Innes St. Fin.	Gaston Fed.	$37.9	63.7%	61.2%	65.6%
6/25/01	Datron	Titan Corp.	$46.6	14.3%	10.3%	30.6%

*Dollars in millions

Market Trading Analysis

If publicly traded, the historical market prices of the company's common stock based on an analysis of closing prices and trading volume for some relevant time period are analyzed. The lowest traded price and the average trading price over the period are reviewed relative to a proposed or estimated valuation.

Leveraged Buyout Analysis

Another relevant estimate of value is a determination of what value could be paid for a company if the company were acquired in a leveraged buyout, i.e., a transaction in which a company is purchased primarily by means of borrowed funds. This method requires a sufficient familiarity with the mechanics of leveraged buyouts and the appropriate capital structure. It also necessitates an awareness of the current market conditions, which dictate the ability to borrow funds, the cost of the borrowing, the amortization of the debt, and the rate of return requirements of private equity investors.

Valuation Weighting

Investment bankers typically do not attribute a precise weight to any method, analysis, or particular factor; instead, they tend to make qualitative judgments about the significance and relevance of each one. As a result, any determination of value must be considered as a whole.

Valuations also typically involve numerous assumptions with respect to the relevant company, including its industry performance; general business, economic, market, and financial conditions; and other matters. Actual future results or values will obviously deviate from these predictions. In addition, analyses relating to the value of businesses or securities are not intended to be property appraisals, which, in contrast, are designed to reflect the prices at which a particular asset or piece of equipment may actually be sold.

CONCLUSION

Valuation analysis is perhaps the most critical element in almost every investment banking assignment. Executives and business owners are well advised to seek the services of a qualified investment banker. The right adviser can be selected after reviewing transactional expertise, industry experience (where appropriate), references, and also after considering the personal chemistry between the individuals involved. A good investment banker should prove to be cost effective after considering the savings in management time and the ability to negotiate improved terms.

Proper valuation analysis requires the consideration of a number of factors and calculations. Some of the most prominent factors are taxes, liquidity, cost savings, macroeconomic conditions, and microeconomic factors. The most commonly accepted calculations include Discounted Cash Flows, multiples of comparable companies, and multiples of comparable transactions. No weighting is assigned to any particular method or analysis, but a proper valuation considers all of them together.

Chapter 13
Venture Capital 101

Bruce Taragin

In this chapter I will attempt to effectively distill and convey some of the lessons I have learned as an entrepreneur and venture capitalist. I will address alternative sources of financing, an overview of the venture capital (VC) market, targeting VCs, and how to effectively penetrate this insular group of private equity money managers. It is important to know what you will need to best manage the fund-raising experience, what you should expect from a VC during this courtship, and ultimately what to expect if you decide to choose this path of funding.

To convey the VC process in a few pages is a formidable task. There are many vehicles (VC being one of them) for an entrepreneur to start and grow her or his business. It's crucial to consider one's overall objectives at the outset before embarking on the journey of starting your own company and raising VC funding. Raising capital from a VC is a marriage, and getting a divorce is near impossible, so choose wisely!

BOWLING FOR DOLLARS

When starting a company, there are a variety of options in terms of financing. Many entrepreneurs choose to grow their companies organically, also referred to as "bootstrapping," meaning self-funding. Often, in the initial stages, you might require a small amount of seed capital—to "germinate" the concept—which is normally sought from friends and family. Typically, these represent the least sophisticated and most expeditious avenue for short-term capital. This group usually has limited resources and is sometimes referred to us as "dumb money," because it adds limited value over and above the capital contribution.

Angel investors generally invest hundreds of thousands of dollars, and often contribute with more than just capital, including go to market strategy and key introductions. They're angel investors because they metaphorically lift you on their "wings," and hopefully elevate your company to the next level of growth. You might benefit if your angel is an industry expert and is in a position to spend time with you to develop your plan.

The shortcoming endemic to all of the above-mentioned sources of capital is that they typically lack deep pockets and are not necessarily investing in your company as a full-time endeavor. Rather, at most they are looking to assist and add value where they can. The ideal structure of angel funding would be in the form of a "bridge" to the next round—called "bridge financing"—with a discount[1] provided, with warrants,[2] to the angel investor, depending on the length of time between the bridge and the first round of investment, usually not to exceed 20 percent coverage for the money invested.

For example, if the investor puts in $500,000 in bridge financing and you close the Series A[3] round in six months, it is reasonable to provide the angel investor an additional 20 percent warrant coverage, so if you raise $5 million (including the angel bridge that converts into the Series A) at a $5 million pre-money[4] valuation, the $500,000 would ordinarily buy 5 percent ($500,000/$10 million) of the equity. You would then provide 20

---

[1] The discount pertains to pricing shares below the market valuation offered to investors on the same round, which yields preferential pricing.

[2] Warrants are a form of stock shares similar to options, typically priced below market, with an exercise time and price.

[3] Usually the first professional investor round of funding in a privately held company is procedurally labeled "Series A," the second round "Series B," etc.

[4] The "value" attributed to the company prior to the investment capital, also known as "prefinancing."

percent warrant coverage that would give the angel another 1 percent (20% × 5%). You might tie the bridge to the length of time it takes between when the angel bridges you the money and when you close the Series A; for example, from zero to six months the angel receives a 20 percent discount, from six to 12 months, 40 percent, and so on. You can change terms monthly on a sliding scale as well. This can become quite complicated, and it's probably wise to adhere to the KISS adage: "Keep It Simple Stupid!"

Be careful of bringing angel investors onto the board of directors and giving up too much control too early. At this stage in the life of your company, you do not want to lose control of your destiny to someone who invests only a few hundred thousand dollars and might not be the most experienced, active, or knowledgeable investor. Keep the capitalization table simple in these early stages; complicated capitalization structures may scare off future investors (e.g., excessive debt or warrant coverage, inconsistent vesting schedules, and equity transfers to inactive parties).

Another category of investor is the strategic investor. This can prove to be a wonderful source of capital, provided there is adequate communication and understanding from the beginning. Know the agenda. Often, a strategic investor will invest for a specific objective that might conflict with your goals. Most other investors will have a similar interest/agenda as you; namely, to maximize shareholder value and generate the greatest possible Return on Investment (ROI)[5] possible. Strategic investors, however, may only be interested in leveraging your technology for the benefit of their parent company, which might not always be in the best interests and long-term goals of your company. Often, strategic investors will seek a licensing or distribution agreement from your company with some preferential terms, the ability to purchase you if you achieve success, or they will seek to preclude you from partnering with their competitors.

[5] The annual ROI is net income divided by the average investment (equity) in the company. The firm as a whole has its own ROI, as does each separate investor group, since each investor group makes its own unique deal at its own implicit valuation.

To the extent that you can leverage the strategic investor network and protect yourself from any downside, it can position you advantageously against some of your competitors in the marketplace. A strategic investor might be a vendor or partner you're currently working with on manufacturing or distribution, or an actual customer who would be interested in investing in your company. Be cautious and maintain the proper balance of disclosure and confidentiality between your prospective strategic investor and partner. Limit the control or level of influence a strategic investor can exert by not giving them board representation and by always preserving your right to partner with potential competitors. Never constrain the company from being able to sell, license, or partner with anyone that can add value to the company. Fortunately, strategic investors often provide a global perspective, excellent distribution channels, deep pockets, are less price sensitive, usually prefer a VC to lead the investment, and rarely seek a role on the board.

This leads us to venture capitalists—full-time professional investors with deep pockets, whose sole task is to assist you with the growth of your company for maximum financial return. VCs are price sensitive, active investors who seek board representation and expect you to deliver on your promises. Be careful of what you "sell" before financing, because you will be expected to deliver on those projections after financing in the form of milestones.

Recently, as a result of the burst of the Internet bubble, venture capitalists have been described as having "deep pockets with short arms." This means that many large VC firms (sometimes managing in excess of $1 billion) have become so distracted by existing and legacy portfolio companies that they now have minimal time to investigate new investment opportunities, and even less time to service and assist those existing portfolio companies that need their professional help. Evaporation of the Initial Public Offering (IPO) market and *de minimus* activity on the mergers and acquisitions (M&A) side have caused the average VC to be "stuck" with a number of companies with no viable exit in the near term.

OVERVIEW OF VENTURE CAPITAL

The venture capital community has been experiencing unprecedented change, both positive and negative, in the last decade. From 1998 through 2001, approximately 700 VC firms in the United States raised and invested $200 billion in over 15,000 companies, the majority of them software and communications companies. Roughly 33 percent of all venture investment activity in the U.S. takes place in Silicon Valley, with the next highest regions (Southern California, Texas, and Boston) together comprising another 21 percent. During this period, over 500 companies raised $50 billion through IPOs, and 1300 companies were merged or acquired for approximately $180 billion. On average, it took 3.3 years from when the first venture capital firm invested money into the company until the company's IPO.[6] Needless to say, these were exciting times and many acquired inordinate amounts of wealth.

In spite of the recent and continued downturn in the overall U.S. and global economies, the challenge of starting a company—office space, recruiting talent—has never been less expensive. As Warren Buffett, renowned investor and head of Berkshire Hathaway, likes to quote his mother as saying, "Buy low and sell high." Moreover, if you are successful in raising venture capital, it is less likely that you'll see as many competitors being funded as you might have in the past. Nonetheless, the standard/threshold has gone up on what is getting funded. Gone are the days of funding a great (or even okay) idea with no defined business model, no viable path to profitability, and significant barriers to entry.

On the negative side, it is a challenging time to sell technology to an enterprise. Many of the Fortune 500 companies have been impaired over the last few years by dedicating dollars and internal resources to early stage startups that have gone out of business. As the saying goes, no one ever got fired for buying IBM. Many enterprises were tantalized by the exciting technologies being developed in Silicon Valley and abroad

---

[6] Venture Capital Industry Report, VentureOne, www.v1.com.

by young, visionary entrepreneurs and were enticed to spend many resources on implementing these cutting edge technologies—only to see the companies disappear, leaving them frustrated and exposed. Once burned twice shy.

This hesitance to be burned again has been coupled with the dramatic reduction of Information Technology budgets. (One CIO of a large financial institution admitted that his 2002 budget was reduced 15 percent from 2001 to $1.5 billion.) As a result, it's difficult for young startups to get traction from the typical early adopters of technology and to allay the fears of more established companies that want to know that the startups will be financially viable in the future to service, maintain, and support the technology they are selling. With IT budgets reduced to cut costs, enterprises are pushing hard to see a more rapid payback, which also means a higher ROI. Historically, it might have sufficed to demonstrate a payback over 24 to 36 months. Now, expectations are six to 18 months. Naturally, this can wreak havoc on pricing models and revenue expectations for the early stage companies trying to penetrate the market.

Make sure you are developing a product that is a "must have" and not a "nice to have" type of product. According to a recent Giga CIO survey, some of the spending priorities include short-term and clear ROI, Internet security, integration, and outsourcing.

TARGETING THE RIGHT VENTURE CAPITAL FIRM

Do your homework before you meet with a venture capitalist. This means knowing in advance as much as you possibly can about his firm, background, prior board seats, and existing investments. Time is money. Come prepared and on time. Keep your presentation short. Typically, you will have less than one hour. If you can't convey your message in 30 minutes, you're not ready for prime time. If you're making a physical presentation, bring everything you need, including hard copies in case you have computer problems or the projector doesn't work.[7] Convey your message in 15 slides or less, discussing each of the following: agenda, team, vision, value proposition, barriers to entry, technology, products, competition, size of market, financials, use of funds, capitalization table, customers, and exit comparables.

Notably, VCs tend to invest at different stages in the life of a company. Blumberg Capital is a seed/early stage VC, and usually among the first professional investors (a.k.a. Series A) on a deal. Next, there are middle and later stage VCs that prefer to invest in the Series B, C, and D rounds. Finally, there are mezzanine, late stage, and pre-IPO funds that prefer to invest in the final rounds before an IPO. One key differentiator is risk versus return for the different stage VCs. The earlier the VC tends to invest, and the greater inherent risks remaining—technology, competition, team, execution, future financing, customers—the higher return the VC will expect to achieve. An early stage Series A VC expects a 10 times multiple, while a mezzanine investor will be happy with a two to four times return. Similarly, an early stage VC expects to wait four to seven years to exit via M&A or IPO, while a late stage investor expects an exit in less than two years.

Do not target just one VC and expect to raise capital. Arrange as many meetings with as many appropriate VCs as you can. Nothing will better position you to negotiate favorable terms than having a variety of financing options. Try to keep the VC process at similar stages, so one group doesn't get much further ahead than another, thereby forcing you to make a decision prematurely. Ideally, you should strive to have a few VCs culminating their diligence at the same time, so you might actually receive multiple term sheets and have alternative options. This will also provide an opportunity to create a syndicate. And you should try and improve your presentation as you go along, learning from each meeting to enhance your presentation and communication skills.

---

[7] Parenthetically, do not invest in a $3000 projector. All VCs will have one, and you can always present slides in hard copy for the time being. Be frugal. You never have enough cash. Everything costs more and takes longer than you planned.

Moreover, it's important to realize that not every startup is appropriate for VC funding. You must be willing to bring partners into your company and share in the governance and key decisions, direction, and vision of your company. We look for opportunities where the company forecasts annual revenue growth in excess of 100 percent in the early years after investment and can achieve annual revenues in excess of $50 million by Year Five. The company also should be focused on reaching an exit—IPO or M&A—during this time period.

If you're looking to run your own business, to remain privately held, and aren't interested in reporting to a discerning board of directors, then VC is not for you. If your business has been growing at a slower pace but you believe that your market is ripe for incredible, as yet untapped, growth, you might consider approaching a VC.

Sources of Deal Flow

The number one source of deal flow for most venture capital firms is the existing network of entrepreneurs they have funded previously. The second most valued source is other venture capital firms. The third most reliable source is general service providers that work in the industry (accountants, lawyers, bankers, etc.).

You will be hard pressed to get much attention from most venture capitalists without having an introduction through one of the abovementioned sources of deal flow.

I can't emphasize enough how important it is to attempt, where possible, to have your business plan submitted to the targeted venture firm through a "friendly" introduction or referral.

Evaluating Your Needs

Here are some questions you should ask yourself before you decide whom to approach for investment capital:

1. Are you looking to grow the management team?
2. Do you have customers that are ready to purchase from you in the near future?

3. Are you in need of marketing talent that can help you hone your message?
4. Are you looking for passive investors?
5. Is your board of directors in need of more experienced industry experts?
6. How much capital do you need to break even?
7. Do you expect to open up satellite offices?
8. What key alliances do you need to form over the next 12 months, and how will you best achieve these?
9. Have the investors you are approaching founded, funded, or exited a company similar to yours in the past?

As an example of the last question, if you want to sign an original equipment manufacturing (OEM) or channel agreement with a firm like Sun Microsystems, BEA, Intel, Amazon, or Mercury Interactive, have the venture capital partners done this in the past? Have they sold companies to the abovementioned firms? Maybe they even funded Sun, BEA, or Intel when they were startups! It's common for VCs to do exhaustive, analytical analysis of a particular segment in the market where they are interested in making an investment. The VCs often will attempt to meet with all the companies in that particular realm and try and glean the "best of breed" for an investment. Ask the VCs if they are invested in, shareholders in, or evaluating something that might in any way be perceived as competitive.

Another essential consideration for an entrepreneur contemplating funding from a VC is for the founder to appreciate what the VC can "deliver" on behalf of your company other than investment dollars. It is crucial, in these nascent stages, for the startup to have investors that can facilitate introductions to prospective customers on behalf of the company. You must find a champion. This person will drive the process internally, will find the budget to pay you, and will act as a reference to other potential customers and investors. Without a champion, you won't close the deal.

Getting the attention of a prospective customer is challenging at best, and agonizing, time consuming, or impossible at worst—even in good times, and all the more difficult in hard times. Find as many champions as you can, because large organizations constantly go through restructuring. It's common to go through six months of meetings, pitches, and negotiations, to be on the verge of signing a proof of concept,[8] pilot,[9] or beta test,[10] only to discover that your champion was fired, left for another group, or underwent a reorganization—and you're back to step one—except you've been "burning your cash" without getting closer to the sale. Try to have as many points of contact and as many champions as you can, and keep as many opportunities alive, because this will happen.

This being the case, the ability of a VC to pick up the phone and contact the right person at the right company, a C-level person (CEO, CIO, CTO, CFO, etc.) who has the authority to drive the process and assist with getting you presented to the right team, is invaluable. Time to market is synonymous with survival. Hopefully, these initial beta customers will become your first paying customers, provide crucial feedback about the feature set within your product, and assist you with prioritizing your ongo-

---

[8] The Word Spy online dictionary (www.wordspy.com) defines proof of concept as " . . . an object that proves that a particular design concept can be implemented." A similar, second definition is "evidence that demonstrates that a business model or idea is feasible." In software, this might mean a "quick-and-dirty" program that shows a more sophisticated and elaborate program could be developed, even if this one is unpolished and not ready for potential customers to see.

[9] According to the Cambridge University Press Online dictionary at http://dictionary.cambridge.org/, a pilot [program] "describes a plan, product or system that is used to test how good something is before introducing it." In this context, it means early-stage software that is still in the testing phase that is not sufficiently developed and tested to be deployable commercially. It may be used in a department, but it is too "rough" to be sold or even to be used throughout an entire business.

[10] Merriam-Webster's online (http://www.m-w.com) defines a beta test as a "field test of a prototype version of a product (as software) especially by testers outside the company developing it that is conducted prior to commercial release." The three terms are in chronological order. A proof of concept is very early stage, before there is any product. The pilot test, though, does require at least a rough product. It may be what is also known as an "alpha test", or it may be pre-alpha test. The beta test is the last test before the product is ready to be sold commercially.

ing product development. You must be cautious to balance your needs, resources, and objectives with the customers' needs, since they will obviously have their own agenda. Again, to avoid disappointment, set the expectations up front for everyone.

Your decision whether to seek venture capital should be based on a calculation of the costs versus the benefits, that is, (1) dilution of ownership and control of the business in return for (2) the increase in the value of the company that arises from greater speed to market and size. The financing, connections, and wisdom the VC brings must weigh that balance in your favor for you to pay the price.

The CEO

It is worthwhile to discuss the CEO position. This is a very delicate and sensitive issue. Often, the existing CEO does not have all the skills to drive a company forward to an eventual IPO or M&A. The question is timing. Typically, the existing CEO company founder is usually either very technical and/or entrepreneurial, but will invariably have flaws and be deficient in some areas, such as finance, sales, marketing, etc. Together, the VC and founders should discuss this important issue prior to funding to avoid undue pain and suffering. Lack of communication can derail any company—all the more so for a startup.

Everyone must set realistic expectations. The entrepreneur must be honest with what he can contribute in what period of time, and the VCs should set candid expectations for what they can contribute in the overall process. Many of us, possibly with the best intentions, overpromise and underdeliver, which is damaging to all parties. Most VCs have a number of viable candidates to take the helm in their *kerietsu* (network), some of whom might even assist the VC in its due diligence process, thereby also providing an opportunity for the founders, VC, and prospective CEO to interact.

A CEO prospect who has come through the ranks over the decades and has deep experience both technically and in sales can be well-suited for the position, because he or she is a "fellow" engineer who earns respect from the founders and obviously can understand and empathize with the team, while having a unique ability to contribute on all levels. It is common for a VC to collaborate with the founders and an outside recruiting firm focused on CEO searches in a particular discipline, stage, sector, etc. The key is to maintain lines of communication at all times and to monitor expectations.

Getting to a Meeting

A typical $100 million venture capital firm receives at least 1500 business plans per year. Of those about 100 (6.7 percent) will be invited to meet with the partners. Perhaps 50 (3.3 percent) will result in serious due diligence, 10 (0.7 percent) will be offered a term sheet (see below), and five (0.3 percent) will ultimately obtain funding.[11] Most VC firms this size will have three to five investment professionals and will likely have the resources to execute one or two deals per professional per year.

The statistics of obtaining funding dramatically improve if you get that first meeting. In that case your odds of getting funding increase from 0.3 to over 10 percent. These statistics demonstrate why it is crucial *how* you get to your VC, because you're more likely to get a meeting if your materials reach the VCs desk through a trusted and friendly source.

On the communications side, be responsive and follow up. This sounds obvious and straightforward, but you would be surprised. If a VC asks you for more information, provide it as quickly and effectively as possible. Always try to get a face-to-face meeting!

THE VENTURE PROCESS

Talk to someone who has been through this process to get a sense of what to expect. VCs vary in their speed of funding, depending on the stage, but expect the process to take one to six months from the first meeting to having money in the bank, with an average of three months. VCs tend to be extremely busy multitasking and are constantly traveling and working with portfolio companies; do not take a lack of a response as a neg-

[11] These numbers are only an estimate.

ative or a personal insult. It is often just a question of time. There are absolutely not enough hours in the VC's day. Try to follow up in a friendly manner, e-mail being the ideal form of communication.

Start the process with a personalized, friendly, short introductory e-mail with a three- to five-page summary attached. In the text of the e-mail, state how you came to contact this VC and why you believe this opportunity is appropriate for this person, firm, etc. In one paragraph or less convey your value proposition, barriers to entry, team, advisers, customers, and anything else you think will entice the VC to open your attachment. At a later date you should be prepared to forward a full business plan, financial model with assumptions and comparables, a PowerPoint presentation, white papers, and marketing reports or customer references that validate your business plan. Good collateral materials address issues (the Five T's, below) in a clear, concise, and focused fashion.

Nondisclosure Agreements

VCs will not sign nondisclosure agreements. We receive so many plans each week that if we signed every NDA request, we would quickly be overwhelmed with legal documentation. Our reputation depends on our professionalism and on our ability to maintain your trust and confidence. Conversely, at some point in time you should absolutely insist on one from strategic investors/partners.

Term Sheets

A term sheet is a document that puts forth a summary of the terms and conditions that will apply if the venture capital firm and the entrepreneur hope to consummate a transaction. Typically, it is nonbinding, subject to further due diligence, and is the necessary step before having counsel draft final, detailed documents. This is the document that contains the proposed valuation of the company, along with many other essential terms that are equally if not more important, such as governance, control, etc. Many significant terms are not addressed in the term sheet, but are typically left for the initial drafting of the full set of final documents.

Entrepreneurs always seem to have angst over valuation, so let's take a few moments to discuss the perceived drivers of valuation, both traditional and from the perspective of a venture capitalist.

Valuation

Be careful about providing a valuation. If your valuation is based on a discount to a market leader, do not assume in your financial model that you will surpass the most successful companies in your realm. You will lose your credibility, which will impact negatively on your valuation. A VC will respect a well thought out financial model, *with reasonable but aggressive assumptions*, as long as you can defend it. What can be helpful in the nascent stages—and much more so as the company matures—is a professional valuation (do not try this at home!) based on comparables in the industry, with some level of discount.

Traditional methods used to value a privately held company are Discounted Cash Flow, analysis of market comparables, or some analysis of a company's net present value. In the early stage of a startup it is almost impossible for an amateur to apply the DCF analysis. Discounts to future cash flow are challenging on many levels. When you are contemplating investment in a company that doesn't expect to even have a product for 24 months, let alone significant revenues for at least another 12 months, expect serious critique and "push back" from the VC on both your assumptions and your perceived valuation.

This is very sophisticated work that needs to be well grounded, with realistic assumptions, market research that accurately quantifies the size of the market, and realistic expectations of market share over a specified period of time. The latter exercise (analysis of market comparables) is slightly more applicable, although often equally difficult to leverage. As an example, VCs often access VentureOne (www.v1.com) to review companies that are in a similar sector, to provide perspective. For example, how much capital did these companies need to raise? At what valuations did they raise the capital? And how much capital was needed to achieve a liquidity event?[12] This is helpful, but it cannot be applied in a vacuum. Market conditions and volatility, availability of capital, and macroeconomic and microeconomic conditions are only a few of the drivers that will significantly impact valuations.

Advisory Board

How do you obtain a "friendly" introduction to a VC? How do you find a "champion" at your first customers? You are in the relationship business. Leverage your network of relationships to open up doors, to find your "friends and champions" and, if it's feasible, make them advisers. Try and build a value-added advisory board with industry experts that can add credibility to complement your management team, especially if you are an early stage company. Advisers should be able to assist you with VC meetings, customer introductions, market and strategy, recruiting a key management team, and other critical functions.[13]

Due Diligence

The due diligence process can be painstaking, expensive, and incredibly time consuming for entrepreneurs and VCs alike. Think of this as an opportunity to review your strategy, financial model, business development and sales efforts, future product development, etc. As part of their due diligence, most VCs will introduce you to prospective customers and possibly some C-level management to determine their level of interest in your product. Is this a luxury purchase for the CIO, or a "must have" over the next 12 months? These are reasonable questions, the answers to which you should also want to know before you start this journey. It is in everyone's best interest when an investor can help accelerate this "truth seeking" process to collectively arrive at a decision whether to invest or not.

---

[12] While you might be able to glean some information from their site, full access requires a subscription that costs in excess of $15,000 per annum.

[13] Advisory board compensation might be 0.1 percent warrants with a three-year vesting period. This may represent 25,000 shares, so it is significant.

Due diligence can be broken down into a number of broad categories: technology, market, financial, legal, team, comparables, competition, and exit strategy. Being a venture capitalist is not rocket science. For the most part it is being thorough and reviewing the above checklist of items. Many funds, depending on the stage of investment, are not willing to take some of these risks. Some later stage funds (expansion capital) do not take technology or market risk, and as such, prefer to invest in companies with a proven technology, many reference customers, and significant revenues. Accordingly, an investor might prefer to invest in a small team of 50 people that expect to achieve annual revenues in excess of $10 million. This stage of investment still contains ongoing execution risk, questions on the exit strategy, changing market conditions and the like. Of course, the valuation of the company, the dollars it needs, and the inherent skill sets of the varied investors are not the same things at all.

The Five T's

Team. Timing. Theme. Terrain. Technology. Each of these elements will drive your valuation and determine whether you will get funded.

Team

This is the most important aspect. The first section I go to in reviewing an opportunity is the biographies of the team. I would rather fund a B technology or market with an A team. Great teams win. It's not just the people—it's the team. The key is that the talent of the individuals combines to form a superb team. Always look to recruit really smart people who can contribute. Most of the teams we fund are deep on the technology side and thin on the business, sales, and finance side. As long as the core team is strong, you can continue to grow from there and attract further talent in other disciplines.

The deeper and more experienced the team, the higher the valuation you can expect. A number of strategic investors have conveyed to me that they would buy early stage technology companies for $1 million per head. Ironically, one of our portfolio companies was so efficient that their head count was low and their sales price was not truly indicative of their tremendous value. The CEO was an individual with a great deal of integrity, and she refused to hire "heads" just to increase her sales price. In the end, she sold the company quite successfully for approximately 10 times the future 12 months of revenue, which was impressive, especially in the current market.

Timing

Probably the only thing worse than being too late to market is being too early. Timing is everything. Blumberg Capital helped launch Check Point Software in the United States and Japan. One of the keys to its success was that the Internet was just penetrating the corporate market, and every CIO who wanted to go online was concerned about obtaining a simple, "shrink-wrapped" firewall solution to protect the enterprise.

Theme

This relates to the sector you are in. For example, my firm uses the moniker N.E.W.S., which represents Networking, Enterprise software, Wireless infrastructure, and Security to describe our sector focus. Therefore, anyone sending us a business plan for a medical device company will not likely make it very far in our process. Focus. Like an entrepreneur, the VC needs to remain focused in its areas of expertise. VCs meet regularly with CIOs of Global 2000 companies to understand where, how, and why they are spending their IT budgets.

Terrain

This refers to the size and growth of the market you are attacking. Most venture funds look for multibillion dollar markets that are growing annually at double-digit rates with low penetration. A total market opportunity of $200 million growing 5 percent annually is unlikely to attract venture capital, even though it might create a wonderful niche market for you to dominate. VCs are looking for very large untapped markets with low penetration and very high compounded annual growth rates (CAGR). Finding these unique opportunities is challenging.

Technology

Technology really defines the potential barriers to entry. Have you filed any patents? How many man-years might it take for others to replicate what you have done? Technology relates to funding a paradigm shift and not just a mild improvement. When the first person found ice and used it to store food, a pickaxe and shovel were great inventions to help break the ice. VCs would not be excited about investing in a pickaxe with a sharper head, but probably would be very excited by the first refrigerator, which allows significantly longer food storage. The refrigerator was a paradigm shift and at least an order of magnitude more efficient than prior methodologies. That is exciting.

The Four E's

Jack Welch, retired CEO of General Electric, was one of the most renowned CEOs of the last few decades. He likes to describe the crucial ingredients found in a successful manager with "the four E's of GE leadership."[14] These are Energy, Energize, Execute, Edge. Then you need to connect the four E's with one P: Passion.

Top performers need high *energy*. It's the playoffs, and the true all-stars bring their game up another notch. Moreover, you need to somehow elevate the play of everyone on the team, and this means the ability to *energize* others on your team to do the same. You will be faced with difficult choices, and you need to possess the *edge* to make difficult yes and no decisions—even if you might sometimes be wrong; some managers are simply incapable and suffer from "analysis paralysis"—and the ability to *execute* and deliver on your projections. Being an entrepreneur is very demanding, and without the *passion* to create something from nothing, you will not thrive.

Marc Andreeson, cofounder of Netscape Communications and one of the leading figures of the Internet boom, sums it up: "What really counts in getting through a tough period like this is a sheer level of energy and willpower. You need a group of people who are willing to walk through brick walls."

---

[14] Jack Welch, *Straight from the Gut*, Warner Books, New York, 2001, p. 158.

The Day After . . .

Congratulations. You have closed on your investment from a venture capital firm, have cash in the bank, and you're feeling pretty darn good about yourself. Now what?

First, celebrate with your team. There is nothing wrong with a little indulgence after all the hard work you and the team have undoubtedly gone through over the last six months to reach this point. Your team should be rewarded and given the opportunity to celebrate, and it's important for you as CEO to set the proper tone and balance of "work hard, play hard." Moreover, this fosters and promotes an *esprit de corps* that will be essential in the coming months. This does not mean you should buy a Ferrari the next day, fly your team to Sun City, South Africa (with spouses or significant others), and sponsor a concert featuring the Rolling Stones in Pacific Bell Park. You get the point.

And second: Don't spend it too fast.

Think of the newly formed board of directors as an extension of your existing network. Try to balance your board with industry experts who can add value at the board level, and communicate with them frequently. Follow the advice of Robert Duvall in *The Godfather*: "I have to go to the airport. The Godfather is a man who likes to hear bad news immediately." This means *no negative surprises*. VCs can wait to hear the good news, but need to hear the bad news right away. As John Smale, former CEO of Procter & Gamble and onetime chairman of General Motors, put it: "Directors know relatively little apart from what management tells them."

CONCLUSION

Hopefully, you have an overview of the financing options your company has, with an emphasis on venture capital. If you choose the VC route, make an effort to get an entrée through the right source, and be brutally honest about your needs and aspirations as the CEO and in your overall presentation to investors. Avoid some of the common mistakes made by many who embark on the venture process and you will dramatically improve your odds of "getting to a meeting" and successfully completing the diligence process. Work with professionals to negotiate your term sheet and valuation, and remember to enjoy the honeymoon, because this is the first day of the rest of your life.

Try to have fun. Know how to laugh at yourself. Life is too short, so don't take yourself too seriously all the time. If you don't love what you do, it's time to move on. Always make time to be with the ones you love. Never do anything that you would be ashamed to tell your mom. Everything in moderation. Set expectations. Give back when and where you can. Be humble. But as Golda Meir, former prime minister of Israel, once said to a visiting diplomat: "Don't be so humble. You are not so great."

Chapter 14

Selling Your Business: Tax Considerations and Strategies

David C. Boatwright

This chapter will touch upon certain relevant tax principles and a number of strategies that should be considered for forming and eventually selling a business, including taxable as well as tax-free and tax-deferred strategies.[1] The principal goal of this chapter is to provide you with information and ideas about the relevant issues and opportunities involved in your deal. This should help you better negotiate the terms of your deal, and, if you are the owner of the business, enable you to better select and manage qualified counsel to represent you.

STRUCTURING A SALE

The methods and strategies of structuring the sale of a business are many and varied, as are the tax consequences associated with each particular method. For example, the consequences of an asset sale can be very different than the consequences of a sale of the outstanding equity interests in the business; and the

[1] This chapter focuses almost exclusively on principles of U.S. federal income tax law in effect when this book was published (all of which are subject to change, even retroactively, after the date of publication). However, other taxes that may be material in determining the owner's after-tax return from forming, owning, and selling his or her business should also be considered.

use of buyer equity interests as acquisition currency may produce different tax consequences than the use of cash or other property—often with surprising results (sometimes good, sometimes bad).

Let's begin with the following principles of tax law that are important to know in order to understand how a transaction may be taxed, and the amount of the potential tax liability from the transaction.

Taxes on the Sale and Exchange of Property

Income tax law presumes that gain or loss results upon the sale or exchange of property. This gain or loss must be reported on a tax return, or returns, unless a specific exception set forth in the "Code" or the Treasury Department's income tax regulations provides otherwise. A number of these exceptions will be discussed later in the chapter.

Computing Taxable Gain or Tax Loss

When a transaction is taxable under applicable principles of income tax law, the seller's taxable gain is determined by the following formula: the *amount realized* over the *adjusted tax basis* of the assets sold equals *taxable gain*. If the adjusted tax basis exceeds the amount realized, the seller instead has a *tax loss*. The amount realized is the amount paid by the buyer, and it includes any debt assumed by the buyer. The adjusted tax basis of each asset sold is generally the amount originally paid for the asset, plus amounts expended to improve the asset (which were not deducted when paid), less depreciation or amortization deductions (if any) previously allowable with respect to the asset. Taxable gain is generally decreased, and a tax loss is generally increased, by transactional costs and expenses paid by the seller.

The adjusted tax basis of a share of stock in a C corporation—a corporation with respect to which an election to be governed by the provisions of Subchapter S of the Code is not in effect—is usually what the owner paid for the specific share, although an inherited share has an adjusted tax basis equal to the value of the share on the decedent's death (which is usually determined by reference to the decedent's estate tax return). If an owner of stock acquired the stock in different blocks for different prices, and certain but not all of the shares are subsequently sold, the adjusted tax basis of the specific shares sold must be used to compute taxable gain or tax loss. *This is known as "specific identification" and should be used to save taxes on a sale of shares by selling the shares with the highest adjusted tax basis unless the seller has other losses available to offset the gain from a sale of lower-basis shares.*

The adjusted tax basis of a share in an S corporation—a corporation with respect to which an election is in effect to be governed by the provisions of Subchapter S of the Code—and an interest in a partnership or a limited liability company (LLC)—each a *pass-through* entity—is generally what the owner paid for the share or interest plus (1) the income and gains allocated to the owner from the entity with respect to the share or interest and (2) any contributions by the owner to the entity with respect to the share or interest, less (3) tax losses allocated to the owner from the entity with respect to the share or interest and (4) any distributions from the entity to the owner with respect to the share or interest.[2]

Character of Gains and Losses: Ordinary vs. Capital

The character of a taxable gain or a tax loss can and usually does affect the amount of tax due upon sale of an asset or assets, often materially. By "character" of taxable gain, I mean whether the gain is classified as so-called ordinary income under federal income tax law, which is usually subject to the maximum rate of tax, or as *capital gain*, which occurs when the gain

---

[2] Technically, the basis of an interest in a partnership or an LLC includes the holder's allocable share of the entity's indebtedness; however, the amount realized on a sale of such an interest also includes the holder's allocable share of the entity's indebtedness, so I have chosen to simply ignore a holder's allocable share of entity debt, since it generally will not affect the taxable gain or tax loss computation. The only exception is if the holder has a negative tax basis capital account, in which case he or she will have a gain on a sale of the interest equal to the amount realized (without regard to his or her share of the entity debt) plus the amount of the negative tax basis capital account.

derives from sale of an asset considered a *capital asset* under Code Section 1221 or Code Section 1235 (which sets forth special rules for patents). When a capital asset has been held for more than one year, it is a *long-term capital gain* and qualifies for taxation at a much lower federal tax rate (currently, less than half what is applicable to ordinary income). If a taxable gain derives from a capital asset held for less than one year, it is a *short-term capital gain*, which is generally taxed like ordinary income.[3]

The character of tax loss under federal income tax law is also important, but unlike taxable gains, it is generally better for tax losses to be "ordinary" in nature than "capital." Ordinary tax losses may be offset against both ordinary income and capital gains. If during a taxable year ordinary tax losses exceed all income and gains against which they may be offset, the excess ordinary tax losses may generally be "carried back" to certain prior years' returns (and refunds of taxes paid in those years sought), and then "carried forward" to certain future years for offset against income and gains earned in those years. Capital losses, on the other hand, may only be offset against capital gains, and only up to a very limited amount of ordinary income. Excess capital losses may generally be carried forward. The rules covered in this paragraph are sometimes referred to as the "netting rules."

The key, then, is that if a transaction will result in taxable gain, the seller should generally endeavor to maximize the amount that will be characterized as long-term capital gain; but if the transaction will result in a tax loss, the seller should generally endeavor to maximize the amount that will be characterized as ordinary loss.

There are a number of strategies for achieving the above italicized objectives, including an agreement between seller and buyer as to an allocation of the sales price in a way that, within

[3] Assets that have been held for more than one year and are depreciable are so-called "Section 1231 assets." Gain on sale of a Section 1231 asset is ordinary income to the extent of certain prior depreciation deductions claimed and thereafter is long-term capital gain. Loss on sale of a Section 1231 asset is an ordinary loss.

reason, minimizes or even eliminates ordinary income and maximizes capital gains, or maximizes ordinary loss and minimizes or eliminates capital losses. Another approach is to defer the sale of one or more assets if doing so will result in the taxable gain from sale of the asset(s) ultimately being long-term capital gain.

The concern with the "character" of a taxable gain or tax loss is much less significant for a C corporation, which is subject to identical federal income tax rates on its ordinary income and capital gains. However, capital losses of C corporations still may only be offset against capital gains, and they're subject to far more restrictive carry-back and carry-forward provisions than ordinary losses. So, if a C corporation has excess capital losses during a taxable year (or capital losses that have been carried forward from an earlier year), the corporation would prefer capital gains over ordinary income, because the excess capital losses may be used to offset the capital gains (but could not be used to offset ordinary income). The same is true for individual taxpayers with excess capital losses, that is, they would prefer to have capital gains (even short-term capital gains), so that the capital losses may be used to offset them.

Sales Price Allocations for Multiple Assets

In selling multiple assets, the sales price should be contractually allocated among each asset to determine the taxable gain or tax loss from the sale of each asset, as well as the aggregate net taxable gain or tax loss. This allocation may impact the seller's tax liability, depending on the character of each of the assets sold for income tax purposes and the amount allocated to each of the assets. To the extent that certain assets are subject to transfer taxes, the allocation may also affect the amount of transfer taxes due by either allocating more or less value to such assets.

Usually, the buyer will have different objectives than the seller with respect to a sales price allocation. This is known as "tax polarity," and where it exists between a buyer and a seller, a sales price allocation agreed to by them normally will be respected by the IRS and the courts. To the extent justifiable under the facts and circumstances, the general rule for sellers is to allocate value to each of the following types of assets up to, but not in excess of, their adjusted tax basis:

- Noncapital assets, whose sale for more than their adjusted tax basis would give rise to ordinary income
- Capital assets that have been held for one year or less at the time of the sale, the sale of which for more than their adjusted tax basis would give rise to short-term capital gain
- Assets that have been subject to prior depreciation or amortization deductions, the sale of which requires the prior depreciation and amortization deductions to be "recaptured" by the seller as ordinary income to the extent the value allocated to them exceeds their adjusted tax basis

Any remaining sales price could then be allocated to capital assets held for more than one year, such as goodwill (which may now be amortized for income tax purposes over a 15-year period), the sale of which would result in long-term capital gains.

The buyer, on the other hand, generally would want as much value as possible allocated to assets that have the shortest possible depreciable or amortizable lives (i.e., assets with lives less than the 15-year life of goodwill) for income tax purposes, so that it may recapture a portion of the purchase price as soon as possible through depreciation and amortization deductions. The buyer generally would also prefer to allocate full retail value to inventory (a noncapital asset) rather than just the seller's adjusted tax basis in the inventory, in order that the buyer not have any taxable income upon sale of the inventory. These differing objectives can cause some tension in the negotiations, particularly depending on the relative bargaining power of the parties, but willing buyers are usually accommodating.

Computing Tax Liability

Assuming that no exceptions to the presumptive taxation of a transaction are available, a seller's income tax liability may be estimated—after the net taxable gain or tax loss has been determined using the principles set forth above—by multiplying the seller's net taxable gains and income (taking care to separate gains by their character, differentiating between long-term and short-term capital gains, and following the netting rules) by the seller's combined effective federal, state, and local income tax rate applicable to each source of gain and income from the sale.[4]

Transfer Taxes

The sale of a business may generate state and local transfer tax liability (e.g., liability for sales taxes) where certain types of property are transferred. These taxes can be material, usually in the range of 5 to 10 percent of the gross value of each asset being transferred.

CHOOSING A SALE STRUCTURE

A number of factors will affect the decision about which structure to use to sell a business, including the owner's objectives, the form of the entity currently conducting the business, the buyer's objectives, and the relative bargaining power of the seller and the buyer.

The Form of the Business

The choice of entity decision made upon formation of a business may well play the most important role in determining how the

[4] At the time of publication, the maximum federal rate applicable to ordinary income and short-term capital gains was 35 percent, and the maximum federal rate applicable to long-term capital gains and dividends was 15 percent. State rates vary. To compute the maximum combined effective federal and state rate applicable to a transaction, add to the federal rate applicable to the transaction (1) the applicable state rate multiplied by (2) one minus the maximum federal rate of the seller for the year of the transaction (i.e., even if greater than the federal rate that applies to gain from the transaction). This assumes that the seller's state taxes for the year of the transaction will be prepaid during such year and will therefore offset the seller's income for such year. This also assumes the seller will not be subject to the alternative minimum tax. If local taxes apply, apply the same formula set forth in (1) and (2) to determine the effective local tax rate.

business is to be sold and the consequences of the sale; for example, whether the business may be sold without current taxation or sold on a basis that otherwise minimizes the tax burden arising from the sale.

C Corporations and the Double Tax

The principal tax disadvantage of a C corporation is what is referred to as the "double tax." A C corporation is a taxable entity and must pay tax on its taxable income and gains. In addition, distributions to its shareholders are not deductible by the corporation and are normally taxable to the shareholders.

There are strategies for avoiding or reducing the double tax with respect to operating profits of a C corporation—such as paying reasonable salaries to shareholder employees to reduce or zero out the corporation's taxable income—but these strategies are often not available (or would be imprudent) with respect to gains from the sale of a corporation's assets and the subsequent distribution of the sales proceeds to the shareholders.

Due to the double tax, a C corporation usually is not the entity of choice for a startup business. *The rule of thumb is that a pass-through entity is the preferred entity in which to conduct a business*, at least until the business becomes a public company or is financed by a person (e.g., a venture capital firm) that insists on investing in a C corporation.

It's usually possible to convert, on a tax-free basis, a pass-through entity into a C corporation. The converse is generally not true. The conversion of a C corporation into an LLC or a partnership usually will give rise to a double tax problem, because the conversion is treated as if the corporation sold its business and assets for Fair Market Value and then distributed the proceeds to the shareholders. Although a qualifying C corporation may be converted free of tax to an S corporation by making an appropriate election, a subsequent sale of assets by the S corporation within 10 years of making such election will give rise to an entity-level tax at the time the assets are sold to the same extent the sale of such assets would have been taxed had they been sold on the effective date of the S election for their Fair Market Value. (This is sometimes referred to as the "BIG Tax.")

However, there are certain tax advantages to businesses conducted as C Corporations. These depend in particular on the likely exit or liquidity strategy for the business. For example, for those who plan on reinvesting the proceeds from the eventual sale of the business in another business, use of a C corporation may be advisable if the corporation constitutes a "qualified small business corporation." A corporation qualifies if it actively conducts a qualifying business and meets certain asset constituency and other tests set forth in Code Section 1202. Gain on the sale of the stock in a qualified small business corporation may be deferred if the proceeds of the sale are reinvested in another qualified small business corporation within 60 days. And even where the proceeds of stock are not reinvested, up to 50 percent of the taxable gain from sale of the stock may be excluded from tax (subject to a number of limitations that can render this benefit illusory).

Another potentially material benefit of using a C corporation is that only a business conducted in corporate form may be acquired by another corporation for stock of the acquiring corporation in a tax-free reorganization. This will be discussed later in the chapter.

Buyer Issues That Affect Pricing

To avoid the double tax problem, shareholders of a C corporation will almost invariably prefer to sell their stock instead of having the corporation sell its assets and then distribute the sale proceeds to its shareholders. But there is a potential problem with this approach for the buyer. If he or she buys the corporation's assets, virtually the entire purchase price can be deducted over time through depreciation and amortization deductions; but if the outstanding stock of the corporation (a nondepreciable or amortizable asset) is bought, the buyer will be limited to deducting depreciation and amortization based on the adjusted tax basis in the corporation's assets immediately prior to the acquisition, in which case the portion of the purchase price over the existing adjusted tax basis of the corporation's assets will be lost for purposes of depreciation and amortization.

The foregone deductions essentially mean that the government will fund less of the purchase price through future tax savings for the buyer, which, of course, usually means that the buyer will want to pay less for the stock of the corporation than he or she would want to pay for the corporation's assets. This is generally not an issue for an S corporation, because, except to the extent it is subject to the "BIG Tax," it may sell its assets, pass through the gains to its shareholders, and then distribute the proceeds of the sale on a tax-free basis to the shareholders.

S Corporations

An S corporation is generally not subject to federal income tax, and its income, gains, and losses pass to its shareholders annually, who are then required to report such items on their personal income tax returns. An S corporation may then make cash distributions to its shareholders, up to the amount of income and gains that were previously passed through to them, without causing the shareholders to incur additional tax liability. This pass-through of income, gains, and losses—the principal advantage of an S corporation over a C corporation—essentially avoids the double tax and pricing issues that face the shareholders of a C corporation that is for sale, and it also affords a benefit not available to C corporations: the ability to offset losses against the shareholders' income from other sources, subject to certain limitations.

Like a C corporation, an S corporation can be acquired on a tax-free basis in a reorganization transaction (discussed later in this chapter); but unlike a C corporation, an S corporation cannot be a qualified small business corporation.

Partnerships and Limited Liability Companies

Partnerships are not subject to federal income taxation at the entity level. This is also true of an LLC with more than one member, unless the LLC elects to be taxed as a corporation. An LLC that has not made such an election and that has only one member is disregarded for federal income tax purposes; in other words, its business and assets are treated as if they were owned by its member, and no separate income tax return is required for the activities of the LLC.

When a partnership or an LLC earns taxable income or gain, the owners must report their respective shares of the income or gain and pay taxes on them. On the other hand, if the partnership or LLC has a taxable loss for any given taxable year, the owners are entitled to claim their respective shares of the loss and, subject to a number of potential limitations, may use the loss to offset their income from other sources. This pass-through of income, gains, and losses essentially avoids the double tax and pricing issues facing the shareholders of a C corporation that is up for sale, and the ability to offset losses against the owners' income from other sources also affords a benefit not available to C corporations.

As a general rule, partnerships and LLCs are subject to fewer restrictions than S corporations and are considerably more flexible. *Therefore, the rule of thumb is that a partnership or an LLC is the entity of choice when compared to an S corporation*, unless the most likely exit or liquidity strategy for the business is acquisition by a public company.

"Hot Asset" Rules

As with sales of stock in a corporation, gain or loss from sale of a partnership or LLC interest is generally a capital gain or loss. If the LLC only has one member, however, it will be treated as having sold the assets of the business directly, and the character of its gain or loss will derive from the allocation of the sales price among the assets and the character of such assets. Also, where a partnership or an LLC with more than one member owns certain "hot assets," gain from sale of a partnership or LLC interest may be deemed partially or wholly ordinary income. Hot assets include certain receivables and appreciated inventory.

To the extent that the value of a partnership or LLC consists of hot assets, a proportionate amount of the gain from sale of a partner's or member's interest will be ordinary income, not capital gain. A strategy for addressing this issue is to agree with the buyer on a valuation of the assets of the partnership or LLC that, within reason, reduces the value allocated to the hot assets.

Buyer Issues That Affect Pricing

These are almost always avoided when the business being sold is conducted in a partnership or an LLC. The buyer may acquire the assets of or all of the equity interests in the business—in which case the gain or loss from the sale will be free of entity-level income taxes, and the buyer will obtain the desired increase in the tax basis of the assets acquired.

Principal Transaction Structures: Taxable

These include the sale of assets and the sale of the equity interests.

Sale of Assets

In an asset sale, the buyer agrees to purchase all or a select group of assets from the selling entity, usually subject to all or certain liabilities of the business. If both the acquirer and the selling entity are corporations and the sales price is solely voting stock of the buyer, the transaction may constitute a tax-free reorganization (discussed later in this chapter). Otherwise, unless the proceeds of the sale are reinvested in a transaction qualifying as a "like-kind exchange" under Code Section 1031 (which is unlikely), the selling entity will recognize taxable gain or tax loss with respect to the sale of each asset equal to the difference between the amount realized for each asset sold and its adjusted tax basis.

If the selling entity is a C corporation, it will pay federal and state income taxes on the net taxable gain from the asset sale. If the corporation then wants to distribute the proceeds to its shareholders, each shareholder will be taxed on the amount distributed to him or her. If the distribution is a dividend, the amounts distributed to the shareholders will be taxable as such (subject, in the case of corporate shareholders, to a special exclusion known as the "dividends received deduction"). If the distribution is in liquidation of the distributing corporation, each shareholder will recognize taxable gain equal to the difference between the amount distributed over its adjusted tax basis in his or her stock in the distributing corporation.

If the selling entity is a pass-through entity, it will determine its gain or loss for each asset sold, determine the character of the taxable gain or tax loss for each asset, and allocate the gains and losses out to its owners. If the selling entity is an

S corporation, it will not owe any federal income taxes as a result of the sale, except perhaps the "BIG Tax." The owners will then report their allocated gains and losses on their personal tax returns and bear the income tax consequences. If the selling entity then wants to distribute the proceeds of the sale to its owners, it may generally do so on a tax-free basis.

Here are some strategies to consider regarding the sale of assets:

- To avoid the double tax and to minimize or avoid transfer taxes, a C corporation should avoid asset sales. Instead, the owners should seek to sell their stock.
- Pass-through entities should avoid asset sales. The buyer will be able to obtain an increase to the adjusted tax basis of the assets of the business in any event, and structuring the sale as a sale of equity should minimize and may even avoid transfer taxes.
- If a sale of multiple assets is to occur, the seller should endeavor to have the buyer agree to a favorable allocation of the sales price among the assets to be sold.
- Consider negotiating for the buyer to pick up the tab for all or a portion of the transfer taxes, which is customarily done.

Sale of Equity Interests by Owners

In a sale of equity interests, the buyer agrees to purchase all or a portion of the outstanding equity interests in the business from one or more of its owners. If both the acquirer and the entity to be sold are corporations, and the sales price is to be paid all or substantially in the buyer's voting stock, the transaction may be a tax-free reorganization (discussed later in this chapter). Otherwise, each seller will recognize taxable gain or tax loss equal to the difference between the amount realized by it from the buyer and its adjusted tax basis in the interests sold.

Generally, subject to the hot asset rules and certain other potential exceptions, the character of a seller's gain will be capital, which may be short term (with respect to interests held for one year or less at the time of the sale) or long term (for interests held for more than one year at the time of the sale).

Elective Treatment as an Asset Sale

In certain instances, the buyer and seller may jointly elect to treat a purchase and sale of stock as an asset purchase for income tax purposes. The election is made pursuant to Section 338(h)(10) of the Code. The benefit of this is that the buyer will obtain an increase in the adjusted tax basis of the assets of the corporation, and may be willing to pay more for this benefit (assuming willingness to acquire the stock without regard to the election). The election is generally not taken into account under state transfer tax regimes, and it may be a way to avoid transfer taxes that would have been payable had the transaction been structured as an asset sale.

Here are some strategies to consider regarding the sale of equity interests:

- If the stock being sold is qualified small business corporation stock, consider whether the seller may be able to defer the payment of tax on the gain from the sale by investing the proceeds from the sale in another qualified small business corporation.
- In the event of a sale of a partnership or an LLC, to avoid or minimize the effect of the hot asset rules, attempt to have the buyer agree to the value of each of the entity's assets, and to further agree not to take any position for tax or financial reporting purposes inconsistent with such valuation.
- In the event the entity being sold is an S corporation or a corporate subsidiary of another corporation, consider whether making a Section 338(h)(10) election would be beneficial to the buyer, perhaps rendering the buyer willing to pay more for the company than he or she would without such election. If the above election is to be made, agree with the buyer on an allocation of the sales price among the assets of the corporation, and request the buyer to indemnify you for any tax liability

you incur as a result of the election that would not have been incurred by you in a straight stock sale.

Seller Financing

Under certain circumstances the seller can use the "installment method" of reporting gain to defer recognition of taxable gain on a sale of assets or stock if the seller takes back a note for all or a portion of the sales price. Under the installment method, the seller determines what portion of total sales proceeds represent taxable gain, which is the percentage of each payment received from the buyer that is taxable at the time the payment is made. If available, the installment method can be used to enhance a seller's investment yield from a sale. This is because the seller would not be taxed on the gain from sale of the stock until the principal amount of the note is paid and would receive interest payments with respect to the amount of tax that would have been paid in an all-cash transaction.

Use of Options

Options can be used effectively to achieve deferral and even elimination of taxable gain. Payments made by those to whom the option is granted (the "grantee" of the option, i.e., the buyer of the business) are nontaxable to the grantor of the option (i.e., the seller) until the option is exercised by the buyer or otherwise terminates. So, the seller can accept a fairly handsome upfront payment and continued option payments thereafter and, provided the total payments are not so substantial that the arrangement starts to look more like a sale than an option, pay no tax on the payments until the option is exercised by the buyer or terminates.

Use of an option can be particularly useful where a "seller" of an asset (including an interest in a business) is of advanced age and does not want to pay taxes on the gain inherent in his or her position to be sold, because such gain would effectively "disappear" upon his or her death, due to the rule that the adjusted tax basis of the asset owned by a decedent is "stepped up" to its Fair Market Value at the time of the decedent's death. Use of the installment method if a note is used instead of an option will not achieve this result, because the gain deferred by the installment method is taxable to the decedent's estate when the note is paid.

Principal Transaction Structures: Nontaxable

These structures are generally only available to corporations (including C and S corporations). However, there are techniques for effectively structuring tax-free combinations where the entity to be sold is a partnership or an LLC. An owner who wants to do this should consult with qualified counsel.

Tax-Free Reorganizations

Code Section 368 sets forth a number of tax-free transaction structures known as "reorganizations." To qualify as a reorganization, a transaction must meet certain requirements, which vary greatly depending on the form of the transaction. If all applicable requirements for a reorganization are met, shareholders of the acquired corporation are not taxable on the exchange of their shares for shares of the acquiring corporation. Conversely, if a single requirement for a reorganization is not met, the entire transaction is taxable, including the receipt by the selling shareholders of stock in the acquiring corporation.

Hedging

Although a reorganization may hold tax appeal, it's critical that the sellers first determine if the stock to be issued to them from the acquiring corporation is an attractive investment opportunity. If the sellers think otherwise, there are certain measures he or she should consider. It may be possible, for example, for the seller to hedge against the prospect of the shares falling in value by using *put* and *call* options. The hedge will usually take the form of a right to put (or sell) the shares to a third party at a specified price for a period of time if the shares' value drop below a particular target. This costs money, but the seller may be able to structure a "costless" hedge by simultaneously selling a call, permitting a third party to acquire the seller's shares if they rise over a specified target value, and then using the proceeds from sale of the call to buy the put.[5]

Straight Merger

This is simply a merger of one corporation into another corporation pursuant to applicable state law. This is a relatively flexible form of reorganization because:

1. Shareholders of the entity being acquired may receive stock or a combination of stock and other consideration, such as cash).
2. Shareholders receiving both stock and nonstock consideration are not taxable on the stock consideration.
3. Shareholders do not have to be treated equally, so, for example, certain shareholders may take stock, others cash, and still others a combination of stock and cash.
4. Straight mergers are not subject to certain restrictive provisions applicable to other forms of reorganization.

As a general rule, in a straight merger, some or all of the shareholders of the corporation being acquired may receive as much as approximately 60 percent of the sales price in cash or

[5] These arrangements are usually structured by investment bankers, and, if structured properly, will not result in a deemed sale of the stock by the hedging party for income tax purposes. Sometimes such hedging arrangements are not available or feasible, in which case the seller should consider attempting to obtain a put right from the acquiring corporation, which, if structured properly, would not affect the tax-free nature of the reorganization. Although not technically a hedge, another possibility would be to request that the acquiring corporation issue convertible preferred stock rather than common stock to the sellers pursuant to the reorganization. The convertible preferred stock would have liquidation rights superior to the holders of the corporation's common stock, thereby hedging the sellers' investment risk by essentially requiring the holders of common stock in the acquiring corporation to bear losses to the value of the acquiring corporation to the extent of the value of the outstanding common stock before the preferred holders would have to bear any losses—yet it would allow the sellers to "ride" the upside of owning common stock through the conversion feature. If this route is pursued, however, care must be taken to ensure that the applicable reorganization requirements are met and the stock is not considered "nonqualified preferred stock" pursuant to Code Sections 351 and 354.

other nonstock consideration without being taxed on the stock portion of the consideration.

A potential nontax problem with this form of reorganization is that the acquirer directly assumes the liabilities of the acquired corporation in the merger, which can pose a risk to the acquirer's other existing businesses and assets.

Stock for Stock

This type of reorganization involves the acquisition of at least 80 percent of the stock of the corporation to be acquired solely in exchange for voting stock of the acquiring corporation. The acquiring corporation may not pay a single dollar of nonstock consideration. Though less flexible than a straight merger, in this type of reorganization the acquirer does avoid the problem of assuming the liabilities of the acquired corporation. This is so because those liabilities remain encapsulated in the acquired corporation (which becomes a subsidiary of the acquired corporation). This same result may be accomplished, however, through use of a subsidiary merger (discussed below), which is generally more flexible and therefore preferable to stock-for-stock reorganizations.

Stock for Assets

This reorganization involves the acquisition of "substantially all" of the assets of the selling corporation solely in exchange for voting stock of the acquiring corporation. Although, like the stock-for-stock reorganization, this requires that "solely" voting stock of the acquirer be used, there is a special rule that permits nonstock consideration to be used so long as the total nonstock consideration given by the acquiring corporation (including the assumption of liabilities of the acquired corporation) does not exceed 20 percent of the total consideration given (including liabilities assumed).

Stock for assets offers the acquirer the benefit of not having to assume the unknown or contingent liabilities of the acquired corporation (either directly or by taking the acquired assets subject to such liabilities, as in a merger and a stock-for-stock reorganization).

Subsidiary Mergers

These are accomplished when the acquiring corporation forms a subsidiary corporation and either merges the corporation to be acquired into the subsidiary under state law (a "forward subsidiary merger") or merges the subsidiary into the corporation to be acquired under state law (a "reverse subsidiary merger"). Although the merger is between a subsidiary and the corporation to be acquired, stock of the corporation that owns the subsidiary (its "parent") is given as consideration to the shareholders of the corporation to be acquired.

The reverse subsidiary merger is the usual form of reorganization chosen, because:

1. It protects the acquirer from the liabilities of the acquired corporation by keeping those liabilities separately encapsulated in the acquired corporation (which becomes a subsidiary of the acquirer).
2. It avoids having to transfer legal title to assets, which can trigger transfer taxes.
3. It often avoids anti-assignability provisions in the contracts of the corporation to be acquired.
4. It permits up to 20 percent of the transaction consideration (without taking into account liabilities of the corporation to be acquired) to be paid in nonstock consideration, which is considerably more generous than available in the stock-for-stock and stock-for-assets formats.

The one drawback to the reverse subsidiary merger, compared to the straight merger and the forward subsidiary merger, is that the latter two permit as much as about 60 percent of the transaction consideration (without regard to the liabilities of the corporation to be acquired) to be paid in nonstock consideration. However, this advantage is of limited benefit since, subject to applicable securities laws and any contractual restrictions that may be imposed by the acquiring corporation's investment bankers, a shareholder of a corporation acquired by a public company may usually dispose of all or a portion of the public company shares received in the reorganization through market transactions immediately afterward.

Tax Attributes and Benefits from a Transaction

Loss and credit carry-forwards of a C corporation can be a valuable asset in the hands of an acquiring company, since they may be available to offset the income and gains of the acquired business following the acquisition and, in certain limited circumstances, may offset the income and gains of the acquirer's other businesses. A seller should work with counsel to determine what value, if any, an acquirer may obtain from acquired tax loss and credit carry-forwards, and seek additional sales price for some portion of that value. In computing the value tax loss and credit carry-forwards to a buyer, the seller and his or her counsel should take into account applicable limitations on the acquirer's ability to use the losses and credits, for which it will be necessary to make present value calculations. The principal limitations to be taken into account are set forth in Code Sections 382 and 383.

An entity being sold may be entitled to extraordinary deductions in the year of sale, and care should be taken to make sure the seller gains the benefit of these deductions. The most notable extraordinary deduction that can arise is the deduction to which an entity is entitled equal to the "spread" between the value of interests subject to options of the acquired entity that are exercised at or about the time of sale and the exercise price payable under the options to acquire the interests. This deduction results without any cash outlay by the entity being acquired and can be very large, which is why an acquirer will often attempt to take steps to obtain the benefit of the deduction. Counsel's input here is critical.

Deliberately Avoiding Nontaxable Structures

The nontaxable structures outlined above are mandatory. In other words, if a transaction meets the requirements of a reorganization, the seller must report the sale accordingly. This means that a seller who would otherwise have had a deductible tax loss cannot take the loss currently. In this latter instance, planning should be considered to intentionally fail to meet the requirements of a reorganization.

CONCLUSION

The considerations involved in forming and later selling a business are varied and complex. Both tax and nontax considerations are important in creating a structure that is operationally feasible and also maximizes the owner's after-tax Return on Investment from owning and later selling the business or "taking it public." The involvement of qualified counsel throughout the process is often imperative to achieving these objectives.

Chapter 15

Valuation Controversy: An IRS Perspective

Howard A. Lewis[1]

The modern tax audit is a true partnership between the taxpayer, his or her representatives, and the Internal Revenue Service. Recent organizational, policy, and procedural changes implemented at the IRS have resulted in a workforce that is receiving better training and becoming more focused on customer satisfaction. The IRS views understanding, solving, and preventing taxpayer problems as critical to enhancing customer satisfaction. In the context of the type of audits of valuation issues discussed in this book, collaboration between the parties can go a long way toward making this a reality and, in the process, truly reducing the burden on the taxpayer.

In this chapter I will discuss several ways of making this happen. I will focus on the parties and their roles and responsibilities, with a special emphasis on your role as the business owner[2] (often overlooked in the audit process). I will discuss ex-

[1] The content of this chapter is the opinion of the writer and does not necessarily represent the position of the Internal Revenue Service.

[2] I refer here to the business owner of small- to medium-size entities. I would not expect the president or CEO of a Fortune 100 company to take an active role in a tax audit, except under perhaps the most extraordinary circumstances.

perts and their roles, pointing out the problems that arise when experts (for either side) stray over to the side of advocacy. I will talk about strategies for collaboration, problems that can develop if the process breaks down, and how to solve those problems. Throughout, as I said, the focus will be on the business owner. An expanded focus on the roles, responsibilities, and issues involving the numerous other parties discussed is better left to other forums.

SETTING THE STAGE: THE CAST OF CHARACTERS

Tax audits have gotten vastly more complicated over the last two decades. Valuation specialists generally serve as team members on audit teams consisting of Internal Revenue agents, IRS estate tax attorneys, and/or others. When I began as a valuation specialist, my role generally consisted of single-handed responsibility for "my" issues, under the interested, but not very active oversight by the agent, estate tax attorney, or other person to whom the audit was primarily assigned. I did my own research, developed my own plans, interacted independently with taxpayers and their representatives, and came to my own conclusions, presenting my findings and resolving any conflicts as best I could. I've worked directly with the business owner many times, providing frequent briefings, engaging in useful debates, and resolving many of the issues as they arose.

Now, teams of examiners may be involved in one audit. Numerous specialists and many managers may have a role. The process has grown in size, scope, and time.[3] I do, however, often yearn for those days when I could sit down with the business owner, have a cup of coffee, and discuss the issues with both of our minds focused on the earliest possible resolution. In this chapter I call for a return to the best practices from those now long gone days.

---

[3] Of course, the complexity of issues, taxpayers' operations, and the entire world economy has contributed significantly to these changes.

Who's Who Now?

You are ably represented by any number of others, each playing their own role in the process. The most significant are corporate staff members, accountants, attorneys, consultants, and valuators. The IRS is represented by audit teams consisting of managers, coordinators, and team members, including valuation specialists. Team coordinators are responsible for day-to-day administration of the audit. Team members may include specialists in valuation, computer audit, financial products, and other areas. The team may seek advice from technical advisers and counsel, among others, and the IRS may also contract with outside experts to assist at the audit, appeals, or litigation levels. Ordinarily, however, the decision to hire an expert will be made only after it is determined that an IRS specialist is not available, due either to workload, urgency, or specific expertise.

You, the business owner, are doubtless the one person most interested in the outcome of the tax audit, and yet often you're the one who is least involved in the audit process. While understandable, since you have a business to run and highly competent staff, representatives, and experts to assist you, I believe, in the interest of progress, that you should consider playing a greater role: expediting activities, identifying problems, and facilitating early resolution. You can do this personally or, with equal effect, through the efforts of those other representatives.

Roles and Responsibilities

There are two major problems a business owner can have a significant impact in solving. The first problem is that the parties on each side do not work together closely enough. The second is that the two teams do not work together closely enough. The first problem is one of internal communication and work practices. The second is more substantial. It may require major cultural change and significant intervention in order to happen.

THE AUDIT PROCESS

The modern audit process is, ideally, more a collaboration than an interrogation. An audit is definitely more successful when there is a good working relationship between the parties. Evidence of this includes excellent communications, a spirit of trust, and a commitment on both "sides" to enable the process to work in a timely, productive, and effective manner.

Once the IRS has introduced its team to the taxpayer and his or her representatives, the steps in the audit are consistent—no matter what the type of return or issue is being examined. Generally speaking, the IRS will conduct an initial review of the tax return and the issue. It would be helpful for the taxpayer to assist in this process by explaining the process by which the return was prepared.

Next, the IRS will ask questions and request information, usually using a form such as the "Information Document Request." The most important thing the parties can accomplish at this step is to ensure a mutual understanding of the questions asked and information requested and to agree on an acceptable date by which it can be expected that the request will be fulfilled. Regular status reports will enable both parties to stay on track with the process. If either side encounters a delay, it would be most beneficial to have a meeting or discussion about the situation and, if necessary, arrive at a revised completion date. This element of the process may be repeated several times during the course of the audit.

Once all the necessary information has been exchanged, the IRS will review and consider it, have further discussions with the taxpayer, and ultimately come to a conclusion as to the correctness of the item. During this stage, effective communication continues to be essential. Seek clarity in all discussions. Ensure that both parties understand their respective conclusions. Resolve differences quickly. Do not hesitate to ask questions.

Once a conclusion has been reached, the IRS will share it with the taxpayer. This can take place in a meeting, via written communication, or both. It is a critical point in the audit process, an opportunity for seeking clarification and mutual understanding. Questions and answers are more than appropriate (from both parties). Differences should be resolved. It is most important to resolve any factual differences. Ultimately, the parties may disagree about the conclusion, but at a minimum the facts should be agreed upon. Preferably, the parties can reach an agreement as to the issue as well as the facts, but if not, an agreement as to the facts enables subsequent decision makers to more easily resolve (or at least understand) the differences.

In particularly difficult problem areas, it may be wise to ask the IRS to involve its first (or upper) level of management in the process. The IRS is committed to enabling its field personnel to make decisions at the lowest possible level, but recognizes that on occasion management intervention is desirable or necessary to facilitate issue resolution. In addition, some types of issues may be appropriate for the new IRS issue resolution programs, such as Prefiling Agreements, Industry Issues Resolution, or Comprehensive Case Resolution.

What Can the Business Owner Do?

You can surely facilitate a better team working environment on the taxpayer's side. The IRS is working hard at enhancing team building on its side. It is in enhancing the collaborative environment between the teams in which the greatest impact can be made. I find it interesting that each of the parties employs the same professionals on its "side." Yet these individuals rarely work with each other. They may meet from time to time, but usually in an adversarial relationship, not a collaborative one.[4]

There is no reason why the two parties cannot work more collaboratively. Attorneys can discuss legal issues together. Valuators can discuss concepts, models, theories, and data together. We can work out problems together. We can agree on approaches, even if we ultimately disagree on results. The more we reframe our mind-sets toward collaboration and common interests, the more productive we will be, the better service we'll provide to ourselves and the public, and the more satisfied all parties will be with the process. We will even find ourselves becoming more satisfied with the results.

You are in a unique position to make this happen. You can surely express expectations to your team and interact more fre-

[4] The IRS recently initiated several "issue management strategies" for many taxpayers, including Prefiling Agreements, Industry Issue Resolution projects, and others. These collaborative methodologies have been very successful and have great promise.

quently and visibly with the IRS team. You can make clear to all parties that the best outcome will occur with greater collaboration and communication, and with more trust. You can set the stage and affect the ideals and the practices of all the parties.

Your unique abilities arise from several sources, including the experience with executive decision making, marshaling resources successfully, setting agendas and the tone and context of important transactions, and bringing out the best in people. Just imagine the improved effectiveness and satisfaction that can be achieved from essentially a controversial and adversarial process such as an audit when these characteristics are injected into the process.

THE NATURE OF EXPERTS IN TAX VALUATION

An expert may be defined[5] as "one with the special skill or knowledge representing mastery of a particular subject." Valuation matters require experts, since those generally responsible for accounting, tax, business management, and operational matters are not well versed in the arcane subtleties of the subject. While the business owner is in the best position to "know" the value of a business, when it comes to stating it in accordance with principles of appraisal and valuation, to the satisfaction of a tax auditor, appeals officer, or court, the owner is not necessarily the most qualified choice.

The Internal Revenue Code, for example, requires most valuations to be conducted by a "qualified appraiser," a term, defined in regulations, which generally requires such a person to be an "expert." An expert has the training, experience, knowledge, skill, and ability to "master" a particular subject. Valuation experts may have accreditations, licenses, advanced degrees, court experience as an "expert witness," or any number of other accomplishments to speak of.

Once the expert is engaged to provide an opinion of value to either the taxpayer or the IRS, the expert is thrust into what frequently may become a very adversarial process. The expert

[5] All definitions taken from *Merriam-Webster's Collegiate Dictionary.*

has a responsibility to avoid the appearance of partiality. He or she is the subject matter expert and must leave the advocacy to others. Failure to adhere to this role is often an important obstacle to issue resolution. In order to grasp this, one must understand the differences between experts and advocates.

The Expert and the Advocate

An advocate may be defined as:

1. "One that pleads the cause of another; specifically one that pleads the cause of another before a tribunal or judicial court."

   or

2. "One that defends or maintains a cause or proposal."

Note the differences between the expert and the advocate. The definitions alone represent a stark contrast between them. Experts are masters in a field. Advocates plead or maintain a cause. These are two significantly different professions, and in tax matters experts and advocates must remain at a distance. The process must demand this, lest the credibility of one suffer greatly. Both taxpayers and the IRS have a long way to go to improve on this aspect of the process.

An advocate may argue; the expert should explain. An advocate may defend; the expert should document. An advocate may strategize; the expert should outline. The differences are significant and compelling. The interesting thing to me is that the IRS is not an advocate and doesn't employ them during the audit. Audit team members, including valuation specialists, may advocate for the correctness of their conclusions, but not for another goal, such as "more tax for the treasury." The taxpayer, however, may advocate for his or her best tax position and the best tax outcome consistent with the law.

The taxpayer may legitimately advocate for the minimum tax possible given the law and facts at issue, while the IRS may not advocate for the converse (the highest possible tax). This is a fundamental policy of tax administration, well documented in the Internal Revenue Manual.

However, when I say that the taxpayer may legitimately advocate for the minimum tax possible, given the law and facts at issue, this privilege does not extend to the taxpayer's expert. There's the rub! The expert must remain in the role of a subject master. This pertains to both the expert representing the taxpayer and the expert representing the IRS.

This is the single most important fundamental concept to understand. And beyond mere understanding, you must ensure that the experts from both parties also understand and abide by these principles. Once it is assured that they do, the other representatives can do their jobs and facilitate the audit process through an accurate and satisfying conclusion. The experts may well play an important and visible role in this process, but they must remain subject masters and not advocates. Then the communications will be materially enhanced, because both parties' experts will spend more time discussing professional issues and clarifying professional areas of disagreement, thereby enhancing the resolution process.

THE BUSINESS OWNER'S ROLE IN THE AUDIT

The business owner has an exceptionally important and interesting role. I have already outlined many things you must be aware of and specific actions you may take. An audit involving valuation issues may arise as a result of a specific business transaction (purchase, sale, merger, gift, or others). Let me discuss a few additional roles in three different contexts: prior to the transaction, after the transaction, and during the audit.

Before the Transaction

You will be very busy if you decide to take a more active role in audit-related activities involving valuation-impacted transactions. There are several steps the business owner should take.

Understand the Process

First and foremost, you should understand the process. Obviously, you understand the business process. Study some of the issues outlined in this chapter. Know the roles and responsibilities of all parties involved. Ask your attorneys for a briefing of recent court decisions involving similar cases and potential disputes. Learn as much as you can about the IRS process involving valuation issues. Who are the principle players, what can you expect from them, what kind of problems are you likely to encounter along the way, and how have others solved some of those problems efficiently and effectively?

Identify a Strategy

We call this preplanning when we relate it to tax audits. Negotiating details of a transaction may well have intended or unintended tax results. Consult with your own advisers and learn enough about the world of valuation matters so that decisions you make today do not surprise you negatively tomorrow. This is where you ensure that your staff engages the best valuation expert.

Anticipate Everything and Seek Competent Advice

Ask questions unceasingly. Your own advisers and consultants are paid to answer them. The IRS will be happy to answer questions about procedural and technical matters, sometimes informally, other times formally.

Use the resources at your disposal, both internally and externally. I get calls frequently from practitioners who want to know about possible outcomes, the IRS position, procedural matters, organization issues, and many others. While I obviously cannot dispense tax advice, I am always happy to answer questions to make the process a little smoother for someone who asks. Common questions include: "What does the IRS think about Revenue Ruling X?" or "If we claim a 40 percent discount, will the IRS allow it?" Obviously I would not be able to comment on specific discounts or values, but I am more than happy to discuss rulings, procedures, policies, and similar issues that taxpayers wish to discuss. Think through possible consequences. Test assumptions. Ask, ask, ask.

Prepare to Negotiate

My friend and first supervisor had a tendency to repeat himself. I guess he did that when he felt he wasn't getting his point across the first time (or the 10th time, for that matter). One common theme I remember him expressing (no mean trick, since it was about 28 years ago) was that every audit has a beginning, middle, and an end. I think his point focused on the fact that the audit has an end, since the issue always seemed to be related to the question: "When are you going to be finished with this case?" The point is just as well taken in the context of managing an audit process as in planning to negotiate.

You might wonder why I put this element in the "Before the Transaction" section. The reason is, the negotiation of valuation-related tax audit matters begins even before the audit begins, and in fact before the transaction is executed. Prepare to negotiate outcomes before you complete the transaction. It's all part of strategy. Negotiating strategies that tend to withhold information and spring surprises at the last minute are never productive. They tend to generate hard feelings on both sides and probably result in hardening positions rather than lessening tensions.

Hold Everyone Accountable

I have another friend who has a number of famous sayings, one of the most important being, "Hold everyone accountable." Learn about everyone's role and responsibility. Realize who the decision makers are. Realize where the power lies. Most important, though, realize that everyone's role is vital to the whole, and only if everyone does his or her own job will the end result be rational, reasonable, and satisfying.

Who can hold everyone accountable? Well, each person can, in his or her own way, but the business owner has a special role. You should certainly hold your own staff and consultants accountable to you, but you should also realize that you have every right to hold the IRS parties accountable as well. We are accountable to our management and to the public at large. You are a member of that public at large, and in that sense we are accountable to you.

After the Transaction

Your role after the transaction becomes a lot simpler if you optimized your role before the transaction. If all goes well, the most important role you have after the transaction is to mobilize the resources you have identified in planning your strategy.

During the Audit

Believe it or not, if you've done all of your homework, as discussed earlier, the audit will be a piece of cake. Well, not really. But that doesn't mean it has to be a nightmare either. Review all of the information in this chapter. Remember who the key players are and their roles and responsibilities. Now the audit begins. What do you do?

It's simple. You lead. You take all the information at your disposal and you mold it together into a productive, effective, and efficient process. Work with the audit team manager. Delegate, certainly. Rely on your staff and your consultants. But don't abdicate your own responsibility. Take the role of a leader. Make it happen. Hold them accountable. Demand excellence. Provide feedback where you are unhappy and frustrated, but also feedback where you're pleased and comfortable. Communicate and collaborate. You will be surprised how satisfying the audit can be.

MISTAKES AND HOW TO CORRECT THEM

Everyone makes mistakes. Blackboards come with erasers. So do pencils. The computer I am writing on has a delete key and a reset button. Mistakes can and will occur. The question is always how best to take advantage of them. My wife always looks forward, never backward. She learns from mistakes and always finds positive value in the process. The audit environment can provide a similar opportunity. Anticipate mistakes to try to prevent them, but do not despair when they occur, just take action to redirect the energy to a positive track.

Mistakes Owners Make

Owners make plenty of mistakes. That's why we have low PE ratios, isn't it?[6] In the world of valuation and tax matters,

[6] Author's note: To clarify, a low PE ratio means that the company has a high discount rate (meaning it is a high-risk firm), has low expected growth, or both. In other words, a low PE ratio means a low-performing firm. JBA

though, mistakes take on another form. How should we define mistakes? I define a mistake in this context as the act that leads to an unsuccessful outcome. An unsuccessful outcome might be an unagreed audit. It might be a tax deficiency greater than expected or greater than the ability of the company to pay. It might be nothing more than a frustrating experience, where, although the monetary outcome was not unacceptable, the relationships between the parties was less than satisfying.

Failing to Prepare

I've devoted a considerable portion of this chapter to collaboration, planning, and preparing for transactions and audits. There are only two things that can result from failing to prepare adequately, as outlined above. The first would be a convenient and coincidentally successful result. Yes, they do happen, but not often enough. If you don't prepare to understand, plan, mobilize, strategize, anticipate, engage, and do all the other things I've been talking about, you might still have a successful outcome, but I tend to doubt it.

More likely the second outcome occurs: frustration, litigation, and expense. These are not good outcomes. Only about a third of the cases involving valuation issues that my staff handles are "agreed." That means that two-thirds of the cases are not agreed, meaning they go on to the appeals function or to litigation. The expense involved to taxpayers, the IRS, and society is much greater than we can legitimately afford. One way to increase the rate of successful agreements is to prepare more effectively.

Failing to Mobilize

Valuation issues in federal tax matters involve huge amounts of money and require enormous investments of time and other resources on the part of both the government and taxpayers. Human resource requirements are substantial, with numerous players, including staff, managers, experts, consultants, and advisers. When either side fails to put these resources together in an optimal fashion, failure becomes more likely. You should spend sufficient energy ensuring that your resources are ready for the preaudit and audit activities, and focus on the collaborative strategies that both parties may engage in to enhance the probability of a successful outcome. Call your advisers together. Brainstorm likely actions. Anticipate questions and resource requirements.

Failing to Lead

I love my father and mother. I hated when they told me, "You have no one to blame but yourself." I must say they were always right, even when I didn't realize it most of the time. If you don't lead your team into a collaborative environment with the IRS team, I may send my mother after you. No doubt she will remind you that you have no one to blame but yourself.

I have seen so many experts, consultants, staff, and other role players drag out an audit with countless disagreements, most of which could have been resolved in minutes rather than months if there were proper oversight and leadership. That should come from both parties, but as the business owner, you have a responsibility to your company and yourself to ensure that such a role is fulfilled. If you have to do it yourself, then by all means do so. You wouldn't want to tangle with my mother.

Failing to Intervene on a Timely Basis

I remember one of my first audit experiences. We had a number of significant issues and valuation disputes. The meetings dragged on interminably over a period of many months. We had some interesting debates but just couldn't break the ice. The audit was in Buffalo in the middle of the winter. I was the youngster in the group, and my manager had a strong preference to stay out of the cold. He fulfilled this by sending me to Buffalo every winter. I was too young or naive to argue. After all, he was the boss.

One winter day, I remember arriving at the company's offices and entering the conference room. The players were different. The company's accountants were not at the table. The appraiser was missing. There was a new face I didn't recognize. I soon learned it was the president of the company. He told me an interesting story. He said he came to the conclusion that the accountant was not solving problems, and he wanted to conclude the audit as quickly as possible. He thought I had made some good points, but there were a few things he thought I didn't understand about the business. He proceeded to explain to me some of the issues involving competition in that particular market.

We agreed to resolve our differences before lunch that afternoon. I learned a great deal from that president. I trusted him, and he acknowledged me. He added an element to the process that was missing, and he solved the problem of leadership that was missing by intervening when he thought he should.

Being Inadequately Briefed

There's really no excuse for this error. Your job is to be informed. The real cause of this problem is that the business owner usually does not know what to ask for, nor does he know the proper questions to be used as follow-ups. Once you learn more about the process, you will be prepared to have regular and detailed briefings to keep you adequately informed of status, progress, problems, and concerns.

Delegating Too Much

This is the opposite of being adequately informed. If you delegate excessively, you run the risk of falling into the same trap in which the Buffalo company found itself. Until the CEO intervened during that final conference, he was not fully informed of the problems and had relied on his consultants excessively.

Mistakes Experts Make

Experts make subject matter errors. We all do. Those are easy to detect, can usually be corrected after peer review, and only occasionally give rise to a greater level of problems. Experts can make other mistakes, though, that have much graver consequences for the client and for the overall process. I have identified four categories of those mistakes.

Failing to Be Objective and Independent

One need look no further than the savings and loan debacle of the 1980s to find the best example of lack of objectivity and independence. Experts have a role to fulfill, which I described earlier. Experts must retain independence in order to be experts. Otherwise, they can fall into the trap of advocacy, which I discuss next.

Becoming Advocates

Experts are subject masters. Advocates may argue a position or an outcome. And never the twain shall meet. Or, never should the twain meet. Unfortunately, experts on both sides often forget their valid roles and slide into the realm of the advocate. Experts may advocate their opinion. That's it. You should take care that your expert maintains his or her area of specialization and does not stray beyond it. Of equal importance, you and your staff should be wary of any attempt by any expert to do more than the position calls for and more than the profession should allow.

Unwillingness to Assist in Problem Solving

Experts tend to get caught up so much in their own world that they forget or ignore the larger world around them. The only job the expert has is to render his or her professional opinion in the form requested. Problems often arise with the process, as we have discussed, and the experts need to be willing to assist all parties in problem-solving activities. Perhaps this is the antithesis of straying into the realm of advocacy. Experts need to listen effectively to the world around them, answering questions such as: "What is the real problem at issue?" "Why has the dispute risen to the level it has?" How can I offer my services and expertise to the parties in the search for solutions?"

Recognizing Strengths and Weaknesses

In 28 years of practice I have yet to see the perfect valuation report. Many have come close. Most have weaknesses one can live with, but perfection—that is another story. Yet, having engaged in thousands of audits and thousands of valuation problems, one thing is eminently clear: Each report has its own strengths and weaknesses, and its authors need to "fess up," that is, grow up and act responsibly.

Take the masks off. Recognize your own limitations. Contribute to the valid search for a reasonable conclusion. Explore possible differences. Admit the pros and cons of approaches. Most important, business owners need to understand that no valuation report is perfect—even those produced by their own consultants. You need to realize that valuation is an art, and not a science, and facilitate the search for responsible compromise.

Seeing a Battle Rather Than a Negotiating Opportunity

This problem is related to many of the preceding issues. Experts are not perfect. Experts are not advocates. The audit is not a battle but, hopefully, a responsible collaborative search for reasonable conclusions. In this context, experts can contribute greatly.

Mistakes the IRS Makes

This one's easy. The IRS never makes any mistakes, because it is always right. Sure. If that were the case, we wouldn't have the Tax Court or have tax matters in other courts.

The IRS makes mistakes everyday—just like other normal people. The reason is simple: The IRS is comprised of normal people just like you, and we all make mistakes every day. The IRS makes as many mistakes of the same nature as other experts. Furthermore, the IRS hires some of the same outside experts you do. It makes another mistake that only it can make, and that's the one I will focus on next.

Failing to Understand Its Mission Statement

The mission of the IRS is to "provide America's taxpayers top quality service by helping them understand and meet their tax responsibilities and by applying the tax law with integrity and fairness to all." The admitted focus on enforcement of prior years has been adjusted to reflect the importance of enforcement, while at the same time reflecting the ideals of service. It has been an adjustment that all employees were carefully educated about, and it has been the focus of constant attention and reenforcement over the last several years. Still, it is a challenge to integrate taxpayer service and customer satisfaction in the admittedly difficult and frequently adversarial world of audit disputes.

Now, to the mistake. It's very hard to draw the line between legal aggressive tax minimization—the acknowledged right of all taxpayers—and that which crosses the line in an area as subjective as valuation. Valuation is a gray area to begin with: the art, as opposed to the science I mentioned earlier.

Valuation operates on a continuum. There is rarely one "right answer." Taxpayers and their consultants and experts are allowed to select answers, consistent with law and ethics that legitimately structure their tax positions in a most favorable fashion. IRS experts do not have this option. We are obligated to search for the objective correct "right" answer to every problem, most of which do not have a "right" answer, while at the same time the taxpayer's experts, consultants, and other staff are frequently engaged in assertive advocacy for that "best result" position. So what's the mistake I am referring to? It is engaging in adversarial debate, which might border on or even become the same kind of advocacy we are trying so hard to avoid.

What's the solution? It's simple to state but difficult to implement. Study all of the principles and guidelines I have discussed in this chapter, and strive constantly to search for ways to facilitate collaboration, enhanced communication, and the objective search for a reasonable resolution of these very difficult problems. Your role in this is to help everyone get on track, stay on track, and stay informed throughout the process.

CONCLUSION

As I wrote this chapter, I found myself more and more amazed at how complicated a picture this one little area of life really is: tax matters involving valuation issues. I wonder, as I recall that I have practiced in this field for over a quarter of a century, why we all have not found more lasting solutions to these problems. I conclude that we haven't tried hard enough. Business owners need to help the rest of us keep a focus on the issue and maintain a constant search for solutions. After all, that's what you do best.

List of Abbreviations

CAGR	Compounded Annual Growth Rates
CAPM	Capital Asset Pricing Model
CE and Cap Exp	Capital Expenditures
CF	Cash Flow
CRSP	Center for Research in Security Prices
D and Depr	Depreciation
DCF	Discounted Cash Flow
DFD	Discounted Future Dividends
DFNI	Discounted Future Net Income
DLOM	Discount for Lack of Marketability
EBIT	Earnings Before Interest and Taxes
EBITDA	Earnings Before Interest, Taxes, Depreciation, and Amortization
ERP	Equity Risk Premium (for CAPM)
ESOP	Employee Stock Option Plan
FASB	Financial Accounting Standards Board
FMV	Fair Market Value
GAAP	Generally Accepted Accounting Principles
GC	Guideline Company
GMM	Gordon Model Multiple
GPCM	Guideline Public Company Method
IPO	Initial Public Offering
LLC	Limited Liability Company

M&A	Mergers and Acquisitions
MM	Miller & Modigliani, i.e., Merton Miller and Franco Modigliani
MVIC	Market Value of Invested Capital
NWC	Net Working Capital
NYSE	New York Stock Exchange
P/BV	Price to Book Value Ratio
PE	Price Earnings Ratio
POR	Payout Ratio
PPE	Property, Plant, and Equipment
P/S	Price to Sales Ratio
PVF	Present Value Factor
REIT	Real Estate Investment Trust
ROA	Return on Assets
ROE	Return on Equity
ROI	Return on Investment
RR	Retention Ratio
SEC	Securities Exchange Commission
SIC	Standard Industrial Classification (Code)
SYD	Sum of Years' Digits
t	Time, usually denoting the current time period, usually the current year. We denote the prior and first forecast year by $t - 1$ and $t + 1$, respectively

Glossary

The following definitions are based on the *International Glossary of Business Valuation Terms,*[1] except for the definition of Gordon Model multiple and where otherwise noted.

Appraisal. See *Valuation.*

Arm's length. A transaction in which the parties to the transaction are financially unconnected. For example, a transaction between two subsidiaries of the same parent organization could only be said to be at arm's length if it could be shown that the deal had been carried out at current market prices with no preference of any kind being shown in the trading terms.[2]

Asset Approach. A general way of determining a value indication of a business, business ownership interest, or security using one or more methods based on the value of the assets net of liabilities.

Beta. The measure of relative risk compared to the market, used in the Capital Asset Pricing Model (see Chapter 5). The market itself has a beta of 1.0. Thus, a firm with a beta of 1.0

---

[1] Available on the American Society of Appraisers' Web site, http. //www.bvappraisers.org/glossary/. Click on "BV Glossary."

[2] *Dictionary of Business Oxford University Press,* Market House Books Ltd., 1996. Quoted at www.xrefer.com/.

is, on average, equally as volatile as the market. A firm with a beta 1.2 is 20 percent more volatile than the market, and a firm with a beta of 0.8 is 20 percent less volatile than the market.

Capital Asset Pricing Model. A model for calculating discount rates. The discount rate equals the risk-free rate (usually the 30-year Treasury bond rate), plus beta times the equity risk premium (see Chapter 5). CAPM is widely used in valuing publicly held firms. Its use in valuing privately held firms depends on the reasonableness of its underlying assumption that the investor is diversified against all forms of nonsystematic risk, including size-based risk. This is usually an unwarranted assumption in valuing most businesses worth less than $10 million, and often unwarranted until the business is worth several tens of millions of dollars. It typically results in discount rates that are substantially lower than the logarithm-size model.

Cash Flow. Cash that is generated over a period of time by an asset, group of assets, or business enterprise. It may be used in a general sense to encompass various levels of specifically defined cash flows. When the term is used, it should be supplemented by a qualifier (for example, "discretionary" or "operating") and a specific definition in the given valuation context.

Control premium. An amount or a percentage by which the pro rata value of a controlling interest exceeds the pro rata value of a noncontrolling interest in a business enterprise, to reflect the power of control.

Discounted Cash Flow Method. A method within the income approach whereby the present value of future expected net cash flows is calculated using a discount rate.

Discount for lack of control. An amount or percentage deducted from the pro-rata share of value of 100 percent of an equity interest in a business to reflect the absence of some or all of the powers of control.

Discount for lack of marketability. An amount or percentage deducted from the value of an ownership interest to reflect the relative absence of marketability.

Discount rate. A rate of return used to convert a future monetary sum into present value.

Equity risk premium. The additional rate of return that a prudent investor would require for investing in equity rather than debt. In the Capital Asset Pricing Model, it is typically the excess returns of equities over the long-term Treasury bond returns (see Chapter 5).

Fair Market Value (FMV). The price, expressed in terms of cash equivalents, at which property would change hands between a hypothetical willing and able buyer and a hypothetical willing and able seller, acting at arm's length in an open and unrestricted market, when neither is under compulsion to buy or sell and when both have reasonable knowledge of the relevant facts.

Fair Value. The standard of value used in financial statement accounting for publicly traded companies in determining whether there has been any impairment of goodwill. It is also the standard of value in shareholder dissolution suits. When one or more shareholders are suing to dissolve a corporation, Fair Value is the standard of value. This definition, however, will vary as interpreted by state case law. Usually the critical issue is whether to permit a discount for lack of control.

Gordon Model multiple. The present value of each dollar of a perpetuity with constant growth. One then multiplies the GMM by next year's forecast cash flow to obtain the value of the perpetuity. The formula for the end-of-year form of the GMM is mathematically the simpler form, which is $GMM = 1/(r - g)$, where r is the discount rate and g is the perpetual growth rate. If $r = 25\%$ and $g = 5\%$, $GMM = 5$, which means that the present value of the right to receive one dollar at the end of every year forever is \$5.00, and if the perpetuity starts at \$1 million next year, the present value of the perpetuity is $5 \times \$1$ million = \$5 million. The formula for the mid-year Gordon Model multiple, in which we assume that cash flows on average occur halfway through the year, and which is generally the appropriate assumption in valuing businesses, is

$GMM_{\text{Mid Year}} = \dfrac{\sqrt{1+r}}{r-g}$. See Chapter 6 for a detailed explanation of the Gordon Model.

Income Approach. A general way of determining a value indication of a business, business ownership interest, security, or intangible asset using one or more methods that convert anticipated economic benefits into a present single amount.

Investment Value. The value to a particular investor based on individual investment requirements and expectations.[3]

Marital value. The standard of value for valuing the family business in divorce cases in San Diego County. The author does not know if there are any other counties in the U.S. that have their standard of value for divorce valuation purposes.

Market Approach. A general way of determining a value indication of a business, business ownership interest, security, or intangible asset by using one or more methods that compare the subject to similar businesses, business ownership interests, securities, or intangible assets that have been sold.

Minority discount. Discount for lack of control applicable to a minority interest.

Minority interest. An ownership interest of less than 50 percent of the voting interest in a business enterprise.

Present value. The value, as of a specified date, of future economic benefits and/or proceeds from sale, calculated using an appropriate discount rate.

Rate of return. An amount of income (or loss) and/or change in value realized or anticipated on an investment, expressed as a percentage of that investment.

Standard of value. The indication of the type of value being used in a specific engagement; e.g., Fair Market Value, Fair Value, Investment Value. A standard of value is a definition of value and a statement of the context in which it applies—whether implicitly or explicitly.

---

[3] In Canada the definition is "value to the owner."

Valuation. The act or process of determining the value of a business, business ownership interest, security, or intangible asset. Synonymous with "appraisal."

Valuation Approach. A general way of determining a value indication of a business, business ownership interest, security, or intangible asset using one or more valuation methods.

Valuation Method. Within approaches, a specific way to determine value.

Value. *Webster's Dictionary*[4] has two relevant definitions: (1) "A fair return or equivalent in goods, services, or money for something exchanged"; and (2) "the monetary worth of something, i.e., its marketable price." The ASA's *International Glossary of Business Valuation Terms* defines valuation as the act or process of determining the value of a business, business ownership interest, security, or intangible asset.

[4] www.m-w.com/cgi-bin/dictionary.

Resources

As has been noted often in the text, the articles on my Web site, www.abramsvaluation.com, listed under this book are supplementary to this book. These articles are all worthy of being included, but the book would then have grown to an inappropriate size for the "trade book" market.

THE SUPPLEMENTAL CHAPTERS

To reiterate information that can be found in the Introduction and elsewhere, Part One of *How to Value Your Business and Increase Its Potential* is the technical valuation material you need to know in order to value your business—whether or not you are planning to sell it in the near future. Chapter 9, which ends the first part, is about valuing your business as of a future date and, more important, understanding from the future valuation equation how you can manage your business to maximize its value in the future. Part Two of the book is about selling or financing your business and the valuation issues that result.

The supplemental chapters on my Web site are the logical continuation of the book. They fall into the following categories:

1. Increasing the value of your business

2. Personal financial planning, including how to increase your resources in retirement by use of proper exit strategies
3. Additional valuation chapters

I will describe the articles below. For the moment, let's categorize them, so you understand how they fit into the overall picture. The articles by Linda Feinholz, Jim Ward, and Daniel O'Connell and Jim Stump[1] are about increasing the value of your business. They provide the link between efficient management of people and cash flow and the results on value. While there are thousands of books and articles on management, you will read these articles with "valuation lenses" in your glasses.

The articles by Ed Shuck and Penelope Roeder fit into personal financial planning—mainly, how to exit your business and plan for retirement. Where Part Two of the book deals primarily with selling your business to third parties, these articles are more about transferring all or parts of your business to your children, or selling to your employees through an ESOP—although they also cover estate planning aspects of selling to third parties.

The additional chapters, written by me, are "The Valuation Effects of Entity Form" and "Accuracy of the Valuation." The former is about how your choice of entity form—C corporation, S corporation, LLC, etc.—affects the value of the business. The latter chapter is important because it's crucial that you understand the limitations of your own accuracy in a "do it yourself," as compared to a professional, valuation.[2]

How They Enhance the Book

There are books of much greater length and that go into greater depth about the topics the contributing authors discuss in the amount of space allotted to them. Linda Feinholz's article, for instance, does not replace the need for books about manage-

[1] This article also covers some topics that cross over into personal financial planning for a business owner.
[2] This chapter also covers the limitations of professional valuations.

ment. However, books about management do not address the theme of how management affects the value of the firm, as does Linda's excellent article. Here you have the opportunity to read about these various topics while wearing glasses with "valuation lenses." Hopefully, after reading this book and the supplemental chapters, you will never think about valuation, management, taxation, estate planning, and the other areas in the same way. You should have a "valuation thinking cap" to apply to all business decisions.

For example, instead of just listening to a suggestion of changing the structure of an organization from a pure management perspective, after reading this book you should be asking questions that will enable you to see the valuation implications of the change, such as:

- How will this change affect income and expenses (and thus, net income)?
- What will the change do to the risk of the firm?
- Will it make net income more or less volatile over time?
- Will it make net income more or less dependent on the owners?
- Will this change require a different level of investment that will change my balance sheet structure and thus influence cash flow?
- What will this change mean for the growth rates of sales and cash flows?

If you read this book and the related articles and change the questions that you ask and the way you think, you can change the destiny and the value of your business.

The Articles

In her article, "Managing for Profitability," Linda Feinholz discusses management techniques that should make your business more profitable and your life more enjoyable. Implementing her suggestions and making them a lifelong habit should greatly enhance the value of any business.

Managing cash flow is one of the fundamental methods of managing value. My approach to the topic in Chapter 4 is valuation-oriented and more technical than Jim Ward's article on the subject, which is written in an entertaining style and is more "hands-on."

"Employee Benefit Planning and Tax Preferences," a collaboration between Daniel O'Connell and Jim Stump, is about employee benefit planning, issues such as pensions, health insurance, and life insurance for the business owner, which fit with the theme of personal financial planning. It also deals with the same topics for employees, and offers some excellent strategies for cost containment, which enhances the value of the business.

Penelope Roeder's article, "Succession and Estate Planning," provides an excellent overview of the many issues one must deal with in business succession and estate planning. Some of the issues are psychological, and very important, but the majority are technical aspects of estate planning that you must know in order to develop a cogent plan to transfer wealth to your heirs.

Ed Schuck and Penelope Roeder's chapter, "ESOPs," discusses Employee Stock Ownership Plans as one specific type of exit strategy, which also happens to be an employee benefit plan. ESOPs can be a complex, confusing topic, and Ed and Penelope do an excellent job of guiding and educating the reader.

About the Contributors

DAVID BOATWRIGHT

David Boatwright practices in the areas of transactional business and tax matters, including mergers and acquisitions, partnership, joint venture and limited liability company arrangements, international transactions, equity and debt offerings, executive compensation arrangements, real estate acquisition, development, finance, exchange and sale, and state taxation. David is a member of the Bar of the states of California, Colorado, and Oregon. He is certified by the California Board of Legal Specialization as a Specialist in Taxation Law and has been a frequent author and speaker regarding transactional and tax matters. He is a partner in the San Diego law offices of Latham & Watkins and can be reached at david.boatwright@lw.com or 619-236-1234.

LINDA FEINHOLZ

For over 20 years Linda Feinholz has been a consultant to the leaders and management teams of evolving businesses, helping them improve their results and execute their businesses more profitably and productively. Through Feinholz & Associates general management consulting, executive coaching, and courses,

Linda transfers the tools and skills used in Fortune 100 companies to privately held and publicly traded businesses. She has worked with UCLA Medical Center, Avon Products, Walt Disney Imagineering, the Los Angeles Metropolitan Transit Authority, and WorldVision and consulted to small- and mid-size companies as they grow, change strategy, and create new value. Her clients have included manufacturers, software developers, professional services firms, and executives changing careers. Linda can be contacted at www.feinholz.com.

MICHAEL KEANE

Michael Keane is a managing director with Wedbush Morgan Securities and a lecturer on Corporate Finance at the University of Southern California's Marshall School of Business. He has an MBA in Finance from the University of Chicago, a JD from the University of Texas, and a BA from the University of Southern California. He is a David S. Boren Fellow of the Defense Department's National Security Education Program. He can be reached at mkeane@marshall.usc.edu.

JIM LEVY

Jim Levy is a managing director with Townsgate Associates Inc., a mergers and acquisitions firm located in Beverly Hills, California. He has completed transactions in a variety of industries and sectors, including manufacturing, distribution, real estate management, and other business services. Mr. Levy represents sellers of small- to middle-market companies, branches and divisions, and corporate clients that retain him for acquisition search assignments. He publishes articles and speaks on M&A topics to industry and professional groups. He received a BA degree in Business from Linfield College in Oregon. Mr. Levy can be reached at (323) 951-1600 or jlevy@townsgate.com.

HOWARD A. LEWIS

Howard A. Lewis is the Engineering Program Manager at the Internal Revenue Service. In this position, Howard has responsibility for all engineering, appraisal, and valuation services for federal tax audits. Howard has been with the IRS for 28 years and has held various technical and management positions in Engineering and Valuation, as well as mid-level management and quality assurance functions. He looks forward to working and collaborating with taxpayers and practitioners in building better working relationships and building models for resolving valuation disputes. Howard holds bachelor's and master's degrees in Engineering from New York University, is accredited as a valuation analyst by the National Association of Certified Valuation Analysts, and is certified as an appraiser by the state of Georgia.

DANIEL H. O'CONNELL

Daniel H. O'Connell has a BS degree from the University of Oregon, a JD from the University of California at Berkeley, and an LLM from New York University. Formerly a professor and assistant dean at the University of Arizona College of Law, he is certified as a tax specialist by the State Bar of Arizona Board of Legal Specialization. He has lectured at various tax workshops and has published several articles and coauthored books on tax-related matters. His law firm, O'Connell & Bouman, P.C., is in the taxation section of the Bar Register, which lists the top-ranked law firms in the United States, and, under Trusts and Estates, he appears in the Best Lawyers of America, a listing of the top attorneys in the nation selected by their peers. For further information, see www.aztaxplan.com. Mr. O'Connell can be reached at dan@aztaxplan.com or 520-615-9802.

PENELOPE C. ROEDER

Penelope C. Roeder is president of Strategic Support Services, Inc., a management consulting firm in Playa del Rey, California. She has assisted organizations and their executives in making complex strategic and financial decisions for more than two decades. Ms. Roeder holds an MBA in Finance as well as a PhD in Human and Organization Systems, with an emphasis on decision-making processes, group dynamics, and leadership. She is also a Certified Financial Planner™. She can be reached at Penelope@StrategicSupports.Com.

EDWIN G. SCHUCK, Jr.

Edwin G. Schuck, Jr., is a partner in the Tax Department of McDermott, Will & Emery, Los Angeles office. Mr. Schuck has extensive experience in both tax controversy and tax-oriented transactional work. He has handled mergers and acquisitions, joint ventures and alliances, leveraged leases, project finance, employee stock ownership plans, and financial products. Mr. Schuck earned his bachelor's degree, his MBA in Finance, and his JD at Columbia University. His e-mail address is eschuck@mwe.com.

JAMES RICHARD STUMP

Mr. Stump is an Assistant Attorney General with the Commonwealth of the Northern Mariana Islands. In this capacity, Mr. Stump serves as the Chief Legal Counsel for the Department of Finance and has responsibility for all tax enforcement in the Commonwealth. In addition to his legal background, Mr. Stump has 12 years of experience as a human resource director and is currently a candidate for an LL.M-Taxation Degree from the University of San Diego, School of Law. Mr. Stump can be contacted at JRStump@CNMILaw.com.

BRUCE TARAGIN

Bruce Taragin is a partner at Blumberg Capital (www.blumbergcapital.com), an early stage venture fund located in Silicon Valley. He has 15 years experience as a venture capital investor, entrepreneur, technology investment banker, and corporate attorney. He has held several senior management positions within technology companies. He also structured and managed early stage technology transactions at Hambrecht & Quist, Mayer Brown & Platt, and Bankers Trust Company. A native of New York, Bruce earned his BA in Finance and Communications, cum laude, from Yeshiva University, and his MBA and JD from Fordham University.

JAMES K. WARD

James K. Ward is a senior executive of Brandlin & Associates, an accounting corporation located in Los Angeles (www.brandlin.com). Mr. Ward's practice concentrates in the areas of corporate due diligence, restructuring, insolvency, business bankruptcy and litigation. Prior to joining Brandlin & Associates, he was a partner in the accounting firm Parks, Palmer, Turner & Yemenidjian, LLP. Mr. Ward is a graduate of California State University at Northridge and is both a CPA and a certified insolvency and restructuring adviser.

OTHER CONTRIBUTORS

Some of the above contributors have written articles that appear on the www.abramsvaluation.com Web site. They are listed in the Resources section.

About the Author

Jay B. Abrams, ASA, CPA, MBA, a nationally known authority in valuing privately held businesses, is the author of *Quantitative Business Valuation: A Mathematical Approach for Today's Professionals*, published by McGraw-Hill in 2001, the most advanced book in the valuation profession. He has published numerous seminal articles in the American Society of Appraisers' *Valuation* journal, *Business Valuation Review*, and *The Valuation Examiner*.

He has an MBA in Finance from the University of Chicago, where he also took graduate courses in the Department of Economics. He received his bachelor's degree in Business Administration from California State University at Northridge, where he received the Arthur Young (now Ernst & Young) Outstanding Accounting Student Award in 1972.

Mr. Abrams has spoken in a variety of different professional and public forums about valuing privately held businesses, including the American Society of Appraisers, the American Institute of Certified Public Accountants, the National Center for Employee Ownership, and the Anthony Robbins Mastery University. He has taught valuation seminars for the University of Southern California, University of California at San Diego extension classes, and numerous continuing legal education seminars.

In 1992, Mr. Abrams published the mathematical solution to a 500-year-old problem—how to pinpoint the source of an accounting transposition error. It is one of dozens of inventions attributed to him, many of which are valuation formulas and models that appear in *Quantitative Business Valuation*. The April 2002 issue of *CFO* magazine highlighted one of these inventions—the Periodic Perpetuity Factor (PPF)—whose applications go beyond valuation. The PPF can enable firms that make large capital purchases of long-lived, expensive equipment (e.g., ships, airplanes, biomedical equipment, fleets of trucks or automobiles, etc.) to decide whether to buy new or used equipment and how long to keep the equipment before selling it.

Mr. Abrams was a project manager at Arthur D. Little Valuation, Inc., in Los Angeles, where he performed the valuations of Columbia Pictures, Dr Pepper, Purex, MCO Geothermal, and many other large firms. He is currently the principal of Abrams Valuation Group, a firm that specializes in business valuation, with headquarters in North Hollywood, California, and offices in New York. He can be reached at 818-505-6008 or jay@abramsvaluation.com. The company Web site is www.abramsvaluation.com.

He lives in the Los Angeles area with his wife and five children.

Index

Page numbers followed by italic *n* refer to a specific text footnote on that page.